Keys to Content Writing

Joan Sedita

Contributing Editors:
Shauna Cotte
Lisa Klein

Keys to Literacy®

319 Newburyport Tpke, Suite 205
Rowley, MA 01969
978-948-8511 **www.keystoliteracy.com**

ISBN 0-9786106-4-4
Printed in the United States of America
Published and Distributed by

Keys to Literacy®

319 Newburyport Tpke, Suite 205
Rowley, MA 01969
978-948-8511
www.keystoliteracy.com

Dedication

To all of the writers whose words have instructed, enlightened, and entertained me for more than 60 years.

Acknowledgments

I started teaching basic writing skills to struggling readers and writers in 1975 at the Landmark School. The drive these students had to learn to write, despite the extreme challenges they faced, made me realize how fortunate I was to have the ability to communicate with written language. Thank you to these students for showing me that learning to write is not natural and that teaching writing is not easy. Thank you to the many educators I have met who have taken on the challenge of writing instruction because they recognize the power they can give students when they teach them to write. Educators' requests for a writing professional development program is what encouraged me to develop *Keys to Content Writing*.

I would like to give special thanks to Shauna Cotte and Lisa Klein who were instrumental in developing the content of the *Keys to Content Writing* professional development. Donna Mastrovito also contributed to the final stages of development. Writing instruction is a huge professional development topic, and it was sometimes a challenge to narrow down the topic of content writing. All of the Keys to Literacy trainers deserve thanks for their patience as we made adjustments until the program met our goal of helping teachers of all subjects embed writing instruction with content instruction.

Joan Sedita
Program Author
Founding Partner, Keys to Literacy

TABLE OF CONTENTS

Introduction

Classroom Scenario

In a social studies class, students are writing about several pieces of text: a primary source, a textbook section, and a magazine article. The assignment is to write an informational piece that synthesizes information from these three sources. The goal of the assignment is twofold: to master the content material and improve content writing skills. The teacher provides a writing assignment guide that describes the purpose and type of writing, suggested length of the piece, and specific requirements for content and text structure. The teacher has differentiated the assignment to meet the needs of students with a variety of writing abilities. Scaffolds, such as a pre-writing template, have been provided for students who struggle with planning strategies. The teacher has provided models of good writing samples, and students have opportunities to collaborate at various stages of the writing process. In this classroom, the teacher is both teaching students to write <u>and</u> using writing to help them learn content.

Like reading comprehension, writing skill is a strong predictor of academic achievement, and it is essential for success in the workforce and post-secondary education. Students need and use writing for many purposes: to communicate and share knowledge, to support comprehension and learning, to explore feelings and beliefs, and many others. Writing is also increasingly necessary for success across a range of occupations (The National Commission on Writing, 2004).

There are far too many students in the United States today who simply do not write well enough to meet grade-level demands. The 2011 National Assessment of Educational Progress (NAEP) writing assessment scores for grades 8 and 12 indicate that the number of students who are not proficient for their grade level remains alarmingly high: 73% of eighth graders and 73% of twelve graders. About a third of high school students intending to enter higher education do not meet readiness benchmarks for college-level English composition courses, and among certain groups, the percent is higher: 50%. Once in college, 20% of first-year college students require a remedial writing class, and more than half of them are unable to write a paper relatively free of errors. At least a quarter of new community college students enroll in remedial writing courses. Compounding the problem, remedial enrollments appear to underestimate the number of students with reading and writing difficulties. (ACT, 2005; Graham, MacArthur, & Fitzgerald, 2007; National Center for Education Statistics, 2012 and 2003)

The good news is that we know **what** students need in order to **become** strong writers; a significant amount of research reviews effective writing instruction. The Common Core State Standards (CCSS) for literacy place considerable emphasis on teaching students in all subjects **to write** and **to use writing to learn** (Common Core, 2010). The key to doing this effectively is conveying strong instructional strategies to teachers, including teachers of science, social studies, math, English and other content areas.

The *Keys to Content Writing* professional development program incorporates essential instructional practices for teaching students the necessary content writing skills and the use of writing as a comprehension strategy.

Who Should Participate in *Keys to Content Writing* Training?

Teachers of any subject area that requires students to write benefit from participation in *Keys to Content Writing* professional development. Elementary teachers of multiple subjects learn strategies for extending writing instruction beyond the literacy block, using social studies, science, and other subject area instruction as an opportunity to practice writing skills. Middle and high school content teachers learn to intentionally and productively reinforce writing skills taught by writing teachers, and – more importantly – to use writing for content instruction. English language arts and writing teachers learn to support their fellow content teachers as they incorporate a school-wide, consistent set of basic writing practices.

Although *Keys to Content Writing* professional development complements and reinforces many writing instruction practices that English language arts and writing teachers already use, the program is not designed to be a complete stand-alone writing curriculum. Because it focuses on writing to learn using informational and argument types of writing, the teacher training does not cover narrative writing or basic "learning to write" skills such as sentence and paragraph writing, conventions (spelling, punctuation, capitalization, grammar), or handwriting/keyboarding. It is also not intended to be a writing curriculum for advanced writing skills, such as those that might be taught in high school advanced placement (AP) writing courses.

Keys to Content Writing Training Book

This training book is for use with professional development for the *Keys to Content Writing* program. During training, trainers ask participants to focus on examples and activities in the book, organized as follows:

- **Chapters 1 and 2** present an overview of *Keys to Content Writing* and its alignment to the CCSS; define content writing and the writing process; and review effective, research-based instructional practices for teaching writing to students in grades 4-12.

- **Chapter 3** suggests and explains the use of "quick writes" to support content learning and improve writing skills.

- **Chapter 4** presents the three types of writing (argumentative, informational, narrative) and discusses teaching basic text structures such as introductions, conclusions, and body organization.

- **Chapter 5** presents strategies to write from sources, including gathering information, taking notes, and using notes to write a first draft.

- **Chapter 6** explains the use of writing models and mentor text to support student writing.

- **Chapter 7** describes and models the use of scaffolds to support students at all stages of the writing process.

- **Chapter 8** suggests ways to provide students with feedback on their writing and opportunities for revision.

- **Chapter 9** presents a writing assignment guide (WAG) for use in planning a writing assignment in any subject area.

Chapter 1: What is *Keys to Content Writing?*

Keys to Content Writing is a professional development program for teachers of all subjects in grades 4-12. The instructional practices presented during training can be used with all students as Tier 1 content writing instruction. Educators who provide Tier 2 supplemental instruction to students who have difficulty writing can also use *Keys to Content Writing* by providing more explicit instruction and guided practice during intervention instruction.

The ability to write is as essential to learning as the ability to read. *Keys to Content Writing* focuses on *writing to learn,* that is, using writing as a tool to promote content learning. Content teachers assign writing activities to help students learn subject material, clarify and organize their thoughts, and improve retention of content. Writing-to-learn tasks can be based on reading, classroom discussion, teacher presentation, multimedia presentations (i.e., video), or hands-on activities. The program focuses on informational and argument writing types.

During training, teachers learn to assign short, informal quick writes and longer, more formal writing assignments based on content reading and curriculum topics. Teachers also learn to teach and reinforce writing skills that are associated with learning to write. This includes encouraging students to apply all the stages of the writing process by using Keys to Literacy's *The Process Writing Routine: Think, Plan, Write, Revise.* In these steps, students learn to

- incorporate basic text structures;
- differentiate between the three types of writing (i.e., argument, informational, narrative);
- be aware of audience, task, and purpose when writing; and
- write from content sources.

A Consistent Instructional Routine for Teaching Content Writing

Professional development for *Keys to Content Writing* is designed to support a consistent approach to teaching content writing as students move from grade to grade and subject to subject. It supports vertical articulation for writing instruction across grades. Figure 1A summarizes the major instructional practices.

Teachers should aim to incorporate as many of these five instructional practices into daily lessons as possible. Consider them a set of instructional tools to be applied opportunistically as you incorporate explicit writing instruction into your teaching.

Figure 1A

Keys to Content Writing Instructional Routine

Instructional Practice	Description
Quick Writes Common Core Writing Standard #10, Reading Standard #2	• Use common terminology and short writing tasks to consistently incorporate informal writing to help students learn content. • Use a consistent set of quick-write activities. • Routinely ask students to write about their reading, including summarizing, generating questions, and taking two-column notes.
Writing Process Common Core Writing Standard #5	• Use *The Process Writing Routine* (THINK, PLAN, WRITE, REVISE) to guide students through all stages of the writing process. • Display the writing process stages in classrooms using a common visual (e.g., poster, handout).
Basic Text Structures Common Core Writing Standards #1, #2, #3 Reading Standard #5	• Use consistent terminology to teach the similarities and differences between the structures of the three types of writing: argument, informational, narrative. • Explicitly teach basic text structures (introductions, conclusions, body paragraphs, transitions) and the specific text components for argument and informational writing.

Writing From Sources
 	
Common Core
Writing Standards #7, #8, #9
Reading Standards #1, #2
	• Provide explicit instruction for skills required to write from sources.
	
	• Teach students to follow the stages of the writing process when they write from sources.
	
	• Provide explicit instruction for the following writing strategies:
	  o Two-column notes, to gather information and evidence from sources
	  o Top-down topic webs, to develop an overall, pre-writing plan
	  o Using notes to generate sentences and paragraphs for a first draft

Writing Assignment Guide (WAG)
 	
Common Core
Writing Standards #4, #5, #10
	• Use Keys to Literacy's WAG to incorporate research-based practices to plan formal writing assignments.
	
	• Use the WAG as a common planning tool to:
	  o Develop content writing assignments that set specific goals about audience and purpose; length & format; due dates; content and text structure requirements; source requirements; connections to subject; and literacy state standards.
	  o Plan scaffolds to differentiate instruction.
	  o Plan writing models to show students.
	  o Identify and plan the opportunities for students to work collaboratively, receive feedback, and revise their writing pieces.
	  o Use the WAG as the basis for a student wrwiting assignment guide.

Gradual Release of Responsibility

The *Gradual Release of Responsibility Model* (Pearson & Gallagher, 1983) is an effective approach for teaching writing. This model is also known as the *I do it, We do it, You do* it model of instruction (see Figure 1B). The teacher is the centerpiece of the "I" stage, which includes explicit instruction with modeling through think aloud. The "We" stage entails individual, small-group, or whole group practice with the strategy. This practice should be guided by the teacher and should include corrective feedback. Eventually, each student reaches the "You" stage, when he or she applies the strategy independently. The gradual release of responsibility model is integrated throughout the *Keys to Content Writing* Program.

Figure 1B

Gradual Release of Responsibility

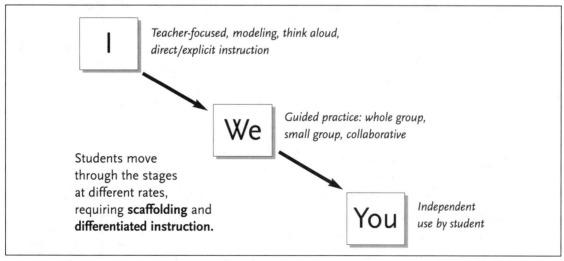

In addition to the five major instructional practices that are the foundation of *Keys to Content Writing*, there is a common instruction sequence that can be applied when teachers introduce any new writing skill or technique. The steps below gradually release responsibility for using the skill to students.

1. **Identify, define, explain the writing skill.** Explicitly teach the skill using modeling and think aloud.

2. **Show the skill in model writing samples.** Show students writing samples that incorporate the skill and analyze how the author applied the skill.

3. **Practice skill-building activities.** Provide opportunities for students to practice the skill. Quick write activities are especially useful for this practice (see Chapter 3).

4. **Modify and revise writing samples.** Have students practice applying the skill to writing samples that are partially completed or that need "fixing". The samples can be generated by the teacher, or they can be anonymous student samples. Have students work collaboratively to apply the skill to improve the samples.

5. **Use the skill in a collaborative writing piece.** Provide opportunities for students to work collaboratively to complete a writing task that incorporates the skill. Give feedback about the use of the skill, and find opportunities for students to revise their pieces using this feedback.

6. **Students use the skill independently.** When students are ready, have them independently complete a writing piece that incorporates the writing skill. Continue to provide feedback and opportunities for revision.

Task, Audience, Purpose

One of the ten writing Common Core State Standards (CCSS) is devoted to awareness of task, audience, and purpose, and *Keys to Content Writing* emphasizes the importance of teaching students to consider these elements when ever they write. Figure 1C provides questions students can ask to become more aware of the task, audience, and purpose.

> **Common Core Connection**
>
> **Writing Standard #4:** Produce clear and coherent writing in which the development, organization, and style are appropriate to **task, purpose, and audience.**

Figure 1C

Task, Audience, Purpose

Task	What is your assignment? What are your being asked to do? What form will your writing take?
Audience	Who is the audience for the writing piece? Is it your teacher or classmates, or is there another, more "authentic" audience? Who will actually read your assignment?
Purpose	What is the purpose for writing this piece? Is it to inform, convince, or tell a story? How might the audience determine the purpose?

Students need to learn that awareness of the task, audience, and purpose for a writing assignment is important because these elements influence a number of decisions that a writer must make, including (McKensie & Tompkins, 1984):

- Tone of the piece (e.g., objective, critical, apathetic, sincere, skeptical, etc.)
- Language and word choice, style, tone of the piece
- Type of information and level of detail to include in the piece
- How to arrange and present the information

Activity

Directions: Review each writing task, then describe who the audience might be and the purpose for writing.

Task: Imagine that your family is trying to decide whether or not to get a pet. Take a position on this subject. Would you like to have a pet or not? Write a letter to members of your family explaining why getting a pet is or is not a good idea.

Audience:

_____

_____

Purpose:

_____

_____

Task: Imagine that a local newspaper reporter has asked you to write about the school talent show that was held last week. Write a short article that will be printed in the newspaper.

Audience:

_____

_____

Purpose:

_____

_____

What is Content Writing?

Quite simply, content writing is a way to promote and deepen content learning. When students write about what they are reading and learning, they are *thinking on paper*. As they write, they concentrate on the information and ideas they are learning and make connections to their existing knowledge. Writing about content also helps students clarify and organize their thoughts, solidify the material they are learning, and place that learning into their long-term memory.

As a result, writing about content is a highly effective comprehension strategy. Lehr, Osborn, and Hiebert (2005, p. 31-32) explain that writing about reading improves students' comprehension in two ways:

- Reading and writing are composing processes – readers compose meaning as they read, and expressing opinions and interpretations in writing helps readers organize their thoughts about a text.

- Writing provides insight about literacy tools – writing enables students to understand how an author's choices about type of writing, vocabulary use, and text structure help make text understandable.

Barbara Walker, former president of the International Reading Association, wrote the following in a letter to President Obama in 2009, wherein she neatly summarizes the importance of teaching students to write about what they are learning:

"As students write about science, math, and social studies, they elaborate and clarify their ideas. It is not just an act of expression of what you know. In the act of writing, students also form new relationships among ideas. Writing helps students integrate their thoughts. Each day, students should write meaningful ideas. Writing is another way to think which often results in deep, complex thinking. When students are involved in writing about crucial ideas, they rethink their understanding and integrate their thinking with new information. They finally look at the idea in a new way, creating multiple ways to think about issues." (p. 16)

Disciplinary Writing

Many content writing tasks are general writing tasks that can be applied in any content area, such as note taking, summarizing, and report writing. However, as students move into high school grades, they also need to learn disciplinary writing skills, which tend to be more unique and specific to certain subject areas (i.e., disciplines). For example:

- Science: experimental lab report; field notes

- History: political speech; analysis of a historical event

- Mathematics: algebraic proof; description of the steps used to solve a problem

- English: literary analysis; poetry; playwriting

In many ways, the content teacher is best suited to teach students to write about content – how to write like a scientist, historian, mathematician, playwright, or novelist.

Writing to Learn and Learning to Write

It is often noted that children in primary grades *learn to read* but shift in or around grade 4 to using *reading to learn*. The same is true of writing. Accordingly, some aspects of writing instruction focus more on learning *how* to write, such as: (1) applying the stages in the writing process (i.e., pre-writing, text production, revising, editing); (2) writing a sentence and then a paragraph; (3) conventions such as spelling, punctuation, and grammar. Learning to write also includes handwriting and keyboarding skills. On the other hand, the focus of content writing instruction is the use of writing to *learn*. That is, how to use writing as a tool to learn subject matter and to extend content knowledge.

Teaching students to write is typically considered the job of English language arts and writing teachers during class time dedicated to writing instruction. However, it is essential that students use writing throughout the school day, in all subjects. First, writing is a difficult task with which students will only demonstrate improvement if they are required to do it often. Second, students need more help learning to write than English language arts teachers alone can provide. Finally, as noted above, it is content teachers who are in the best position to teach students discipline-specific kinds of writing.

Understandably, content teachers can be overwhelmed with all the material they must cover during a school year, which may contribute to the belief that there simply is not enough time to teach writing. Using a plate of food as a metaphor, content teachers may view writing instruction as one more thing to add to an already crowded "plate." However, teaching students to write about what they are learning gives the students a strong foundation upon which they can access and add more content. When students have strong literacy skills, they have a solid plate to hold all of the content to be learned. In other words, writing is not simply another item on the plate; rather, it makes the plate stronger.

Keys to Content Writing: **Aligned With Content Literacy Standards**

Most states have adopted the Common Core State Standards (CCSS, 2010) or a similar version. *Keys to Content Writing* is tightly aligned with these literacy standards. The title of the literacy standards alone emphasizes the major shift that they represent regarding reading and writing instruction embedded in content instruction: *English Language Arts and Literacy in History/ Social Studies, Science, and Technical Subjects*. The standards signal a collective responsibility on the part of all educators to improve the literacy skills of students in all grades, as clearly indicated in the introduction to the CCSS:

> "The Standards insist that instruction in reading, writing, speaking, listening, and language be a shared responsibility within the school. The K-5 standards include expectations ... applicable to a range of subjects, including but not limited to ELA. The grades 6-12 standards are divided into two sections, one for ELA and another for history/social studies, science, and technical subjects. This division reflects the unique, time-honored place of ELA teachers in developing students' literacy skills while at the same time recognizing that teachers in other areas must have a role in this development as well." (p. 4)

Figure 1D identifies the standards most closely addressed by *Keys to Content Writing*, and Figure 1E lists the ten writing and ten reading standards. Note that there are also several standards related to writing skills in the language and speaking/listening categories.

Figure 1D

Literacy Standards Related to Keys to Content Writing

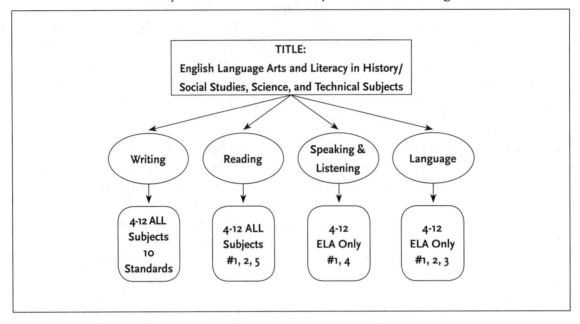

Figure 1E

Writing Anchor Standards

expectations for types of writing	**1**	Write opinions/arguments to support claims in an analysis of substantive topics or texts using valid reasoning and relevant and sufficient evidence.
	2	Write informative/explanatory texts to examine a topic and convey ideas and information clearly.
	3	Write narratives to develop real or imagined experiences or events using effective technique, well-chosen details and well-structured event sequences. *Note: For grades 6-12, the narrative standard is only in ELA standards, although other subjects should try to include narrative writing assignments.*
production and distribution of writing	**4**	Produce clear and coherent writing in which the development, organization, and style are appropriate to task, purpose, and audience.
	5	Develop and strengthen writing as needed by planning, revising, editing, rewriting, or trying a new approach.
	6	Use technology, including the Internet, to produce and publish writing and to interact and collaborate with others.
research to build and present knowledge	**7**	Conduct short as well as more sustained research projects based on focused questions, demonstrating understanding of the subject under investigation.

	8	Gather relevant information from multiple print and digital sources, assess the credibility and accuracy of each source, and integrate the information while avoiding plagiarism.
	9	Draw evidence from literary or informational texts to support analysis, reflection, and research.
range of writing	**10**	Write routinely over extended time frames (time for research, reflection, and revision) and shorter time frames (a single sitting or a day or two) for a range of discipline-specific tasks, purposes, and audiences.

Reading Anchor Standards

key ideas and details	**1**	Read closely to determine what the text says explicitly and make logical inferences from it; cite specific textual evidence when writing or speaking and writing to support conclusions drawn from the text.
	2	Determine central ideas or themes of a text and analyze their development; summarize the key supporting ideas and details.
	3	Analyze how and why individuals, events, and ideas develop and interact over the course of a text.
craft and structure	**4**	Interpret words and phrases as they are used in a text, including determining technical, connotative, and figurative meanings, and analyze how specific word choices shape meaning or tone. Determine the meaning of symbols, key terms and other domain specific words and phrases.
	5	Analyze the structure of texts, including how specific sentences, paragraph, and larger portions of the text relate to each other and the whole.
	6	Assess how point of view or purpose shapes the context and style of a text.
integration of knowledge and ideas	**7**	Integrate and evaluate content presented in diverse formats and media, including visually and quantitatively, as well as in words.
	8	Distinguish among facts; assess the extent to which reasoning and evidence in a text support author's claim.
	9	Analyze how two or more texts address similar themes or topics in order to build knowledge or to compare the approaches the authors take.
range and text complexity	**10**	Read and comprehend literary and informational texts independently and proficiently.

Language Anchor Standards Related to Writing

writing conventions	**1**	Demonstrate command of the conventions of standard English grammar and usage when writing or speaking.
	2	Demonstrate command of the conventions of standard English capitalization, punctuation, and spelling when writing.
	3	Apply knowledge of language to understand how language functions in different contexts, to make effective choices for meaning or style, and to comprehend more fully when reading and listening.

Speaking and Listening Anchor Standards

comprehension and collaboration	**1**	Prepare for and participate effectively in a range of conversations and collaborations with diverse partners, building on others' ideas and expressing their own clearly and persuasively.
	2	Integrate and evaluate information presented in diverse media and formats, including visually, quantitatively, and orally.
	3	Evaluate speaker's point of view, reasoning, and use of evidence and rhetoric.
	4	Present information, findings, and supporting evidence such that listeners can follow the line of reasoning and the organization, development, and style are appropriate to task, purpose, and audience.

Differentiating Instruction to Meet Student Needs

The CCSS identify benchmark writing skills for students to acquire by the time they complete each grade. They do not, however, identify how teachers should teach these skills. Most classrooms have students with a range of literacy skills, and the standards also do not specify how teachers should teach to students with advanced writing skills and those who struggle to write. The introduction to the CCSS provides the following explanation:

> "The Standards do not define the intervention methods or materials necessary to support students who are well below or well above grade-level expectations. No set of grade-specific standards can fully reflect the great variety in abilities, needs, learning rates, and achievement levels of students in any given classroom... The Standards should also be read as allowing for the widest possible range of students to participate fully from the outset and as permitting appropriate accommodations to ensure maximum participation of students with special needs." (p. 9)

During professional development for *Keys to Content Writing,* we suggest scaffolding strategies and writing assignments to differentiate instruction.

Activity

Identify Students With Different Skill Levels

<u>Directions</u>: *The pictures represent students who have grade-level writing skills, are advanced writers, or are struggling writers. Write the first names of students you know who represent these levels. At times in the training when differentiating instruction is addressed, we will ask you to consider these students.*

Struggling Writers   **Grade-Level Writers**   **Advanced Writers**

_____   _____   _____

_____   _____   _____

_____   _____   _____

_____   _____   _____

Chapter 2: Effective Writing Instruction

Beginning in 2007, numerous seminal reports summarized the research on effective writing instruction and strategies to improve student writing skills (Graham & Perin, 2007; Graham & Hebert, 2010; Graham, Harris, & Hebert, 2011; Graham et al., 2012). Three broad findings are consistent across the reports:

- Teach the stages of the writing process.
- Explicitly teach the writing strategies used at each step of the writing process.
- Increase the amount students write – the more they write, the more their writing improves.

Teach the Stages of the Writing Process

Beginning in the 1960s, Hayes and Flower (1980) researched the steps strong writers take in order to better understand how to teach writing. They developed a model of the writing process with three stages: planning, translating, and reviewing. Over the years, the model was informed by new research and modified to include four stages (Hayes, 1996; 2004):

1. **Pre-Writing:** reflection, selecting a topic, planning what to say
2. **Text Production:** writing a draft
3. **Revising:** reflection, making changes to improve the writing
4. **Editing:** proofreading

Today, it is general knowledge and practice that students be taught and follow the stages of the writing process as they write. Not surprisingly, one of the writing Common Core State Standards (CCSS) focuses specifically on the writing process – writing standard #5.

Keys to Literacy has developed an acronym to help students recall the writing process stages. The first letters of the steps, *THINK, PLAN, WRITE,* and *REVISE,* correspond to the first letters in the process title, *The Process Writing Routine.* Figure 2A presents the steps in the routine. Teachers are encouraged to teach the writing process explicitly and provide visual reminders for students by hanging classroom posters and distributing handouts of *The Process Writing Routine.*

> **Common Core Connection**
>
> **Writing Standard #5:**
> Develop and strengthen writing as needed by planning, revising, editing, rewriting, or trying a new approach.

The writing process is dynamic and recursive – writers repeat and revisit the stages several times as they develop a piece of writing. For example, a student may discover while he is writing a first draft that he needs to go back to the THINK and PLAN stages to gather and organize more information about the topic. While revising the draft, the student may discover he needs to change the way he planned to organize the content. The arrow in Figure 2A indicates that writing stages are overlapping parts of a process that may be repeated multiple times as it unfolds. In many respects, a piece of writing is never completely finished

– further thinking and editing can usually lead to further improvement.

Many students assume they should spend the bulk of their time writing a first draft, not realizing that most of their time should be spent at the THINK, PLAN, and REVISE stages of the writing process. Students, especially in middle and high school, should consider appropriating their time as follows (University of Victoria, 2010):

- **spend 40%** of the time planning, reading, gathering, taking notes (THINK, PLAN)
- **spend 20%** of the time draft writing (WRITE)
- **spend 40%** of the time rewriting and revising, including editing (REVISE)

When the primary goal of writing is to help learn content, students may spend less time rewriting and revising, especially if the writing task is a quick write or something intended to simply help a student process thinking through writing.

Figure 2A

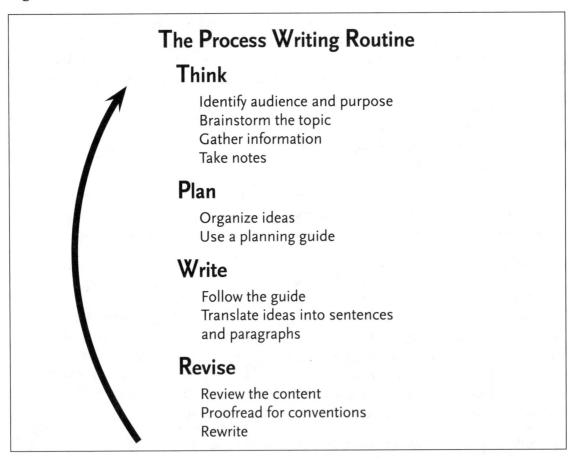

The Process Writing Routine

Think
- Identify audience and purpose
- Brainstorm the topic
- Gather information
- Take notes

Plan
- Organize ideas
- Use a planning guide

Write
- Follow the guide
- Translate ideas into sentences and paragraphs

Revise
- Review the content
- Proofread for conventions
- Rewrite

Explicitly Teach Writing Strategies

When we ask students to write, we make assumptions that they have the basic literacy skills and strategies to be successful at each stage of the writing process. The first and most effective instructional practice identified in *Writing Next* (Graham & Perin, 2007) is explicit instruction of writing strategies. Consider the following examples of skills and strategies that may require explicit instruction:

- At the **THINK** and **PLAN** stages:
    - ✓ Identify the audience and purpose
    - ✓ Brainstorm and narrow down the topic
    - ✓ Read and comprehend the sources
    - ✓ Gather information and take notes
    - ✓ Organize information, notes, and ideas into a logical plan for writing
    - ✓ Use a graphic organizer, writing template, or other type of planning scaffold

- At the **WRITE** stage:
    - ✓ Follow a writing plan
    - ✓ Take into account the audience, purpose and task
    - ✓ Write complete sentences and organized paragraphs
    - ✓ Apply text structures specific to narrative, informational, and argument writing
    - ✓ Write introductions and conclusions
    - ✓ Use transition words and phrases to make connections among sentences and paragraphs
    - ✓ Track sources
    - ✓ Incorporate proper English grammar

- At the **REVISE** stage:
    - ✓ Use specific criteria to evaluate the content and organization of a writing piece
    - ✓ Improve a writing piece by revising the wording, structure, and content
    - ✓ Proofread and edit for conventions (spelling, capitalization, punctuation)

Chapter 7 provides additional information about writing strategies and explicit instruction.

Increase The *Amount* Students Write

Adequate time for students to write is essential to the development of strong writing skills, and that time can occur during content instruction (Graham et. al., 2012). Writing is one of the major strategies to extend critical thinking about a subject-area topic. If schools are to improve students' critical thinking and writing skills, they must offer a broad range of writing activities in content-area classes and promote content teachers' knowledge about the use of writing as a tool to learn (Newell et. al., 2007). Common Core Writing Standard #10 calls for students to write *routinely* in all subject areas. This standard also addresses both short- and long-term writing tasks. Chapter 3 offers suggestions for short, content-based writing tasks for teachers to assign on a regular basis to ensure that students write routinely.

> **Common Core Connection**
>
> **Writing Standard #10:** Write routinely over extended time frames (time for research, reflection, and revision) and shorter time frames (a single sitting or a day or two) for a range of tasks, purposes, and audiences.

Research-Based Writing Instruction

Two reports provide meta-analyses of the existing research on writing instruction: *Writing Next* (Graham & Perin, 2007) and *Writing to Read* (Graham & Hebert, 2010). *Writing Next* identifies eleven elements of writing instruction found to be most effective in helping students in grades 4-12 learn to write well and to use writing as a tool for learning. See Figure 2B. *Writing to Read* summarizes the most effective instructional practices for teaching writing to enhance students' reading ability, listed in Figure 2C.

Figure 2B

Writing Next Findings
(Graham & Perin, 2007, p. 4-5)

Based on a large-scale statistical review of research into the effects of specific types of writing instruction on grades 4-12 writing proficiency, this report identified 11 elements of writing instruction found to be effective for helping students learn to write well and to use writing as a tool for learning.

1. **Writing Strategies,** which involves teaching students strategies for planning, revising, and editing their compositions.

2. **Summarizing,** which involves explicitly and systematically teaching students how to summarize text.

3. **Collaborative Writing,** which uses instructional arrangements in which adolescents work together to plan, draft, revise, and edit their compositions.

4. **Specific Product Goals,** which assigns students specific, reachable goals for the writing they are to complete.

5. **Word Processing,** which uses computers and word processors as instructional supports for writing assignments.

6. **Sentence Combining,** which involves teaching students to construct more complex, sophisticated sentences.

7. **Pre-writing,** which engages students in activities designed to help them generate or organize ideas for their composition.

8. **Inquiry Activities,** which engages students in analyzing immediate, concrete data to help them develop ideas and content for a particular writing task.

9. **Process Writing Approach,** which interweaves a number of writing instructional activities in a workshop environment that stresses extended writing opportunities, writing for authentic audiences, personalized instruction, and cycles of writing.

10. **Study of Models,** which provides students with opportunities to read, analyze, and emulate models of good writing.

11. **Writing for Content Learning,** which uses writing as a tool for learning content material.

Figure 2C

Writing to Read Findings

(Graham & Hebert, 2010, p. 5)

Recommendations: Writing Practices That Enhance Students' Reading

I. HAVE STUDENTS WRITE ABOUT THE TEXTS THEY READ. Students' comprehension of science, social studies, and language arts texts is improved when they write about what they read, specifically when they

- Respond to a Text in Writing (Writing Personal Reactions, Analyzing and Interpreting the Text)
- Write Summaries of a Text
- Write Notes About a Text
- Answer Questions About a Text in Writing, or Create and Answer Written Questions About a Text

II. TEACH STUDENTS THE WRITING SKILLS AND PROCESSES THAT GO INTO CREATING TEXT. Students' reading skills and comprehension are improved by learning the skills and processes that go into creating text, specifically when teachers

- Teach the Process of Writing, Text Structures for Writing, Paragraph or Sentence Construction Skills (Improves Reading Comprehension)
- Teach Spelling and Sentence Construction Skills (Improves Reading Fluency)
- Teach Spelling Skills (Improves Word Reading Skills)

III. INCREASE HOW MUCH STUDENTS WRITE. Students' reading comprehension is improved by having them increase how often they produce their own texts.

Keys to Content Writing: Research-Based

Keys to Content Writing incorporates many of the instructional practices recommended in *Writing Next, Writing to Read,* and other similar research:

> **from the eleven *Writing Next* elements:** (1) writing strategies, (3) collaborative writing, (4) specific product goals, (6) sentence combining, (7) pre-writing, (9) process writing approach, (10) study of models, (11) writing for content learning

> **from the *Writing to Read* recommendations:** (I) have students write about the texts they read, (II) teach students the writing skills and processes that go into creating text, (III) increase how much students write

One of the five instructional practices from *Keys to Content Writing* is the Writing Assignment Guide (WAG). As you will learn in Chapter 9, this writing assignment planning tool incorporates research-based best practices for teaching writing and assigning writing tasks to students. Figure 2D describes these practices.

Figure 2D

Writing Assignment Guide (WAG): Instructional Practices

Set Writing Goals	Identify and clarify the writing task: set specific product goals that include characteristics of the finished product. This includes identifying the audience and purpose, stating requirements about length, the type of writing to be used (e.g., narrative, informational, argument), format, content and text structure requirements, and use of sources.
	Use these requirements as the basis for grading writing assignments.
Show Models	Provide students opportunities to read, analyze, and emulate models of good writing.
	Show models of every step in the writing process.
Provide Scaffolds	Provide additional, targeted support for students in completing a writing task, such as steps to follow, top-down topic webs, two-column notes, or writing templates.
Provide Opportunities for Collaboration	Provide opportunities for students to work with peers or the teacher to plan, draft, revise, and edit their writing. Collaboration engages students more in the writing process because writing is a social activity that is best practiced in a community.
Provide Feedback	The feedback students receive matters as much as the writing instruction they receive. Without feedback, students cannot learn specific ways to improve their writing. • Is the writing *accurate*? • Does it convey the intended message? • Feedback can be from the teacher, peers, or the student (self). • Strong, valuable feedback is more than simply marking mechanical errors on final drafts!
	Specifically, *teachers* should: • Provide feedback throughout the writing process. • Focus on the *content* of the writing first; mechanics should be secondary. • Provide feedback that is descriptive, specific, and based on the student's individual needs. • Use feedback checklists or rubrics.
Provide Opportunities for Revision	Students require time to reflect on self-assessment and feedback from others and then improve their drafts through revision. It is necessary to provide explicit instruction on incorporating feedback to revise writing. Not every writing task has to be revised so it is ready for publication, but students need opportunities to revise based on feedback.

Peer Writing Collaboration

Collaborative writing, or instructional arrangements in which students work together to plan, draft, revise, and edit their compositions, has been identified as a highly effective instructional practice. Significant research shows that student collaboration has a strong positive impact on quality of writing, which is why it is among the eleven *Writing Next* elements (Graham & Perin, 2007). Peer collaboration is also related to Common Core Speaking and Listening Standard # 1.

> **Common Core Connection**
>
> **Speaking and Listening #1:** Prepare for and participate effectively in a range of conversations and collaborations with diverse partners, building on others' ideas and expressing their own clearly and persuasively.

Boscolo and Gelati (2007) suggest a "dynamic" relationship between collaborative and individual writing. Students collaborate to brainstorm ideas before writing, share ideas for organizing before writing, provide feedback on drafts, and help with revision. When writing individually, students express their own thoughts and voices. The relationship between collaborative and individual writing is dynamic because a student's individual writing may be informed by collaborative experiences.

Pritchard and Honeycutt (2007, pp. 34-35) note the following about peer collaboration:

- Writing is a social activity and is best learned in a community.

- Teachers use peer groups across curricula to encourage students to write and revise. Most agree that the social benefits of peer groups support the process approach.

- Specifically, these benefits include:
  - immediate feedback
  - experience with a wide range of writing abilities
  - reduced writing apprehension
  - development of positive attitudes about writing
  - more teacher time for individual attention
  - development of cooperation and interpersonal skills

Activity

Describe a time in your personal or professional life when you collaborated with a peer to write.

_____

_____

_____

_____

_____

_____

Do you think the collaboration improved the overall quality of the writing?

_____

_____

_____

_____

_____

_____

_____

Can you describe a time in your teaching when you provided an opportunity for students to write with their peers?

_____

_____

_____

_____

_____

_____

_____

Do you think the collaboration improved the quality of the students' writing? If so, how? (Hint: If necessary, refer to the list of benefits in the previous section!)

_____

_____

_____

_____

_____

_____

_____

Teaching Students Writing Collaboration

Naturally, it takes time and deliberate effort to create a collaborative environment where students feel comfortable sharing ideas and giving and receiving feedback. Many students need explicit instruction on working with peers. Here are some suggestions for teaching peer collaboration:

- **Model** by conducting teacher-led collaborative sessions.
- Use **role-play** to model appropriate peer discussion.
- Provide specific **guidelines and checklists** for use during collaborative sessions.

Figure 2E lists some additional considerations when managing and making decisions about peer collaboration. Figure 2F shows a sample completed collaboration activity guide, and Figure 2G is a blank copy of the guide for use with your students.

Figure 2E

Managing Peer Collaboration

Options for assigning partners or small groups:

- **Teacher-assigned**
    - *Homogeneous* grouping: students with same skills levels
    - *Heterogeneous* grouping: students with different skill levels (stronger literacy skills with weaker literacy skills)
    - Consider personalities, potential challenges

- **Student choice**
    - Potential benefit: tends to foster more engagement
    - Potential challenge: more difficult to manage

GENERAL TIPS:

- **Plan how students will be grouped ahead of time.**
- **Avoid <u>always</u> using the same grouping; alternate your methods of group selection.**
- **Set clear expectations for behavior, process, goals and final product:**
    - Assign roles (e.g., facilitator, reader, note taker, writer, presenter).
    - Provide interaction and communication rules (e.g., take turns talking, no interrupting, everyone participates, etc.).
    - Provide procedural guidelines and scaffolds (e.g., set of steps, writing template(s), note taking guide, feedback checklist, etc.).
    - Be clear about the *task* to be completed and the *amount of time* for collaboration.
    - Describe and provide models/samples of the expected final product.
    - Post a set of guidelines for collaboration as a poster, or distribute a handout.
    - Model a collaborative session; role play with some students at the front of the class.

Figure 2F

Sample Collaboration Activity Guide

Collaboration Activity Guide

Date: *Tuesday, Jan. 8*   **Time for collaboration:** *40 minutes*

Partner(s):

Group 1	*Group 2*	*Group 3*	*Group 4*	*Group 5*
Paul	*Emma*	*Abigail*	*Luke*	*Jake*
Jack	*J.P.*	*Kaitlyn*	*Allison*	*Natasha*
Olivia	*Jorge*	*Jacob*	*Adam*	*Thomas*

Assign these roles:

- *One person: facilitator (keep the group on track)*
- *One person: mark the text based on group input*
- *One person: fill in the 2-column notes based on group input*

Writing task:

- *Collaborate on the informational writing assignment we introduced yesterday*
- *Read the text source and mark relevant text information (hightlight, margin notes)*
- *Take 2-column notes - invlude at least 3 main ideas in the left column and at least 2 details for each main idea in the right column*

Expected finished product:

- *Hand in your group's marked text*
- *Hand in your group's 2-column notes*
- *If you do not complete the notes, each of you will have to complete them for homework.*

Use these support materials:

- *Use the 2-column notes template.*

Figure 2G

Blank Collaboration Activity Guide

Collaboration Activity Guide
Date: **Time for collaboration:**
Partner(s):
Assign these roles:
Writing task:
Expected finished product:
Use these support materials:

Motivation and Engagement

How do I *motivate* students to write? How can I keep my students *engaged* in writing? Teachers ask these questions all the time. Although there is no single instructional practice to answer these questions, there are several instructional practices which, when combined, have been found to motivate and engage students reliably (Hidi & Boscolo, 2006; Boscolo & Gelati, 2007). See Figure 2H.

Figure 2H

Suggestions to promote student motivation and engagement in writing:

- Assign writing for a real purpose and a real audience.

- Make writing relevant to students' everyday life; incorporate important current events.

- Teach students writing strategies so they feel competent about writing.

- Provide procedural scaffolds to keep students engaged.

- Emphasize successes at *each stage* of the process, rather than focusing only on the finished product.

- Provide opportunities for peer collaboration.

- Give actionable, user-friendly feedback.

- Create and maintain a supportive, nonthreatening classroom environment.

NOTES:

Chapter 3: Quick Writes

> "If you want to be a writer, you must do two things above all others:
> read a lot and write a lot." *Stephen King*

Have Students Write A Lot

As the prolific writer Stephen King notes above, the best way to get better at writing is simply to write a lot. In fact, practice is critical to improving at just about any new skill we want to learn: how to ski, how to play a musical instrument, how to use a software program, how to cook. However, it may not be easy at first to persist in practicing a skill that is difficult. This is partly why students with strong writing skills are often interested in writing more, whereas students who struggle to write avoid it.

The Common Core State Standards (CCSS) expect students at all grades to write routinely, as noted in writing standard #10. However, many content teachers feel that there is not enough time for students to complete lengthy, formal writing tasks on a regular basis, nor is there time for content teachers to review and grade many student papers. Thus, a dilemma arises: How can we have students write more in content classrooms? Part of the solution is to use *quick writes* on a regular basis.

Common Core Connection

Writing Standard #10: Write routinely over extended time frames (time for research, reflection, and revision) and shorter time frames (a single sitting or a day or two) for a range of tasks, purposes, and audiences.

Quick writes are short, informal writing tasks which are limited to 10 minutes of class time or assigned as brief, out-of-class assignments. As one teacher wrote, they are like "sketching with words" (Peha, 2003). Quick writes help the writer to remember, organize, and manage information, and they can be used at any point in a classroom lesson to help students communicate their thoughts, experiences, and reactions to what they are reading and learning. They can also be used as formative assessment to determine how well students have learned content.

See Figure 3A for a list of quick write tasks. Figure 3B provides quick write example assignments from teachers of various subjects and grades. Review these examples for some ideas about using quick writes with your own students.

Figure 3A

Examples of Quick Writes

check if you use	
	admit and exit tickets
	informal notes/scribbles

	margin notes while reading
	list of facts, steps, ideas (e.g., list 3 details you learned today)
	set of instructions or directions
	filling in a graphic organizer, complete a set of notes
	free-writing – having students write on a topic for a short, specified amount of time (can be described as a *brain dump*)
	one-paragraph summary
	generate a question
	KWL Chart (What I Know, What I Want to Know, What I Learned)
	write a definition in your own words
	draw, label, or explain pictures/diagrams
	short-answer questions
	1- to 2-sentence reflections
	sentence combining
	short communication with someone else (note, email, tweet, text message)

Figure 3B

Classroom Examples

Science

- Write out the definitions of weathering and erosion, then describe an example of each.
- In 10 sentences or less, summarize the 5 stages in human development.
- Choose one of Newton's Laws of Motion. Write what the law states. Then write a paragraph that describes the example provided in section 5 of the textbook.
- Label each part of the animal and plant cell diagrams.
- Make a list of all the materials needed to complete the experiment.
- Identify one exhibit you saw during our field trip to the science museum. Do a "brain dump" and write everything you can remember about the exhibit. You have 4 minutes.
- Work with a partner. You have 8 minutes to describe in your own words the Big Bang Theory.
- Using the periodic table, identify which elements belong to the group that includes the most active metals. Then write down the name, symbol, and periodic number for each of these elements.
- Explain the steps required to convert Celsius to Fahrenheit.

- Combine the four short sentences about photosynthesis into one, complex sentence.
- Write a list of the procedures you followed in today's lab.
- Draw a cycle graphic organizer that illustrates the water cycle.
- Admit ticket: in less than 3 minutes, list as many facts that you remember about the star *Polaris*.

Social Studies/History

- Circle the 3 most challenging vocabulary words on the list of terms related to the different forms of government, then complete a Concept Definition Map for the three words.
- Exit ticket: List 4 new, interesting facts you learned today about our region of the country.
- In 5 minutes or less, describe 3 major social reforms of the late Roman republic.
- Describe at least 3 reasons why people immigrate.
- After watching the video of the constitutional debate, choose one side and write 5 sentences about why you think that side was successful in the debate.
- Based on the primary source letter, list 3 to 5 details that show how the mills provided opportunity for the workers.
- Identify what you think are the 3 most important tools for an archaeologist. Then pick one and write a paragraph about why you chose that tool.
- Historical Landmarks: List 3 possible locations for your curating project. Then write a pro and a con for each.
- On the map, label each explorer's route. Include the last name of the explorer, the country he sailed for, and the start date of his voyage. Then pick a voyage you would like to have been on and explain why in a paragraph.
- Answer this question in 8 sentences or less: Why do some people call Reagan's tenure as president the "Reagan Revolution"?

English/ELA

- Admit ticket: describe a character trait you learned about the main character in your reading last night.
- Exit ticket: write out your personal writing goal for the next Writer's Workshop lesson.
- Explain what the literary term "conflict" means. Then write a few sentences that describe a conflict you have faced in your life.
- Write a postcard from Fenn to his grandfather that explains why he doesn't want to return to Westwood. Then write a postcard back to Fenn from his grandfather based on what you think he would write.

- You have 5 minutes to describe everything you learned about the main character in your summer reading novel.
- List the 7 major stages of an epic.
- Organize the 12 sentences into logical paragraphs. Then write a topic sentence for each paragraph.
- Look at the picture on the cover of the book. In 8 sentences or less, describe what is happening and explain what you think this book might be about.
- Exit ticket: List 3 events that impacted Johnny in Chapter 6.
- You have 6 minutes. Write as much as you can remember about how the main character ended up in a life raft (from the novel *Life of Pi*).
- Describe how the two settings in chapter 3 are different and similar.
- Under each sample ad, describe the persuasive writing technique(s) used.

Mathematics

- Write a list of step-by-step instructions for calculating the volume of a box.
- Define 5 properties of a polygon.
- Identify and label each element in the sample coordinate system graph.
- Create a word problem and solution for adding fractions.
- Write the definition of division. Then list the steps used to solve a long division problem with 1 divisor.
- In 3 minutes, complete as many blanks as you can on the handout of multiplication facts.
- Based on our class lesson about probability, describe one thing that you really understand and one thing that still confuses you.
- Exit ticket: generate a question you have about estimating quotients.
- Explain the difference between an obtuse angle and an acute angle. Draw an example of each.
- Math Journal Entry: Use sentences to explain how to find the area and perimeter of a triangle and a square.

Other Subjects/Topics

- Read the article and jot down the main idea of each paragraph in the left margin.
- (For Teachers) At a faculty meeting: In 4 minutes, list all of the opportunities to write that you provided your students this week.
- Based on the sample passage, generate 3 quiz questions at the understanding, applying, and evaluating levels of Bloom's Taxonomy.
- (Business Management) Write a one-paragraph summary of an example when you felt you received excellent customer service. Then write a second summary paragraph of an example when you received poor service.

- Write an ordered list of the procedures you should follow if you need to see the school nurse or use the restroom.

- (Music class) Explain your emotional reaction to each sample of music that was played in class today.

- Write an email to a classmate complimenting him or her on something he or she shared during our class discussion.

- (Art class) Define the term perspective as it relates to drawing. Then explain one technique that can be used to create the illusion of perspective in a drawing.

- (Economics) Summarize what happened during yesterday's supply and demand auction. Conclude by explaining why demand went down.

- Create a top-down topic web that shows the 3 major topics covered in the informational article you read for homework. Then add at least 2 sub-topics under each topic.

Admit/Exit Tickets and Other Templates

A popular quick write is use of an "admit" or "exit" ticket from class. An admit ticket is written at the start of class and can be used to review content covered the day before, connect to homework, activate existing student background knowledge, or preview a lesson. An exit ticket, written at the end of class, can be used to encourage reflection about the lesson, bring closure to the class, or briefly review key information and ideas. See Figure 3C for some sample admit and exit tickets. Full-page versions for use with your students are provided at the end of this chapter.

Figure 3C

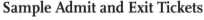

Sample Admit and Exit Tickets

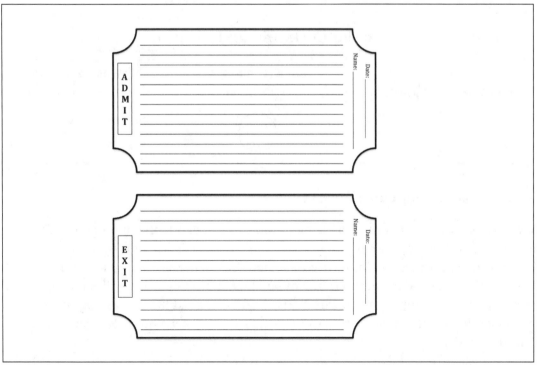

Here are a few other ideas for quick writes. The first is a text message quick write. Figure 3D is a visual of a blank cell phone and a sample text message task. Students write a response to the teacher's prompt as if it were a text message. The second idea is a reflection template such as the example in Figure 3E. The template is organized into space to record reflections related to shape prompts. Full-page versions for use with your students are provided at the end of this chapter.

Figure 3D

Text Message Quick Write

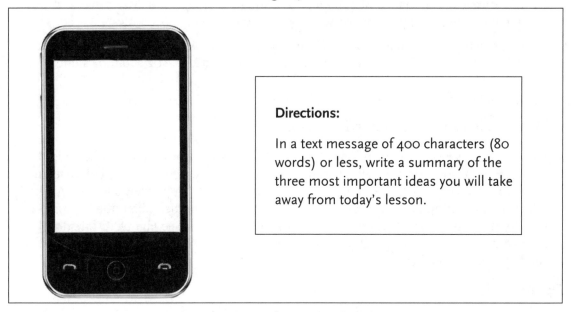

> **Directions:**
>
> In a text message of 400 characters (80 words) or less, write a summary of the three most important ideas you will take away from today's lesson.

Figure 3E

Square, Circle, Triangle Reflection

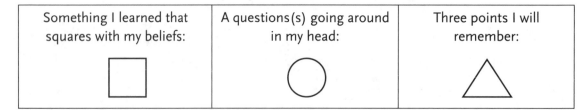

Something I learned that squares with my beliefs:	A questions(s) going around in my head:	Three points I will remember:
□	◯	△

Using Questions For Quick Writes

As we discuss in another of Keys to Literacy's professional development programs, *The Key Comprehension Routine*, generating and answering questions is one of the most effective strategies students can use to improve comprehension (National Reading Panel, 2000). When students respond to questions in writing, their ability to process and remember content information improves (Graham & Hebert, 2010). In addition to asking students content-specific questions, here are some suggestions for general questions that can be used in all content areas:

At the start of class:

- *What was the most important thing you learned from your homework assignment or reading?*
- *What questions do you have about your homework assignment or reading?*
- *What are you most interested in discussing or learning about in today's class?*

At the end of class:

- *What was the most important thing you learned today?*
- *What do you want to learn more about?*
- *What was confusing, or is there something you would like explained better?*
- *Complete the statement (Russek 1998):*
  - *– I learned that …*
  - *– I was surprised that …*
  - *– I discovered that …*
  - *– I was pleased that …*

Asking students to generate their own questions is also an effective quick write. Thinking is driven by questions, and the type of question asked determines the level of thinking required. Based on what they recently read, completed for homework, or learned in class, students can generate a question at one or more of the levels of Bloom's Taxonomy: Remembering, Understanding, Applying, Analyzing, Evaluating, Creating (Bloom, 1956). Figure 3F lists question terms and prompts related to each level of the taxonomy.

Figure 3F

Bloom's Taxonomy

Question Terms		Prompts
Remembering		
• cite • define • find • identify • label • list • locate • match	• name • quote • recall • recite • recognize • retrieve • show	• *Where is…* • *What did…* • *Who was…* • *When did…* • *How many…* • *Locate in the passage/story…* • *Point to the…* • *Give an example of…* • *Restate in own words…*
Understanding		
• describe • discuss • explain • interpret • paraphrase	• retell • review • summarize • translate	• *Tell me in your own words…* • *What does it mean…* • *Describe what…* • *What is the main idea of …*

Applying

• adapt	• interview	• *Give me an example of...*
• apply	• make	• *What would happen if...*
• compute	• operate	• *How would you solve the problem...*
• demonstrate	• practice	• *If you were there, would you...*
• dramatize	• role play	
• draw	• sequence	
• illustrate	• solve	
• implement	• use	

Analyzing

• analyze	• examine	• *What other ways could...*
• arrange	• group	• *What things are similar/different?*
• categorize	• inspect	• *What kind of person is...*
• compare	• integrate	• *What things could not have happened in*
• contrast	• organize	*real life...*
• deconstruct	• probe	• *What caused...*
• detect	• research	
• dissect	• separate	
• distinguish	• sift	

Evaluating

• appraise	• hypothesize	• *Rank the ideas/events in order of*
• assess	• judge	*importance.*
• choose	• justify	• *Select the best... why is it the best?*
• conclude	• prioritize	• *Was... good or bad? Why?*
• criticize	• rank	
• critique	• rate	
• debate	• reject	
• deduce	• validate	
• defend		

Creating

• assemble	• generate	• *What if...*
• compile	• imagine	• *What would it be like if...*
• compose	• invent	• *What would have happened if...*
• concoct	• make	• *Tell/write a different ending/result...*
• create	• originate	• *Design a...*
• design	• prepare	
• develop	• produce	
• devise	• set up	
• formulate		

Question terms from: *The Key Comprehension Routine.* Sedita, J. (2003, 2015). Rowley, MA: Keys to Literacy.
Prompts adapted from: *Checking for Understanding.* Fisher, D.B., & Frey, N. (2007). Alexandria, VA: ASCD

Using Quick Writes to Practice Subskills

In order to write well, students must be able to combine multiple subskills and use them independently. Teachers often assume that students have already mastered these skills or that students need to complete entire writing tasks in order to learn and practice them. However, many of the skills can be practiced using shorter writing tasks to target a specific skill. Quick writes are a great way to practice specific skills. For example:

- Have students review a writing sample and list all the transitions words or phrases.
- Give students a short text with missing transitions, and have them add transitions in the appropriate places.
- Give students a list of topics for informational writing, and have them develop titles and headings for sub-topics.
- Give students a sample body of a text, and have them add an introduction and/or conclusion.
- Give students a list of topics for argument writing, and have them write some claims and counterclaims for the topics.
- Give students sentences or paragraphs of text, and have them paraphrase the information in their own words.
- Ask students to generate a list of possible nonfiction leads for informational or argument writing.
- Give students a list of main ideas for informational paragraphs, and have them develop the topic sentences for these paragraphs.
- Give students a list of reasons that support a claim, and ask them to develop topic sentences for these reasons.
- Focus on sentence writing skills by assigning quick writes that have students combine sentences

What Can Be Done With Quick Writes?

Because the goal of quick writes is to get students writing frequently and informally, it is not always necessary to collect and grade them, which understandably concerns some teachers: "If I don't grade their writing, they won't take it seriously – and some of my students won't do the quick write." To avoid this, consider the following suggestions for promoting student participation:

- Allow students to work in pairs to complete a quick write.
- Have students share their quick write with another student.
- Randomly select a few quick writes to read to the class.
- Randomly select a few quick writes to review and grade.
- Tell students you will collect and review the quick writes to get a sense of what they are thinking, but they do not have to include their names on the quick writes.
- Collect the quick writes, shuffle them, and distribute them back to other students.

Then ask several students to read another student's quick write to the class. Names need not be included.

- Remind students that they will not be penalized for grammar, spelling, and other mechanical errors in a quick write, because it is an informal draft.

Activity

Directions: Use the space below to develop <u>4</u> quick write activities to use with your students. For each quick write, (1) identify related content reading material and/or topic(s); (2) describe the writing task; and (3) describe what you will do with the quick write when students are finished.

Quick Write #1

Content topic/related reading material:

Writing task:

What to do when finished:

Quick Write #2

Content topic/related reading material:

Writing task:

What to do when finished:

Quick Write #3

Content topic/related reading material:

Writing task:

What to do when finished:

Quick Write #4

Content topic/related reading material:

Writing task:

What to do when finished:

Sentence Combining

Sentence combining activities were developed in the 1960's (Strong, 1986). Research consistently finds that sentence combining is an effective method for helping students of all ages, from the elementary grades through college, produce more syntactically mature sentences, and it is one of the eleven instructional practices recommended in *Writing Next* (Graham & Perin, 2007; Saddler, 2012). Sentence combining provides practice with manipulating and rearranging words in sentences, expanding sentences, and clarifying sentence meaning.

Because a sentence combining activity only takes a few minutes, it is a good quick write activity for an admission ticket or during time between other classroom activities. Figures 3G and 3H provide examples of sentence combining activities from various content areas, and Figure 3I offers some additional suggestions for sentence combining activities.

Activity

Simple Sentence Combining Activity

Directions: Combine each pair of sentences into a single sentence.

The girl drank lemonade. The girl was thirsty.

_____

_____

The book was good. The movie was good.

_____

_____

The weather was perfect. The girls were playing soccer.

_____

_____

Activity

Multi-Sentence Combining Activity

<u>*Directions*</u>*: Combine all of the sentences into one, long sentence.*

- Wildlands are lands.

- The lands are public.

- The lands are private.

- The lands support native ecosystems.

- The lands include landscapes.

- A grazed rangeland is a landscape.

- Active timberland is a landscape.

Figure 3G

Subject Area Examples

ELA/Literature

The ants were busy on the ground, big black ones with shiny bodies, and little dusty quick ants. *From: "The Pearl" by John Steinbeck (Gr. 6-8)*

- The ants were busy.
- They were on the ground.
- There were big ones.
- The big ones were black.
- The big ones had shiny bodies.
- There were little ants.
- The little ones were dusty.
- The little ones were quick.

One quiet, Tuesday morning, I woke up to a pair of bright, dazzling shoes, lying right in front of my bedroom door. *From: Grade 4 Student Writing Sample*

- I woke up to a pair of shoes.
- It was Tuesday morning.
- The morning was quiet.
- The shoes were bright.
- The shoes were dazzling.
- The shoes were lying.
- They were lying in front of my door.
- The door was my bedroom door.

Science

The fundamental innovation underlying the astrolabe was the projection of an image of the sky (usually the northern hemisphere, centered on Polaris) on a plane corresponding to the earth's equator. *From: "Circumference..." by Nicholas Nicastro.*
(Gr. 9-10)

- The innovation was the projection of an image.
- The innovation was fundamental.
- The innovation was of the astrolabe.
- The image was of the sky.

- The image of the sky was usually the northern hemisphere.
- The image was centered on Polaris.
- The image was on a plane.
- The plan corresponded to the earth's equator.

<u>History/Social Studies</u>

The fancy exterior decorations on just about every building were carved from wood, then painted to look like stone or marble. *From: "The Great Fire" by Jim Murphy. (Gr. 6-8)*

• The decorations were carved.
• The decorations were fancy.
• The decorations were exterior.
• They were carved from wood.
• They were on just about every building.

• Then the decorations were painted.
• They were painted to look like stone.
• Or they were painted to look like marble.

I have the honor of serving as president of the Southern Christian Leadership Conference, an organization operating in every southern state, with headquarters in Atlanta, Georgia. *From: "Letter from Birmingham Jail" by Martin Luther King, Jr.*

• I have honor.
• The honor is of serving as president.
• I am president of the Southern Christian Leadership Conference.

• It is an organization.
• The organization operates in every southern state.
• Its headquarters are in Atlanta, Georgia.

<u>Math</u>

In this section, we will review the four basic operations of whole numbers – addition, subtraction, multiplication, and division – and discuss the use of exponents and the rule of order of operations in simplifying expressions. *From: "Introductory Algebra – 3rd Edition" by Franklin Wright and Bill New.*
(Gr 7-8)

• We will review four operations.
• The operations will be basic.
• The operations will be of whole numbers.
• The operations include addition, subtraction, multiplication, and division.

• We will discuss the use of exponents.
• We will discuss the role of order of operations.
• The order of operations are for simplifying expressions.

In an isosceles trapezoid, both pairs of base angles are congruent and the diagonals are congruent. *From: "Geometry" – McGraw Hill/Glencoe. (Gr. 10)*

• Both pairs of base angles are congruent.
• The base angles are of a trapezoid.
• It is an isosceles trapezoid.

• The diagonals are congruent.
• The diagonals are of the same trapezoid.

Figure 3H

Fact Sheet: Whales

are among the most intelligent animals
have no ears
use sound signals to communicate
use sound signals to navigate
are the largest living creatures
strain plankton from the seawater
are mammals
can sometimes be found in fresh water
have voices
may become extinct
have teeth
eat fish
have fishlike bodies
have paddle-shaped flippers
range in size from the porpoise to the blue whale
can hold their breath up to two hours
are insulated by a layer of blubber, or fat
are aquatic animals
have lungs, not gills
have horizontal tail fins, unlike fish
are different from fish
have thick, smooth skin
can dive to depths of 4,800 feet
do not see very well
range from 4 feet to 100 feet in length
are social animals
may weigh as much as 150 tons
cannot smell

have nose openings, or blow holes, atop their heads

are hunted for oils in their bodies

live in all of the world's oceans

At level	Students are able to
A	use five facts in no more than four sentences.
B	use ten facts in no more than six sentences.
C	use fifteen facts in no more than eight sentences.
D	use twenty facts in nor more than ten sentences.
E	use twenty-five facts in no more than twelve sentences.

From: "Creative Approaches to Sentence Combining" by William Strong. (1986).
ERIC Clearinghouse on Reading and Communication Skills. National Council of Teachers of English

Figure 3I

Introducing Sentence Combining to Students

adapted from Saddler, B. (2012). Teacher's Guide to Effective Sentence Writing. New York: Guilford Press.

Begin instruction with simple "kernel" sentences.

Examples:

British troops found fighting in America very challenging.
British troops were trained to fight wars in Europe.

Colonial soldiers would hide behind trees.
Colonial soldiers would fire at British troops.

Suggested wording to explain sentence combining to students (Saddler, p. 54-55):

"These sentences sound all right, but we can make them better. We are going to play with these sentences to make them sound better and more interesting. This play is called 'sentence combining.' When we practice combining sentences, we will do these things:

- **Combine** sentences together.
- **Change** words or parts of sentences.
- **Add** words or parts to the sentences.
- **Rearrange** words or parts of sentences.
- **Delete** words or parts of sentences.

Learning how to combine sentences in different ways will help you write more interesting sentences that sound better to readers. Good writers often play with their sentences to make them sound better, just as we are doing. One of the best parts about this activity is that there will usually be more than one solution to many of the practice problems."

This template is also available on Keys to Literacy's website:
http://www.keystoliteracy.com/resources/worksheets/

This template is also available on Keys to Literacy's website:
http://www.keystoliteracy.com/resources/worksheets/

REFLECTION FORM

Name: _____

Something I learned that squares with my beliefs:

A question(s) going around in my head:

Three points I will remember:

This template is also available on Keys to Literacy's website:
http://www.keystoliteracy.com/resources/worksheets/

NOTES:

Chapter 4: Basic Text Structures

Teaching students about text structure supports both writing and reading comprehension. Text structure is the arrangement of ideas and the relationships among the ideas; readers and writers who are familiar with text structure recognize how the information is unfolding (Snow, 2002; Akhondi et al, 2011). Common Core Reading Standard #5 addresses text structure.

As students advance into middle and high school, the text they are required to read and write is increasingly varied in style, vocabulary, text structure, purpose, and intended audience. Content teachers are often best suited to teach students about text structure, simply because they have a unique, expert understanding of how text is written in their discipline.

Authors use structural elements to organize information and ideas and to highlight important parts of the text. Structural elements can be organized into the two categories indicated in Figure 4A, *text features* and *text structures*.

Figure 4A

Structural Elements

Text Features	Text Structures
• title • headings and subheadings • graphics (charts, pictures, maps) • captions • table of contents • index • glossary	• type *(argument, informational, narrative)* • introduction, conclusion • transition words and phrases • patterns of organization: description, sequence, problem/solution, cause/effect, compare/contrast • sentence • paragraph

- **Text features,** such as title and headings, help identify the topic and overall organization of ideas. Headings represent topical sections of text, making it easier for readers to work their way through a longer piece of text in manageable "chunks." Graphics and captions highlight important details and present an alternative visual representation to supplement and support the textual representation.

- The ability to recognize the **type of writing** (i.e., argument, informational, narrative) and **genre** allows readers to access clues about how the text is organized and presented. Introductions and conclusions help readers determine the topic and purpose of the text.

- Although it is often overlooked, the use of **transition words and phrases** is an important structural element. Transitions make connections among sentences, paragraphs, and larger pieces of text.

- Recognition of specific **patterns of organization** (e.g., sequence, compare and contrast) also supports comprehension and retention of information (Akhondi et. al., 2011). Transition words and phrases often provide the reader with clues about patterns of text organization.

- Knowledge of **sentence and paragraph structure** enables writers to develop the individual ideas within sentences, also known as *propositions,* and combine them to develop the main ideas in paragraphs.

Three Types of Writing

The Common Core State Standards (CCSS) identify three major types of writing that students in all grades must learn to write: writing standards #1, #2, and #3. It is important for students to recognize the similarities and differences between argument, informational, and narrative writing, as well as to identify the most appropriate type for a writing assignment. Figure 4B briefly describes each writing type, followed by a graphic organizer that simplifies the purpose of each type. Grade-specific standards and sub-standards are provided in Figures 4L, 4M, and 4N at the end of this chapter.

Students must also learn that writing often incorporates a combination of these types, as noted in the Standards: "skilled writers many times use a blend of these three text types to accomplish their purposes." (2010, p. 24) For example, a newspaper editorial might begin with

> **Common Core Connection**
>
> **Writing Standard #1:** Write opinions/ arguments to support claims in an analysis of substantive topics or texts using valid reasoning and relevant and sufficient evidence.
>
> **Writing Standard #2:** Write informative/ explanatory texts to examine a topic and convey ideas and information clearly.
>
> **Writing Standard #3:** Write narratives to develop real or imagined experiences or events using effective technique, well-chosen details and well-structured event sequences.
>
> *Note: For grades 6-12, the narrative standard is only in ELA standards, although it is suggested that other subjects should try to include narrative writing assignments.*

informational writing to present the basic facts about a topic; it might then use narrative writing to recall a series of events; and finally, the author may make an argument by stating a claim (position) about the topic and providing reasons with evidence to support that claim.

Figure 4B

The Three Types of Text

> ### *Argument Writing*
>
> <u>What it does</u>: gives an opinion or makes an argument to convince the reader that a point of view is valid or to persuade the reader to take a specific action
>
> <u>Examples</u>: persuasive letters, editorials, argument essays, review of books or movies, claims about the worth or meaning of a literary work

Text Structure: organized around specific text components – claim, reason, evidence, counterclaim, rebuttal

Informational Writing

What it does: examines previously learned information or provides new information

Examples: textbook, article, letter, speech, instructions, manual, directions, subject area report, summary of information, workplace memo, job application, resume

Text Structure: organized into sections and sub-sections that include paragraph main ideas; tends to be organized hierarchically

Narrative Writing

What it does: tells a story (real or imagined) of an experience, event, or sequence of events

Examples: diary entry, biography, autobiography, personal narrative, memoir, folktale, fairy tale, fable, myth, creative fictional story, science fiction, poem, play, eyewitness account, plot summary, short story

Text Structure: organized around literary elements such as setting, characters, problem/solution

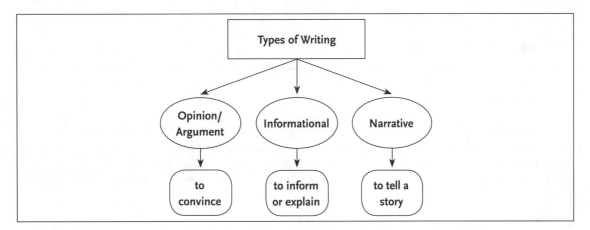

Activity

Identify Type of Writing

Directions: read each paragraph from the passage below. Then label if the paragraph is an example of informational, argument, or narrative writing.

I started to shake as I got towards the platform at the top of the tree. I put on my protection helmet, goggles, and gloves. Then my instructor helped strap me in to the harness. My heart started beating faster at that point! When my harness was clipped to the zip line pulley, I gasped. Suddenly the break was opened and I began to move faster and faster down the zip line, screaming all the way. It was over in less than two minutes, but it was the most thrilling experience I have ever had!

Writing Type: _____

A zip line consists of a pulley suspended on a cable, usually made of stainless steel, mounted on an incline. It is attached at either end to a trees or tall poles. A zip line is designed to enable a user to travel from the beginning of the line to the end, propelled by gravity. The user is attached to the free moving pulley. They come in many forms, and are often used as a means of entertainment. Longer zip lines are sometimes use as a means of accessing remote areas, such as a rainforest canopy. Zip line tours are popular vacation activities found at resorts or adventure camps. The world's biggest zip line was build by action sports athlete Mike Wilson in January, 2012.

Writing Type: _____

Are you afraid of trying a zip line? For the most part, zip line attractions are safe. Statistically, accidents by zip lines are very rare when compared to other types of accidents. Sports such as football and basketball have a higher probability of accidents. If you use an experienced zip line company that conducts regular inspections and mandatory maintenance, and provides safety gear such as a helmet, harness, gloves, goggles, and pads, the risk of getting hurt is minimal. While it is true that some accidents do occur, the majority of them are caused when zip lines are homemade.

Writing Type: _____

Suggested Distribution of Writing Types

The CCSS suggest that students in elementary grades spend equal time on each of the writing types (2010, p. 5). Furthermore, the standards emphasize that this be achieved by incorporating more informational and argument writing during science, social studies, and other content areas to balance out the common emphasis on narrative writing during English language arts.

However, a shift occurs between the middle school grades and high school. By high school, the CCSS suggest that student writing be 40% argument, 40% informational, and 20% narrative (2010, p. 5). The stronger focus on argument and informational writing is made particularly evident in the CCSS' treatment of writing standard #3, regarding narrative writing (see above): this standard is included only in the ELA standards for grades 6-12 and not in those for history, social studies, science, and technical subjects. For these subjects, the CCSS describes writing standard #3 as
"not applicable as a separate requirement" and provides this note:

> "Students' narrative skills continue to grow in these grades. The Standards require
> that students be able to incorporate narrative elements effectively into arguments
> and informative/explanatory texts. In history/social studies, students must be able to
> incorporate narrative accounts into their analyses of individuals or events of historical

import. In science and technical subjects, students must be able to write precise enough descriptions of the step-by-step procedures they use in their investigations or technical work that others can replicate them and (possibly) reach the same results." (2010, p. 65)

Across all grades, teachers of all subjects should find opportunities to note the differences among the types of writing in their content reading material. When the instructional practices from *Keys to Content Writing* are used across a school or district, students hear common terminology about text structures that promotes a consistent approach to writing. *The Glossary of Terms* at the end of this book provides a list of these common terms.

Introductions

The basic purpose of an introduction is to inform the reader about the topic of the writing. Note that the CCSS addresses introductions in the sub-standards for all three types of writing. Figure 4C presents introduction components for use in informational or argument writing. Students should consider the task, audience, and purpose of a writing assignment as they determine which of these components to include in an introduction.

Common Core Connection
Writing Standards #1a, 2a, 3a: Introduce topic, claim; orient the reader

Figure 4C

Introduction Components

topic	• an introduction of the topic must be included in an informational or argument piece • statement of claim (position) in an argument piece must be included in an introduction
nonfiction lead	• a lead captures the reader's interest; sometimes referred to as a hook that draws the reader in; there are several types of leads (see Figure 4D) • can be used in informational and argument writing
preview	• for informational writing: an overview of the central ideas that will follow in the body of the writing piece • for argument writing: an overview of the major reasons presented in the body to support the claim
background knowledge	• presentation of essential information that sets the stage for the writing piece • can be used in informational and argument writing
thesis statement	• succinct statement about what will be discussed in the writing piece – what will be explained or analyzed, the problem and solution to be addressed, or what you believe and what you intend to prove • most often used in argument writing, but can be used for informational writing

There are no precise rules about the "correct" length of an introduction. If the writing piece is relatively short (e.g., a half-page or less), then the introduction might be just a *single sentence*. If the writing piece is lengthy (e.g., a textbook chapter), the introduction might be *multiple paragraphs or pages*. Most informational or argument writing pieces written by students in grades 4-12 will require an introductory *paragraph* that includes the components in Figure 4C.

Nonfiction Leads

The purpose of a nonfiction lead, typically placed at the start of an introduction, is to get the reader of a piece interested enough to want to continue to read. There are many types of leads, and writers can combine several of them in the same introduction. Students must learn both to *use* a nonfiction lead as well as to select an appropriate type of lead based on the task, audience, and purpose of the writing assignment. Figure 4D lists common types of leads, along with some examples.

Figure 4D

Common Types of Nonfiction Leads

Pose a question

- *Have you ever wondered what makes expert skiers go so fast?*

- *How can deer defend themselves against predators?*

- *Did you know that the coffee you drink might be causing damage to the environment?*

Start with a quote

- *"The faster you ski, the less time you are in danger." So jokes the ski instructor!*

- *"Deer have an incredible knack for defending themselves," said the park ranger.*

- *The farmer in Central America now says, "I wish I had kept growing coffee the traditional way. By switching to high-yield coffee growing, I have destroyed my land."*

Present fascinating facts or details

- *Speed skiers regularly exceed 125 mph, which is even faster than the terminal velocity of a free-falling skydiver. In 2006, Simone Origone set the world record by skiing at 156 mph.*

- *A male deer's antlers can grow to be as wide as 16 inches, and a white-tailed deer can run as fast as 30 mph.*

- *The number of bird species in the rainforest has declined by at least 94%, and Central America has lost two-thirds of its rainforests.*

Provide an anecdote (a brief story)

- *It was a beautiful day in France on April 29, 2006. Simone Origone waited at the top of the ski slope. When the starting bell went off, he began the run that enabled him to break the world speed record for skiing.*

- *The baby deer heard the coyote approach. They were all alone. But the coyote walked by and did not realize they were there. They were camouflaged!*

- *It was 1963 at a Colombian coffee plantation. One of the laborers accidentally spilled a barrel of endosulfin, a powerful pesticide. That worker died from the poisonous substance, and 60 of his fellow laborers were injured.*

Describe a memorable image

- *The sky is blue, the air is crisp, and the sun glistens off the snow.*

- *A herd of deer was standing in the field. Suddenly, the adults stuck up their white tails and they all took off!*

- *It is the late eighteen hundreds and the rainforest is beautiful, full of birds, and has coffee plants growing in the shade next to trees. Fast-forward to the late 1900's, and all you see is open fields of coffee plants out in the blazing sun.*

Make the reader part of the piece

- *When you are going down a hill on skis, attempting to go as fast as possible, you will probably try to get your body into the lowest tuck possible. But wait – your position on skis isn't the only thing that makes you go fast.*

- *Have you ever been in trouble and wanted to get out of the way?*

- *The picture may seem familiar. Tumbling out of bed and stumbling around in the kitchen – you beginning your day. But wait, it cannot begin without that daily ritual, the morning cup of coffee.*

Activity

Analyze the Informational Introductions

Directions: Review each sample introduction from informational pieces written by students at various grades. Answer the questions for each introduction.

1. *Did the student successfully introduce the topic?*
2. *Did the student include a lead? Which type?*
3. *Did the student preview the subtopics?*
4. *Did the student include any background information?*

From the student examples:	intro the topic?	lead? type?	preview	back-ground?
Grade 4 Have you ever been in trouble and wanted to get away? The white-tailed deer can swim, run, hide, and fight to stay out of trouble. If you want to know how they do it, read on.				
Grade 8 When you are going down a hill on skis, attempting to go as fast as possible, you will probably try to get your body into the lowest tuck possible. But wait - your position on skis isn't the only thing that makes you go fast, and definitely not the most important. What really makes you go fast is the *camber* and *flex* of your skis, the *structure* of the ski base, and the *waxes* that you use.				
High School The picture may seem familiar. Tumbling out of bed and stumbling around in the kitchen—you begin your day. But wait. It cannot begin properly without that daily ritual, the morning cup of coffee. However, most people don't realize that much of today's coffee is grown in such a way that it damages the environment.				
More examples:	intro the topic?	lead? type?	preview	back-ground?
Grade 4 I would like to introduce you to someone who I admire, his name is Dr. Martin Luther King Jr. He was born on January 15, 1929. If you read the rest of this you will learn that Martin Luther King was a dreamer who was very determined.				
Grade 5 Yumm! A baked apple and you don't even have to run to the nearest restaurant to get a good one. All that you have to do is follow this easy to read recipe on how to make a baked apple. I know that you will love to have one of those wonderful baked apples that your great grandmother used to make. This will show you how to make one right at home.				
Grade 6 Can you imagine hearing the howl of a wolf during the night? A while ago you could hear howls in northern Wisconsin, but now you cannot. The wolf population was eliminated up through the 1950's. Ranchers and the federal government played major roles in eliminating wolves.				
Grade 7 More than any other state, Hawaii is world famous for its beauty and pleasant climate. This is probably why Hawaii, the "Aloha State," is one of the most popular tourist attractions in the world. Besides being a great place for tourists, Hawaii has over one million residents.				

Grade 8				
Captain Kirk of the USS Enterprise beams you aboard. As your molecules come back together, he gives you a tour of the spotless flight deck. It's filled with clean crew members working on equipment that's all in perfect shape. That's TV. The Russian Mir space station is reality, and life there isn't glamorous. Astronauts have to face many struggles while on board *Mir*.				

Activity

Analyze the Argument Introductions

<u>Directions</u>: *Review each sample introduction from argument pieces written by students at various grades. Answer the questions for each introduction.*

1. *Did the student successfully introduce the topic?*
2. *Did the student state the claim?*
3. *Did the student include a lead? Which type?*
4. *Did the student preview the counterclaim?*
5. *Did the student include any background information?*

From the student examples:	intro the topic?	claim?	lead? type?	counter claim?	back-ground?
Grade 5 Even though zoos aren't a perfect solution, we should support zoos because they help protect endangered animals. Sometimes animals are in trouble in the wild. They don't have enough to eat, or they are endangered.					
Grade 6 Think about how much electricity you use every day. Your alarm clock, your radio, your computer, and the lights in your home and at school all use electricity. Now think of all the other people in your community, in your state, and in the country who use as much electricity, if not more. The problem is the process that provides most of this electricity damages the environment. We need to devote more time, energy, and money to develop geothermal energy because it is renewable and a less harmful source of energy.					
Grade 10 Could there really be something schools can serve for lunch that tastes good and is healthy at the same time? Schools should serve chocolate milk. Many kids love it and are happy to see it in their cafeteria. Research shows that, overall, chocolate milk is pretty good for kids.					

More examples:	intro the topic?	claim?	lead? type?	counter claim?	back-ground?
Grade 4 Dear (Principal), My teacher said you are thinking about giving the kids in the early grades only one recess. Please don't do this. We should keep two recesses a day for K-3 students in our school.					
Grade 7 Like Diego, many illegal immigrants come to America every day for a better life and a better education. Whether these illegal immigrants should get the education they came for is very controversial in today's economy. Some Americans think that illegal immigrants shouldn't be eligible for instate tuition, but other Americans think that these illegal immigrants should be eligible for instate tuition. I am one who thinks the illegal immigrants should be eligible for instate tuition.					
Grade 9 John Boyne's story, *The Boy in the Striped Pajamas*, tells the tale of an incredible friendship between two eight-year old boys during the Holocaust. One of the boys is Bruno, the son of an important German commander who is put in charge of Auschwitz Camp, and the other is Shmuel, a Jewish boy inside the camp. Throughout the story their forbidden friendship grows, and the two boys unknowingly break the incredible racial boundaries of the time. They remain best friends until Bruno goes under the fence to help Shmuel find his father when they are both killed in the gas showers of the camp. By comparing and contrasting supporting characters, irony, and the themes in the movie and the book, it is clear that the movie, The Boy in the Striped Pajamas (Mark Herman, 2008) is not nearly as good as the novel of the same title.					
Grade 12 Have you ever wondered why so many students at (name of school) are sluggish and lethargic? Are they just lazy and unmotivated? No, most of them probably suffer from lack of sleep, caused by biological clocks that are set to a different schedule than their classes. Teenagers have a physiological need to stay up later and sleep longer than pre-adolescents, yet the daily schedule of the school runs oblivious to this.					

Conclusions

The purpose of a conclusion is to close a writing piece by wrapping up the important information. It enables the writer to emphasize important information and share any necessary final remarks about the topic. It is also the final opportunity to make an impression on the reader. As with introductions, CCSS addresses conclusions in the sub-standards for all three types of writing.

> **Common Core Connection**
>
> **Writing Standards #1d & 1e, 2e & 2f, 3e:** Provide a concluding statement or section

The conclusion lends both closure and structure by referring back to what has already been said. Naturally, a conclusion's length depends on the length of the writing task itself – it can be as short as a *single sentence,* a *paragraph,* or it can be *a longer section.* Again, students should consider the task, audience, and purpose of a writing assignment to determine an appropriate conclusion.

The Three Main Goals of a Conclusion

- **Rephrase the main topic (informational writing) or claim/position (argument writing) presented in the introduction.**
    - *Do* use different words and phrasing.
    - *Don't* just repeat the same introductory statement.
    - *Don't* begin with obvious transitions, such as "in conclusion" or "to sum up," which can make the writing choppy or awkward.
    - *Don't* wait to introduce the topic or a claim until the conclusion.

- **Summarize key main ideas (informational writing) or reasons (argument writing).**
    - *Do* recap and synthesize the main points that were in the body.
    - *Do* show how the main points fit together.
    - *Do* keep it short.
    - *Don't* focus on just one part of the body.
    - *Don't* repeat sentences from the body word-for-word.
    - *Don't* restate a lot of details.
    - *Don't* introduce new ideas.

- **Leave the reader with a sense of closure, an interesting final impression, or a call to action (argument writing).**
    - *Do* add something that the reader will remember.
    - *Do* pose a question, describe a powerful or vivid image, call for action, explain why a topic is important, or use a compelling quotation related to the topic.

Activity

Analyze the Informational Conclusions

Directions: Review each sample conclusion from informational pieces written by students at various grades. Answer the questions for each conclusion.

1. *Does the writer rephrase the main topic?*
2. *Does the writer summarize the key main ideas?*
3. *Does the writer leave the reader with a sense of closure or interesting final impression?*

From the student examples:	rephrase topic	summarize main ideas	closure, impression
Grade 8 As you have seen, there are many contributing factors to how fast you glide on cross-country skis. The flex, structure, wax, and body position all depend on each other to work properly to make you go fast. A ski that is right for your body weight, a good combination of linear and cross structure, and the right wax for the snow temperature will ensure that you go as fast as possible down the hill.			
Grade 4 Deer stay safe by hiding, swimming, running, and fighting. Whenever you see a deer raise its tail, you know that it has seen a predator.			
High School The switch from traditional coffee growing in shaded rainforests to growing coffee that requires full sun has had an impact on the environment. Farmers have adopted full-sun coffee crops because they yield more beans, but the result has been a loss of rainforest, a decrease in bird numbers, and the need to use more harmful pesticides.			
More examples:	rephrase topic	summarize main ideas	closure, impression
Grade 5 This recipe will help you make your very own baked apple. The time that I made one we had a good time, but we forgot to turn on the timer so it was a little bit burned. It still tasted good!			
Grade 7 Despite the problems of transportation and increased tourism, Hawaii is still a great place to visit or live because of the warm climate and the beauty of the islands. There are so many things to do and see on this group of islands. Every American should visit Hawaii at least once in his or her life.			
Grade 8 Even though life on Mir isn't glamorous and equipment often fails, the Mir astronauts have had lots of success. Like the pioneers, they have found many useful things that help explorers who follow them. But maybe Mir's greatest success is that astronauts from Russia and the U.S., two old enemies, have worked together as friends.			
Grade 10 When you walk into Versailles it is truly an amazing sight. The impact of the palace stays with you for a long time. That is exactly the impact that Louis XIV had on France and then the world. Louis worked hard to make Versailles just as glorious as he was, and it worked. Versailles truly is the grand symbol of the greatness of Louis XIV's reign.			

Activity

Analyze the Argument Conclusions

<u>*Directions*</u>*: Review each sample conclusion from argument pieces written by students at various grades. Answer the following questions for each conclusion in the respective columns to the right.*

1. *Does the writer restate the claim?*
2. *Does the writer summarize the reasons?*
3. *Does the writer leave the reader with a sense of closure, interesting final impression, or call to action?*

From the student examples:	rephrase topic	summarize main ideas	closure, impression
Grade 5 **CLAIM:** Even though zoos aren't a perfect solution, we should support zoos because they help protect endangered animals. **CONCLUSION:** Overall, it seems like zoos are a good idea, as long as they take care of the animals. They can rescue endangered animals, and they can breed them so they won't be so endangered. It would be even better if we could stop destroying their land. But since we're not endangered, that's probably not going to happen.			
Grade 6 **CLAIM:** We need to devote more time, energy, and money to develop geothermal energy because it is renewable and a less harmful source of energy. **CONCLUSION:** Geothermal energy hasn't beaten fossil fuels in any popularity contests yet, but scientists are hopeful that it may one day be a workable substitute to nonrenewable energy sources. The sooner we start exploring how to take advantage of it, the better it will be for our environment and our future.			
Grade 10 **CLAIM:** Could there really be something schools can serve for lunch that tastes good and is healthy at the same time? Schools should serve chocolate milk. Many kids love it and are happy to see it in their cafeteria. Research shows that, overall, chocolate milk is pretty good for kids. **CONCLUSION:** Two government programs, the National Institute of Child Health and Human Development's Milk Matters and the U.S. Department of Health and Human Services' Best Bones Forever, recommend low-fat and fat-free flavored milk as a good option for children. So let's keep serving chocolate milk in schools. It's a good source of vitamins and calcium and kids really like it!			

More examples:	rephrase topic	summarize main ideas	closure, impression
Grade 4 _CLAIM:_ We should keep two recesses a day for K-3 students in our school. _CONCLUSION:_ The students in grades K-3 need two recesses every day so they will get enough exercise to stay in shape and burn off calories from snack and lunch so they don't get overweight. They also need to give their brains a break from thinking. I hope you will agree to keep both recesses. Sincerely, (name)			
Grade 7 _CLAIM:_ Some Americans think that illegal immigrants shouldn't be eligible for instate tuition, but other Americans think that these illegal immigrants should be eligible for instate tuition. I am one who thinks the illegal immigrants should be eligible for instate tuition. _CONCLUSION:_ In conclusion, illegal immigrants should be eligible for instate tuition so, like Diego, they can follow their dreams. If you have to take a side on this issue, I hope you will consider mine.			
Grade 9 _CLAIM:_ By comparing and contrasting supporting characters, irony, and the themes in the movie and the book, it is clear that the movie, _The Boy in the Striped Pajamas_ (Mark Herman, 2008) is not nearly as good as the novel of the same title. _CONCLUSION:_ Based on the analysis of supporting characters, irony, and themes of John Boyne's _The Boy in the Striped Pajamas_ and the movie, it can be concluded that the book is far superior to the movie. Though Bruno's mother is a dishonest woman in the book, her bad character is more realistic for the time when compared to the mother in the movie who is horrified by Auschwitz. John Boyne uses many examples of irony in the book to emphasize Bruno's innocence and to magnify the tragedy of his death. Unlike the movie the irony in the book leads the reader to ponder on the barbarity of the German leaders during the Holocaust. The book's theme of long lasting friendship gives purpose to the story, while the movie's theme of the cruelty of concentration camps does not lead the viewer to delve deeper into the story. It is necessary for the person to read this book in order to understand the true message of friendship and cooperation in the story, a message that a person who had only seen the movie could not even begin to grasp.			

<table>
<tr><td>

Grade 12

    <u>**CLAIM:**</u> Teenagers have a physiological need to stay up later and sleep longer than pre-adolescents, yet the daily schedule of the school runs oblivious to this.

    <u>**CONCLUSION:**</u> Moving _____'s start back an hour would be beneficial to the school. Students would be healthier and do better academically, and, as surprising as it seems, there would be no major drawbacks. Administrators should ask themselves why this isn't happening already.

</td><td></td><td></td><td></td></tr>
</table>

Body Organization and Development

When students write the body of an informational or argument piece, they translate ideas and information into sentences and paragraphs. The CCSS includes body development sub-standards for both argument and informational writing. As always, students should consider the task, audience, and purpose of a writing assignment as they determine how best to develop the body.

Organization of the Body

During the THINK stage of the writing process, students acquire or access background knowledge about the subject, gather information from sources, and develop ideas for an informational or argument piece. During the PLAN stage, students begin to make decisions about the writing's organization and development of ideas. This includes determining how text structures will be used (e.g., introduction, conclusion, sections) and how text features will be used to support those structures (e.g., title, headings).

> **Common Core Connection**
>
> **Writing Standard #1a:** organize and logically sequence reasons, evidence, counterclaim
>
> **Writing Standard #2a:** group related information in paragraphs and sections, include formatting; organize ideas, concepts, and information into broader categories

For informational writing, the body is where students develop the topic, subtopics, and main ideas using facts and details, definitions, quotations, information, and examples. The writer makes decisions about grouping the information into sections and sub-sections as well as the order in which to present topics.

For argument writing, the body is where students develop a claim with clear reasons. It is also where they provide the evidence to support each reason (i.e., facts, statistics, quotations, examples, observations, anecdotes, comparisons, surveys, expert opinion). Students may also present a counterclaim and then a rebuttal, using evidence to refute the counterclaim. The writer makes decisions about how best to present evidence to support reasons, the order in which to present these reasons, and where to include a counterclaim and rebuttal.

Transitions

Transition words and phrases are useful for connecting sentences, paragraphs, or sections in a writing piece. The CCSS also refer to transitions as *linking words,* and they include sub-standards for transitions for both argument and informational writing.

For argument writing in middle and high school, students should use transitions to create cohesion and clarify the relationships among claims, reasons, and evidence for argument writing. For informational writing in these grades, transitions should be used to create cohesion, link major sections, and clarify the relationships among ideas and concepts. Some writers include transitions as they are writing a first draft, but they may also add transitions after the first draft.

Struggling writers are often not adept at using transition words. Many students benefit from access to a list of transitions when they are writing; see Figure 4E. Teachers should consider making these accessible to students either as classroom posters or by distributing handouts. It is imperative to model good writing that incorporates varied transition words and phrases so that students eventually move beyond using basic transitions (i.e., *first, then, next*).

Figure 4E

Transition Words and Phrases

To indicate a time relationship	after, afterward, after that, at first, at this time, before, beginning with, beyond, during, earlier, ending with, eventually, finally, following, from then on, in the meantime, last, later, meanwhile, next, now, since, soon, then, until, while
To indicate spatial placement	below, beside, between, beyond, farther on, here, next to, parallel with
To list or present a series of ideas	after, after that, finally, first, lastly, next, second, third
To add information or continue a line of thought	also, another, besides, further, furthermore, in addition, likewise, moreover, similarly
To summarize or show conclusion	accordingly, finally, in conclusion, in other words, in short, to conclude, to sum up, to summarize
To show comparison	by comparison, compared to, in like manner, likewise, similarly
To show contrast	although, but, however, in contrast, nevertheless, on the contrary, on the other hand, unlike
To repeat or stress a point	above all, in fact, in other words, most important, once again, to repeat
To provide an example or illustrate a point	for example, for instance, such as, to illustrate, that is
To show cause and effect	as a result, because, because of, caused by, consequently, for that reason, that is why, therefore, thus
To state the obvious	certainly, granted that, in fact, most certainly, naturally, obviously, of course, surely, undoubtedly, without a doubt

This template is also available on Keys to Literacy's website:
http://www.keystoliteracy.com/resources/worksheets/

Patterns of Organization

Expository text typically incorporates five common patterns of organization (Shanahan et. al., 2010), and transition words often signal the use of these patterns. See Figure 4F. These patterns of organization are sometimes referred to as text structures, and they are more frequently used in informational and argument text types. The CCSS focus on patterns of organization specifically in the sub-standards for grades 6 and 7. Although a passage may contain just one pattern of organization, text typically incorporates more than one pattern. It is not unusual for one paragraph to follow one pattern (e.g., description) and another paragraph to follow a different pattern (e.g., compare and contrast). Sometimes a single paragraph may use more than one pattern.

> **Common Core Connection**
>
> **Writing Standard #2a, grades 6 & 7:** organize ideas, concepts, and information using strategies such as definition, classification, comparison/contrast, and cause/effect

Some transition words and phrases are associated with certain patterns of organization. When students recognize that transitions provide clues to meaning, they are more likely to recognize a pattern of organization while reading.

Figure 4F

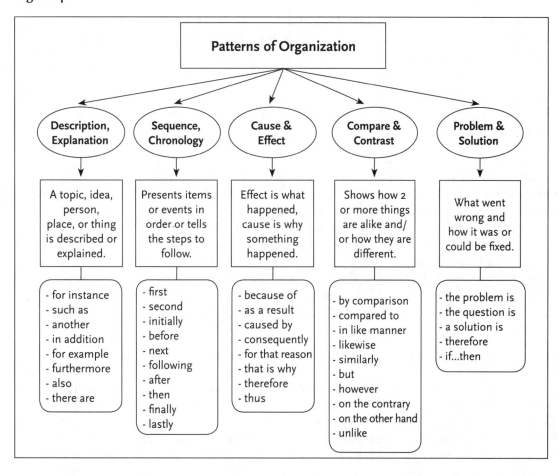

Activity

Patterns of Organization

Directions: *Read each paragraph and identify the pattern(s) of organization: description/ explanation, sequence/chronology, cause and effect, compare and contrast, problem and solution.*

From Grade 5 Student Sample:

When the deer see, smell, or hear something suspicious, they stick their white tails up to signal that danger is near. This causes the lead deer to start to run. The result is that all the other deer follow and avoid trouble.

Pattern(s) of Organization: _____

When a deer is chased to water, it knows what to do. The deer will win this battle. First the deer runs into the water and swims to the deepest part. Next, if the predator tries to follow in the water the deer will kick and thrash. Finally the predator either drowns or swims off wounded.

Pattern(s) of Organization: _____

There is one more way that deer stay out of trouble. Bucks fight with weapons called antlers. These are different from horns because they are attached to the skull, and horns are not. Antlers are made of bone and have vitamins in them. The deer can use its antlers to protect itself.

Pattern(s) of Organization: _____

From Grade 6 Student Sample:

The most important advantage of geothermal energy is that it doesn't produce pollution or contribute to the greenhouse effect. Geothermal plants are almost entirely emission free. The U.S. Department of Energy states that more than 50% of the electricity used in the United States comes from coal. Coal is known to release harmful gasses, such as carbon dioxide, that contribute to pollution. The result is that every time half the households in the country flip a light switch a little bit more pollution leaks into the air. Studies conducted by scientists at the U.S. Department of Energy point that geothermal power plants produce less than 1% of the carbon dioxide released by power plants relying on fossil fuels, such as coal. This fact means that when more and more power plants switch to geothermal energy instead of burning coal, the air in our country will greatly improve.

Pattern(s) of Organization: _____

Some people would argue that taking advantage of geothermal energy is expensive because of the cost of building power plants. But let's take a closer look. Technological changes have been made to make it easier to drill wells that can reach into geothermal pools. Iceland already generates more than 25 percent of its energy from geothermal. The more geothermal energy is used the lower the price will become to build. The chart shows that geothermal is the lowest cost of all heating fuels. It is true that the first costs for building geothermal plants is high, but lifetime costs of geothermal operations are smaller than other kinds of energy. Also the U.S. government has offered tax credits for individuals who use the technology in their homes.

Pattern(s) of Organization: _____

<u>From Grade 8 Student Sample</u>:

    The ski is not flat. There is a bend in the ski that creates an arch, and if you put a ski flat on the ground without any weight on it, there will be a space under the middle of the ski. This bend is called *camber*. The camber flexes and distributes most of your weight on the ski to the tips and tails and leaves a little space under the ski where your foot is. If there were not camber, or too little camber, your weight would push the middle of the ski flat to the ground, creating more friction and making you go slower.

This is why having the right type of ski for your weight is very important. If the ski is just right, meaning the right amount of space under you ski is in the right place, then you will go fast.

Pattern(s) of Organization: _____

<u>From High School Student Sample</u>:

    Americans lead the world in coffee drinking, consuming an average of 3-4 cups per person per day. All this coffee has to be imported because it can only grow in the tropics such as in Mexico, Central and Latin America, Indonesia, and Africa. In addition, coffee fields must be at an altitude between 3000 and 5000 feet with a temperature between 65 and 70 degrees Fahrenheit. Furthermore, for optimum growth, coffee must have shade from nearby trees and overhead growth, but it also requires at least two hours of sunlight each day. These are the only requirements for coffee to grow well.

Pattern(s) of Organization: _____

    However, this took a turn in 1970 when U.S. agricultural scientists decided to develop a new, high-yield coffee plant that grew only in the full sun. At first, farmers were easily convinced to adapt to this modernization because they could produce five times more coffee than before. For that reason, they cut down rainforests to plant the new coffee crops. As a result, over the past 40 years, Central America has lost two-thirds of its rainforests to coffee plantations at a rate of 40 million acres per year. That figure is similar to Mexico. The effect is that these modern coffee plantations are mono-cultural; nothing can grow in the fields besides the stubby coffee bushes. According to Elizabeth Skinner, a director of the Rainforest Alliance, these modern plantations "create ecological deserts" that are growing at an alarming rate.

Pattern(s) of Organization: _____

The Structure of a Five-Paragraph Essay

A classic format for school writing assignments is the five-paragraph essay. The format requires one introductory paragraph, three body paragraphs, and one concluding paragraph. Essays are not limited to five paragraphs, but this format has been a traditional way to teach and reinforce these basic text structures. Figure 4G illustrates the five-paragraph essay structure.

The five-paragraph essay structure is helpful in that it reminds students to include an introduction and conclusion. However, it has limitations for other writing assignments that follow a different form (e.g., letter, brochure, response to a blog post) or that may require more or fewer than three body paragraphs to "get the job done." Striving to adhere to this rigid five-paragraph format for all formal writing may constrain or frustrate students.

As you will see in Chapter 9, it is best to suggest a range for the number of paragraphs you require of student writing and to base that range on content and text structure requirements.

Figure 4G

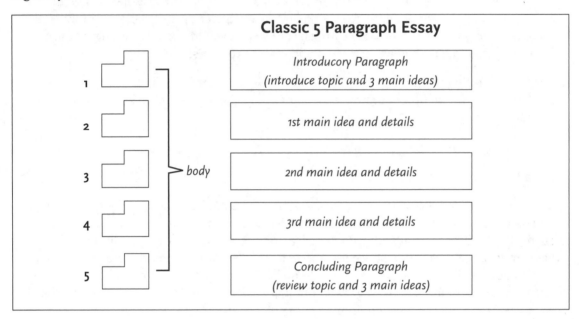

Analyzing Text Structure

Deconstructing and Constructing Text

While we read, the ability to deconstruct the author's building of the text supports our comprehension. Deconstructing a piece of sample text also teaches us how to *construct* text that we ourselves write. Figure 4H suggests some important questions for readers and writers to consider as they deconstruct and construct text.

Figure 4H

Deconstructing Text

- How did the author assemble the basic text structures (introduction, conclusion, body)?
- For informational text, did the author organize information paragraphs into topics and subtopics?
- For argument text, how did the author organize the reason, counterclaim, and rebuttal paragraphs?
- Did the author use transition words and phrases to make links and clarify?
- Did the author use text features (title, headings, sub-headings) to support the structure of the text?

Constructing Text

- What should I include in my introduction and conclusion?

- For informational text, what is the best way to organize my information into topics and subtopics?

- For argument text, what is the best way to organize my reasons, evidence, counterclaim, and rebuttal?

- How can I use transition words and phrases to make links and clarify?

- How can I use text features (title, headings, sub-headings) to support the structure of the text?

Writing Component Cards: Visual Representation of Text

Keys to Content Writing provides a set of writing component cards for use in teaching students about argument and informational text elements. The cards, representing both text features and text structures, can be arranged on a wall or bulletin board to build a top-down topic web that represents a *deconstructed* piece of sample text, or to represent the plan for *constructing* a piece of text. Figure 4I illustrates the writing component cards and provides some guidance for you to make your own classroom set. During training for *Keys to Content Writing*, a trainer will demonstrate how the cards can be used.

Figure 4I

Writing Component Cards

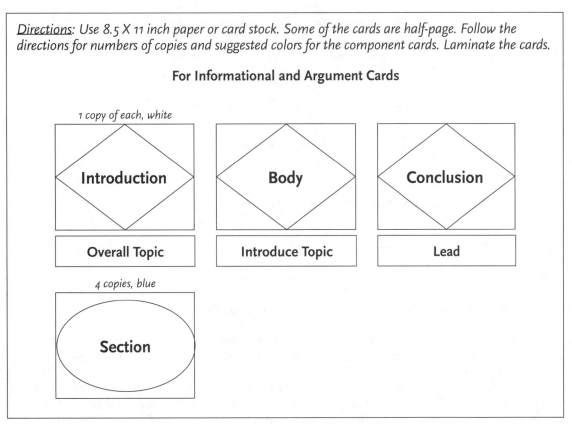

Directions: Use 8.5 X 11 inch paper or card stock. Some of the cards are half-page. Follow the directions for numbers of copies and suggested colors for the component cards. Laminate the cards.

For Informational and Argument Cards

1 copy of each, white

| Introduction | Body | Conclusion |

| Overall Topic | Introduce Topic | Lead |

4 copies, blue

Section

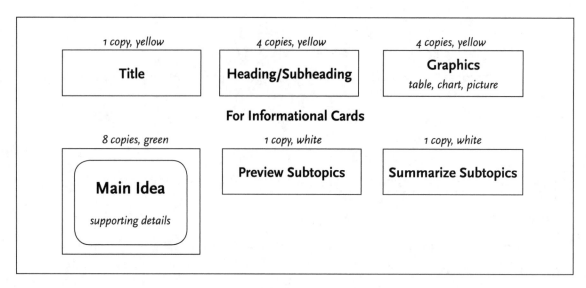

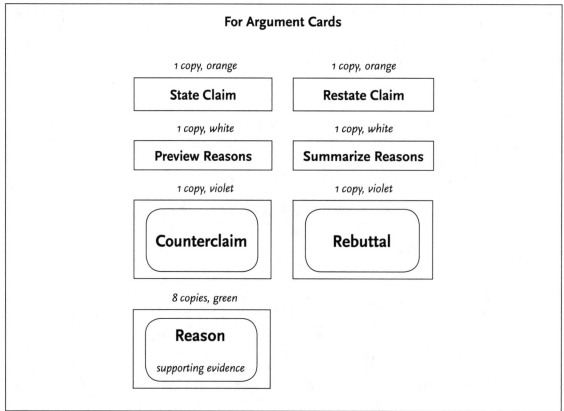

Using Writing Component Cards to Visualize Informational Text

The purpose of informational writing, also called *explanatory* or *expository* writing, is to convey information accurately. The CCSS describe informational writing as follows:

> "This kind of writing serves one or more closely related purposes: to increase readers' knowledge of a subject, to help readers better understand a procedure or process, or to provide readers with enhanced comprehension of a concept... To produce this kind

of writing, students can draw from what they already know and from primary and secondary sources. With practice, students become better able to develop a controlling idea and a coherent focus on a topic and more skilled at selecting and incorporating relevant examples, facts, and details into their writing." (p. 23)

The CCSS explain informational writing techniques and provide examples of content-specific writing genres that incorporate informational writing:

"Informational/explanatory writing includes a wide array of genres, including academic genres such as literary analysis, scientific and historical reports, summaries, and précis writing, as well as forms of workplace and functional writing such as instructions, manuals, memos, reports, applications, and resumes. As students advance through the grades, they expand their repertoire of informational/explanatory genres and use them effectively in a variety of disciplines and domains." (p. 23)

Figure 4J depicts the introduction, body, and conclusion for three informational texts. The first top-down topic web represents a short text (four body paragraphs); the second represents a medium-length piece (seven body paragraphs); and the third represents a longer piece (14 body paragraphs). Consider arranging the writing component cards to resemble these topic webs.

Figure 4J

Informational Text

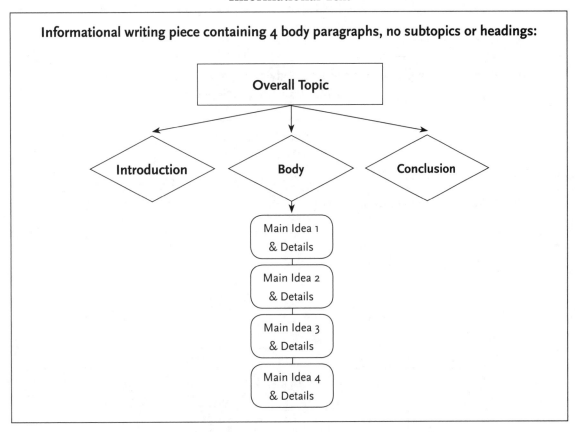

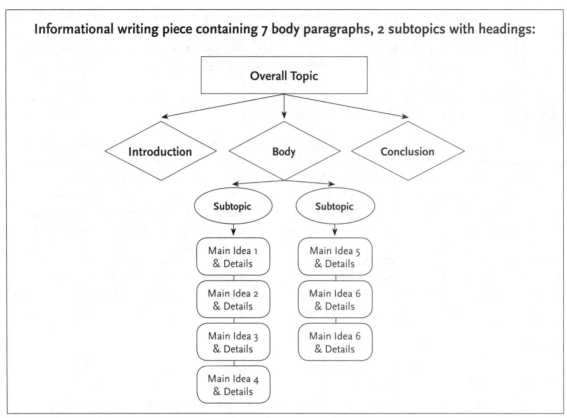

Informational writing piece containing 7 body paragraphs, 2 subtopics with headings:

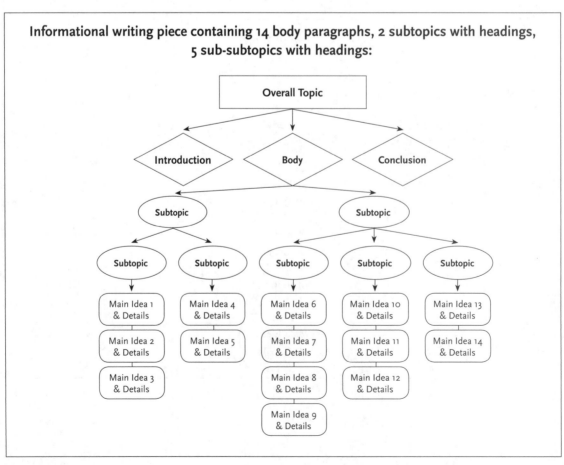

Informational writing piece containing 14 body paragraphs, 2 subtopics with headings, 5 sub-subtopics with headings:

Using Writing Component Cards to Visualize Argument Text

The CCSS identifies argument writing as *opinion* through grade five, and *argument* for grades 6 and up. There is a strong emphasis on argument writing, as noted in Appendix A (2010):

> "While all three text types are important, the Standards put particular emphasis on students' ability to write sound arguments on substantive topics and issues, as this ability is critical to college and career readiness." (p. 24)

Argument writing has several purposes:

- To change the reader's point of view
- To bring about some action
- To persuade the reader to accept the writer's explanation or evaluation of a concept, issue, or problem

An argument, or opinion, is a reasoned, logical way of demonstrating that the writer's position, belief, or conclusion is valid. For some students, the term *argument* connotes controversy or conflict (i.e., fighting). Therefore, it is important to emphasize that *argument* as a formal type of writing is actually unemotional and that topics for argument writing are not necessarily controversial.

Several text components are unique to argument writing:

- Claim: the position taken by the writer; what the writer is trying to *prove* or *argue*
  What *do I think?*

- Reason: provided to support a claim; reasons are supported by evidence
  Why *do I think it?*

- Evidence: used to support or prove a reason; statistics, facts, quotations, surveys, etc.
  How *do I know? What proof do I have?*

- Counterclaim: opposing position, counterargument
  What *is the "other side" to this argument? What is the opposite of my claim?*

- Rebuttal: refutes or disproves the counterclaim; addresses the criticism of the claim
  What *is my response to the "other side"?*

Figure 4K depicts the introduction, body, and conclusion for two argument texts. The first top-down topic web represents a piece that states the claim in the introduction and provides two reasons with evidence in the body to support the claim. The second web presents the claim in the introduction, provides three reasons with evidence in the body, and also includes the counterclaim and a rebuttal in the body. Consider arranging the writing component cards to resemble these topic webs.

Figure 4K

Argument Text

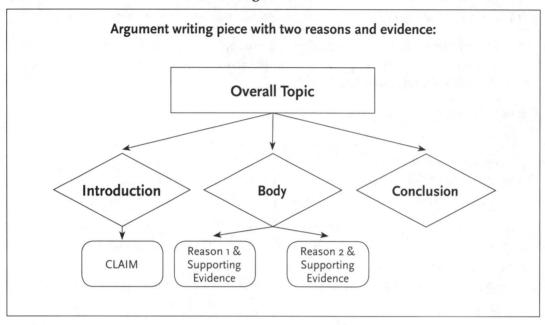

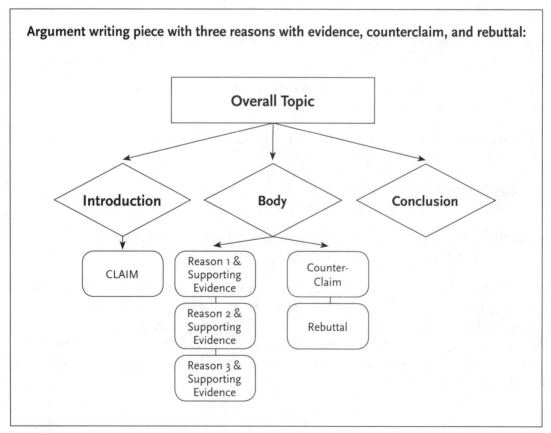

What is the Difference Between Informational and Argument Writing?

Information, often from externally identified sources, is used in both types of writing. However, these two types of writing have fundamentally different purposes: Informational writing presents all relevant information and seeks to inform others in order to help them better understand the topic, whereas argument writing presents some of the information in an attempt to persuade others to accept a position about a debatable topic. Appendix A of the CCSS explains the distinction as follows:

> "Although information is provided in both arguments and explanations, the two types of writing have different aims. Arguments seek to make people believe that something is true or to persuade people to change their beliefs or behavior. Explanations, on the other hand, start with the assumption of truthfulness and answer questions about why or how. Their aim is to make the reader understand rather than to persuade him or her to accept a certain point of view. In short, arguments are used for persuasion and explanations for clarification. Like arguments, explanations provide information about causes, contexts, and consequences of processes, phenomena, states of affairs, objects, terminology, and so on. However, in an argument, the writer not only gives information but also presents a case with the "pros" (supporting ideas) and "cons" (opposing ideas) on a debatable issue. Because an argument deals with whether the main claim is true, it demands empirical descriptive evidence, statistics, or definitions for support. When writing an argument, the writer supports his or her claim(s) with sound reasoning and relevant and sufficient evidence." (p. 23)

What is the Difference Between Persuasive and Argument Writing?

Persuasive and opinion/argument writing are similar in that they both try to convince a reader. Their main difference is the way the writer accomplishes this.

In **persuasive writing**, the writer assumes a personal position about the topic and tries to persuade the reader to agree.

- appeals to the reader's emotions or self-interest
- may include:
  - emotional language, or words that make the writer feel sad, angry, upset, guilty
  - exaggeration, using language that represents information more positively or negatively than reality
  - rhetorical questions not requiring an answer but meant to incite strong reactions

In **opinion/argument writing**, the writer demonstrates a valid, logical, objective argument, without regard for the reader's intention to adopt the same position.

- writer convinces the reader with the merit and soundness of his claim and evidence
- tends to be a more formal style of writing

Activity

Analyze An Informational Writing Sample

Part 1

Directions: Using the student informational writing sample selected by your trainer from the end of this chapter, follow the directions and answer the questions.

1. Bracket the introduction. Did the student clearly identify the topic?

_____

_____

_____

2. Review the body. How is it organized? Are there sections with headings? Are text features included, and do they support comprehension?

_____

_____

3. Bracket the conclusion. Did the student provide closure and sum up the topic or message?

_____

_____

_____

Part 2

Directions: Use the space below to develop a top-down topic web that represents the structure of an informational writing piece. Use the shapes represented on the writing component cards.

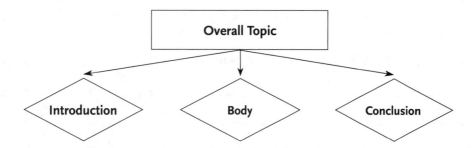

Activity

Analyze An Argument Writing Sample

Part 1

Directions: *Using the student argument writing sample selected by your trainer from the end of this chapter, follow the directions and answer the questions.*

1. Bracket the introduction. Did the student clearly identify the topic and state the claim?

_____

_____

2. Review the body. Place an **R** next to each reason. If there is a counterclaim, write **CC** next to it. If there is a rebuttal, write **RB** next to it. Are text features included, and do they support comprehension?

_____

_____

Bracket the conclusion. Did the student provide closure and sum up the topic or message?

_____

_____

_____

Part 2

Directions: Use the space below to develop a top-down topic web that represents the structure of an argument writing piece. Use the shapes represented on the writing component cards.

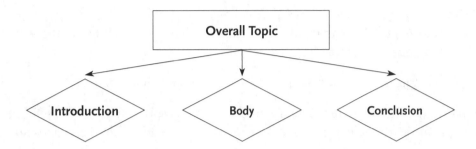

Sentences and Paragraphs

One by one, sentences communicate ideas that combine to make meaning. Sentences related to the same main idea are then grouped into paragraphs. There are two basic types of sentences in a paragraph:

- Topic sentence: states the main idea of a paragraph; located in the beginning, middle, or end of a paragraph; some paragraphs do not include a topic sentence, and the main idea must be inferred

- Supporting sentence: contains details that support the main idea

In written text, the shift from one paragraph to another is represented visually either by an indentation at the start of a new paragraph or a double-spaced line between paragraphs.

Many students in grades 4-12 who struggle to write do so because they have difficulty with basic sentence and paragraph skills. *Syntax* refers to the system and arrangement of words, phrases, and clauses that make up a sentence (i.e., rules of grammar). *Syntactic awareness* refers to familiarity with the rules of grammar in order to grasp the meaning that comes from the interrelations between words in sentences. In the primary grades (K-3), the syntax of most sentences that students read is relatively simple, as are the sentences they write, typically with just one subject and one predicate. However, after grade 4, the sentences in classroom reading material become longer and more complex, and they are expected to write more interesting, longer, complex sentences.

> **Common Core Connection**
>
> **Language Standard #1:** Demonstrate command of the conventions of standard English grammar and usage when writing and speaking.
>
> **Language Standard #2:** Demonstrate command of the conventions of standard English capitalization, punctuation, and spelling when writing.

Efficient processing of sentence structure and good syntactic awareness are necessary for successful reading comprehension and writing. Common Core Language Standards #1 and #2 are related to sentence-writing skills.

Because *Keys to Content Writing* is focused on the use of writing as a learning strategy, this book and the associated professional development program do not emphasize instructional practices for teaching sentence and paragraph skills. However, Chapter 3 provides some guidance about the use of sentence combining activities as *quick write* assignments to develop strong sentence-writing skills.

As with any other skill, another effective strategy to teach students to write longer, more complex sentences is to provide models of these types of sentences. See Chapter 6 for more on the use of models and mentor text.

Informational Student Writing Samples

Grade 4   **Deer Don't Need To Flee To Stay Trouble-Free!**

(1)   Have you ever been in trouble and wanted to get away? The white-tailed deer can swim, run, hide, and fight to stay out of trouble. If you want to know how they do it, read on.

(2)   In early April, fawns (baby deer) are born. After a few weeks, the doe (the mother deer) leaves her fawns to find food. The doe leaves her fawns in a bushy place. The trees and grass can help keep the fawns from being seen by hungry predators. The white-tailed deer has many predators, such as bobcats, dogs, bears, coyotes, wolves, and even humans. Hiding fawns keeps them out of trouble with predators.

(3)   The fawns' camouflage hides them in different seasons. In spring, the fawns' fur is brown with white spots that help them blend in with the new grass and leaves. In summer, the fawns' white spots disappear and never come back. In winter, their fur is gray, which helps them hide in the snow.

(4)   When the deer see, smell, or hear something suspicious, they stick their white tails up to signal that danger is near. This causes the lead deer to start to run. The result is that all the other deer follow and avoid trouble.

(5)   When a deer is chased to water, it knows what to do. The deer will win this battle. First the deer runs into the water and swims to the deepest part. Next, if the predator tries to follow in the water the deer will kick and thrash. Finally the predator either drowns or swims off wounded.

(6) If a deer is in a wide-open field and notices a predator, it will run zigzag to get away. It runs zigzag to confuse the predator. If the deer ran straight, it could become a venison feast.

(7) There is one more way that deer stay out of trouble. Bucks fight with weapons called antlers. These are different from horns because they are attached to the skull, and horns are not. Antlers are made of bone and have vitamins in them. The deer can use its antlers to protect itself.

(8) Deer stay safe by hiding, swimming, running, and fighting. Whenever you see a deer raise its tail, you know that it has seen a predator.

Adapted from: The Write Source – Student Writing Samples
http://www.thewritesource.com/studentmodels/we-deer.htm

Grade 8	**Cross-Country Skis: What Makes Them Go Fast**

(1) When you are going down a hill on skis, attempting to go as fast as possible, you will probably try to get your body into the lowest tuck possible. But wait - your position on skis isn't the only thing that makes you go fast, and definitely not the most important. What really makes you go fast is the *camber* and *flex* of your skis, the *structure* of the ski base, and the *waxes* that you use.

Camber and Flex

(2) The ski is not flat. There is a bend in the ski that creates an arch, and if you put a ski flat on the ground without any weight on it, there will be space under the middle of the ski. This bend is called *camber*. The camber flexes and distributes most of your weight on the ski to the tips and tails and leaves a little space under the ski where your foot is. If there were not camber, or too little camber, your weight would push the middle of the ski flat to the ground, creating more friction and making you go slower. This is why having the right type of ski for your weight is very important. If the ski is just right, meaning the right amount of space under your ski is in the right place, then you will go fast.

(3) Your body position affects the *flex* of the ski. Many people think that getting in the lowest and most forward tuck will make you go fastest. Aerodynamically, that is pretty true, but aerodynamics doesn't play that big a part in how fast you go (Holden, 1998). In terms of flex, you definitely don't want to lean forward (Caldwell, 2003). When you move your body forward, that makes the ski distribute your weight to the front of the ski. This digs the tip of the ski into the snow, slowing you tremendously. The optimal position for gliding downhill is to have your weight centered over the ski, if not putting a little weight back on the heel. This makes the most even distribution of weight to the tips and tails of your skis, without having too much weight on the front (Caldwell, 2003). (See fig. A)

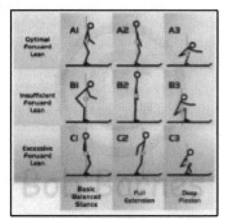

Figure A

Structure

(4) Another factor that affects how fast your skis glide is something called *structure*. Structure, as known in micro grooves, is a series of grooves in the thin layer of plastic that comes in contact with the snow, known as Ptex, that channel the snow particles along the base of the ski.

(5) There are two basic types of structure, linear structure, which are long parallel grooves running all the way along the base, and cross structure which has long grooves but also grooves

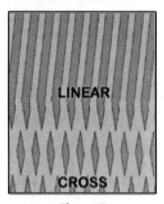

Figure B

that run across the base. (See fig. B) A good combination of these two structure types is the fastest. Linear structure works by reducing friction between the snow and the Ptex by channeling the snow crystals down along the base. Cross structure does the same thing but because of the grooves that run across the base, as the ski slides along the snow, the snow crystals "jump" from groove to groove as they go down the base (Underwood and Alexander, 1998, p. 1). Now remember, all this is happening almost microscopically under the ski. This turbulence helps to break the surface tension and suction between the ski and snow. Once the suction is broken, the ski will travel much faster. Wax also helps do the same thing.

Wax

(6)   As you probably know, wax is melted in to the base of skis to make them go faster in certain snow conditions. But what I bet you don't know is how the wax makes your ski go faster. The Ptex is not completely solid, but has microscopic holes in it called sinters that are in a sort of honeycomb shape. The sinters absorb the wax into the base of the ski. If the base is dry, the sinters close and the wax is not absorbed properly. To prevent getting a dry base, regularly wax your skis.

(7)   The wax works the same two ways as the structure. It either reduces friction between the snow and the ski, or keeps snow and water from creating suction with the base. Wax reduces friction by actually changing the hardness of the base (Caldwell, 2003). There are many kinds of wax, for all different temperature ranges. Warmer wax softens the base for warmer snow conditions and colder wax hardens the base for colder snow.

(8)   As you have seen, there are many contributing factors to how fast you glide on cross-country skis. The flex, structure, wax, and body position all depend on each other to work properly to make you go fast. A ski that is right for your body weight, a good combination of linear and cross structure, and the right wax for the snow temperature will ensure that you go as fast as possible down the hill.

Bibliography

Caldwell, Zach. (2003, February, 6).

Underwood, John and Alexander, Erica. (1998). Skis and Stones Finally Mix.
http://nensa.northcottweb.com/articles/nenn@htm (2/7/03)

Holden, Michael S. (1998, Feb.) "The Aerodynamics of Skiing," Scientific American, Pg. 3.

Adapted from: Vermont Department of Education, November 2003.
http://education.vermont.gov/documents/grade_8_1_8_report.pdf

| High School | **The Effects of Growing Coffee on the Environment** |

(1) The picture may seem familiar. Tumbling out of bed and stumbling around in the kitchen—you begin your day. But wait. It cannot begin properly without that daily ritual, the morning cup of coffee. However, most people don't realize that much of today's coffee is grown in such a way that it damages the environment.

(2) Americans lead the world in coffee drinking, consuming an average of 3.4 cups per person per day (Pennybacker 18). All this coffee has to be imported because it can only grow in the tropics such as in Mexico, Central and Latin America, Indonesia, and Africa. In addition, coffee fields must be at an altitude between 3000 and 5000 feet with a temperature between 65 and 70 degrees Fahrenheit. Furthermore, for optimum growth, coffee must have shade from nearby trees and overhead growth, but it also requires at least two hours of sunlight each day ("Shrinking Shadowland" 60). These are the only requirements necessary for coffee to grow well.

(3) It was in the eighteenth and nineteenth centuries that coffee seeds from the Middle East first took to the fertile soil of Latin America, the Caribbean, and Africa. Millions of acres of rainforest and jungle were planted with coffee trees. Because of coffee's need for shade and its ability to be grown alongside other crops, it didn't originally pose a hazard or threat to the environment. Habitats for animals were not drastically changed; indeed, the tropical ecosystems were much the same as before because the small coffee trees growing near the ground didn't require any forests to be cleared or plants eliminated.

(4) However, this took a turn in 1970 when U.S. agricultural scientists decided to develop a new, high-yield coffee plant that grew only in the full sun. At first, farmers were easily convinced to adapt to this modernization because they could produce five times more coffee than before (Wille 63). For that reason, they cut down rainforests to plant the new coffee crops. As a result, over the past 40 years, Central America has lost two-thirds of its rainforests to coffee plantations at a rate of 40 million acres per year (Pennybacker 18). That figure is similar to Mexico. The effect is that these modern coffee plantations are mono-cultural; nothing can grow in the fields besides the stubby coffee bushes. According to Elizabeth Skinner, a director of the Rainforest Alliance, these modern plantations "create ecological deserts" that are growing at an alarming rate ("Shrinking" 63).

(5) As the rainforests disappeared, this caused animals to also disappear, especially migratory birds. One study found that bird species in coffee plantations have diminished by 94-97 percent since many farmers switched to sun-grown plantations. This is not surprising considering the fact that two-thirds of birds found in shade-grown coffee plantations live in the canopy of the trees, and less than ten percent actually feed among the coffee plants ("Why Migratory Birds" 2). At the turn of the century, there were 65 species of common migratory birds found in Guatemala. Today, the effect of new ways of growing coffee is that only one-third of these birds have stable populations, another one-third seems to be in decline and 25 species are missing (Wille 62).

(6) Full-sun plantations are damaging to the environment in other ways as well. Due to the nature of the hybrid variety, the full-sun coffee plants possess little inbred resistance to pests and disease. In July 1993, 60 laborers on a Colombian coffee plantation were injured and one killed after they were exposed to high levels of endosulfan, a pesticide banned in many developed countries but commonly used on coffee plantations ("Shrinking" 64). These pesticides and fertilizers also kill insects and microrganisms and pollute the water.

(7) The switch from traditional coffee growing in shaded rainforests to growing coffee that requires full sun has had an impact on the environment. Farmers have adopted full-sun coffee crops because they yield more beans, but the result has been a loss of rainforest, a decrease in bird numbers, and the need to use more harmful pesticides.

Works Cited

Pennybacker, Mindy. "Habitat-Saving Habit." Audubon Nov./Dec. 1997: 18-19.

"Shrinking Shadowland." Utne Reader. Nov/Dec. 1994: 72.

"Why Migratory Birds Are Crazy for Coffee." Smithsonian Migratory Bird Center.
1997. Smithsonian Institution. 24 April 2000 <http://www.si.edu/smbc/fxshts/fxsht1a.htm>.

Wille, Chris. "The Birds and the Beans." Audubon Nov./Dec. 1994: 58-64.

Adapted from: The Write Source – Student Writing Samples
http://www.thewritesource.com/studentmodels/wi-kllrbean.htm

Argument Student Writing Samples

Grade 5   Zoos

(1) Even though zoos aren't a perfect solution, we should support zoos because they help protect endangered animals. Sometimes animals are in trouble in the wild. They don't have enough to eat, or they are endangered.

(2) Sometimes endangered animals are in trouble in the wild because there isn't enough to eat. For example, Tom French, who won a Pulitzer Prize as a journalist, studied elephants in many zoos, and he wrote a book about them. It's called *Zoo Story*. It turns out that there are too many elephants in South Africa. There isn't enough food for them and there isn't enough food for the rhino, because the elephants eat all the trees. So when elephants get moved to zoos, it might save their lives and it might help some other animals too. Tom French shows that in good zoos like the one in San Diego, there are clinics with experts who will care for the elephants. The article says "the animal clinic at the San Diego Zoo was better than any hospital in Swaziland."

(3) Another thing that zoos help with is breeding endangered animals. One Fox News program showed how local zoos can help breed endangered animals and then set them back in the wild. That seems like a good idea. If we could use zoos to breed these animals, and then put them back in the wild, maybe they wouldn't be endangered.

(4) On the other hand, animals in zoos don't always live a long time. They seem to live a lot longer in the wild. But the chart that shows how long elephants live in the wild is only counting the elephants who live at all. It doesn't count the ones who die of starvation because there are no trees, or the ones who get shot by poachers. Tom French shows that's what happens to lots of elephants. You might worry about zoochosis, too. That's when animals get lonely and sad in zoos. But it sounds like the San Diego zoo takes good care of its elephants. And it's probably pretty lonely when you face a poacher who wants your tusks.

(5) Overall, it seems like zoos are a good idea, as long as they take good care of the animals. They can rescue endangered animals, and they can breed them so they won't be so endangered. It would be even better if we could stop destroying their land. But since we're not endangered, that's probably not going to happen.

Source: Grade 5 Literacy – Nonfiction Reading and Opinion/Argument Writing.
Common Core-Aligned Task With Instructional Supports, New York City Department of Education.

Grade 6 — Geothermal Energy Now

(1) Think about how much electricity you use every day. Your alarm clock, your radio, your computer, and the lights in your home and at school all use electricity. Now think of all the other people in your community, in your state, and in the country who use as much electricity, if not more. The problem is the process that provides most of this electricity damages the environment. We need to devote more time, energy, and money to develop geothermal energy because it is renewable and a less harmful source of energy.

(2) Geothermal energy is energy that we can capture directly from Earth's heat. Miles and miles beneath Earth's surface hot molten rock heats a part of the Earth's crust. Then the molten rock causes underground water supplies to heat up. They are geothermal pools. Wells are drilled to pump the steam from these pools to use for heat or in power plants to make electricity.

(3) One argument for geothermal energy is that it is a renewable resource. Experts estimate that there is 15,000 times more geothermal energy than all the oil reserves in the world and most of that energy is constantly replenished. This evidence shows that we will never run out of geothermal energy the way we will with oil and gas. Experts estimate that geothermal energy is higher than all the fossil fuels and uranium used for nuclear plants combined.

Table 8.1 Gaseous omissions from various power plants.				
Plant type	CO_2 kg/MWh	SO_2 kg/MWh	NO_2 kg/MWh	Particulates kg/MWh
Coal-fired	994	4.71	1.955	1.012
Oil-fired	758	5.44	1.814	N.A.
Gas-fired	550	0.0998	1.343	0.0635
Hydrothermal – flash-steam, liquid dominated	27.2	0.1588	0	0
Hydrothermal – The Geysers dry steam field	40.3	0.000098	0.000458	negligible
Hydrothermal – closed-loop binary	0	0	0	negligible
EPA average, all U.S. plants	631.6	2.734	1.343	N.A.

N.A. = not available

(4) The most important advantage of geothermal energy is that it doesn't produce pollution or contribute to the greenhouse effect. Geothermal plants are almost entirely emission free. The US Department of Energy states that more than 50% of the electricity used in the United States comes from coal. Coal is known to release harmful gasses, such as carbon dioxide, that contribute to air pollution. The result is that every time half

the households in the country flip a light switch, a little bit more pollution leaks into the air. Studies conducted by scientists at the US Department of Energy point out that geothermal power plants produce less than 1% of the carbon dioxide released by power plants relying on fossil fuels, such as coal. This fact means that when more and more power plants switch to geothermal energy instead of burning coal, the air in our country will greatly improve.

(5) Some people would argue that taking advantage of geothermal energy is expensive because of the cost of building power plants. But let's take a closer look. Technological changes have been made that make it easier to drill wells that can reach into geothermal pools. Iceland already generates more than 25 percent of its energy from geothermal. The more geothermal energy is used the lower the price will become to build. The chart shows that geothermal is the lowest cost of all heating fuels. It is true that the first costs for building geothermal plants is high, but lifetime costs of geothermal operations are smaller than other kinds of energy. Also the U.S. government has offered tax credits for individuals who use the technology in their homes.

Comparing the Cost of Heating Fuels
March 2011

Type of Energy	BTU/unit	Adj Effic	$/unit	$MMBtu
Fuel Oil, gallon	138,200	80%	$3.62	$32.70
Kerosene, gallon	136,600	80%	$3.98	$36.43
Propane, gallon	91,600	80%	$3.39	$46.29
Natural Gas, therm	100,000	80%	$1.55	$19.40
Eletricity, kwh	3,412	100%	$0.15	$43.46
Geothermal, kwh	3,412	400%	$0.15	$10.87
Wood, cord (green)	22,000,000	60%	$180.00	$13.64
Pellets, ton	16,400,000	80%	$247.00	$18.83
Note: MMBtu equals 1 million Btus				

(6) Geothermal energy hasn't beaten fossil fuels in any popularity contests yet, but scientists are hopeful that it may one day be a workable substitute to nonrenewable energy sources. The sooner we start exploring how to take advantage of it, the better it will be for our environment and our future.

Adapted From: *Writing: Literacy in history/social studies, science, and technical subjects –*
science argument essay. Retrieved from
http://macmillanmh.com/ccssreading/treasures/grade6/ccslh_g6_wr_6_1a_tl2.html

Grade 10 — Chocolate Flavored Milk Is Good For You

(1) Could there really be something schools can serve for lunch that tastes good and is healthy at the same time? Schools should serve chocolate milk. Many kids love it and are happy to see it in their cafeteria. Research shows that, overall, chocolate milk is pretty good for kids.

(2) Milk provides nutrients essential for good health. Low-fat and fat-free flavored milk contains calcium, potassium, phosphorous, protein, vitamins A, D and B12, riboflavin and niacin and can help kids meet their calcium recommendations.[4] The 2005 *Dietary Guidelines for Americans* acknowledges milk and dairy foods' contribution to bone health and improvement of diet quality.[6] Milk drinkers, in general, consume more calcium, phosphorus, magnesium, potassium and vitamin A than non-milk drinkers.[7]

(3) Low-fat chocolate milk is the most popular milk choice in schools and kids drink less milk if it's taken away which means they get less nutrients. Flavored milk drinkers consume more milk than exclusively white milk drinkers.[1] According to 2005 USDA data, 66% of the milk chosen by children in schools is flavored.[8] Removing flavored milk from schools has been shown to result in a 62-63 % reduction in milk consumption by kids in kindergarten through 5th grade, a 50 % reduction by kids in 6th through 8th grades, and a 37 % reduction in kids in 9th through 12th grades.[9]

(4) Chocolate milk is much healthier than alternative drinks that students might drink instead. Research shows that flavored milk drinkers drink less soft drinks compared to those who do not drink flavored milk.[1] The American Academy of Pediatrics policy statement *Soft Drinks in Schools* encourages schools to offer low-fat or fat-free white or flavored milk, water or real fruit or vegetable juice as healthful alternatives to soft drinks.[6]

(5) Some people might say that chocolate flavored milk is not as good for students because it has a lot of sugar, fat and calories. However, it turns out that flavored milk drinkers do not have higher total fat or calorie intakes than non-milk drinkers.[1] According to the 2005 *Dietary Guidelines for Americans,* adding a small amount of sugar to reduced-fat milk products helps enhance their palatability and improves nutrient intake without contributing excessive calories.[6]

(6) Two government programs, the National Institute of Child Health and Human Development's Milk Matters[2] and the U.S. Department of Health and Human Services' Best Bones Forever,[3] recommend low-fat and fat-free flavored milk as a good option for children. So let's keep serving chocolate milk in schools. It's a good source of vitamins and calcium and kids really like it!

References

1. Johnson RK, Frary C, Wang MQ. The nutritional consequences of flavored milk consumption by school-aged children and adolescents in the United States. *J Am Diet Assoc.* 2002; 102(6):853-856.

2. NICHD. For Stronger Bones....for Lifelong Health...Milk Matters! Accessed Sept 7, 2009 via http://www.nichd.nih.gov/publications/pubs/upload/strong_bones_lifelong_ health_mm1.pdf

3. HHS, Best Bones Forever. Accessed Sept 7, 2009 via http://www.bestbonesforever.gov/

4. Frary CD, Johnson RK, Wang MQ. Children and adolescents' choices of foods and beverages high in added sugars are associated with intakes of key nutrients and food groups. J *Adolesc Health* 2004;34(1):56-63.

5. American Academy of Pediatrics, Committee on School Health. Soft drinks in schools. *Pediatrics* 2005; 113152-154.

   United States Dept. of Health and Human Services, United States Dept. of Agriculture and United States Dietary Guidelines Advisory Committee, *2005 Dietary Guidelines for Americans.* (6th ed. HHS publications, 2005, Washington D.C.)

6. Murphy MM, Douglas JS, Johnson RK, Spence LA. Drinking flavored or plain milk is positively associated with nutrient intake and is not associated with adverse effects on weight status in U.S. children and adolescents. *J Am Diet Assoc.* 2008; 108:631-639.

7. ENVIRON International Corporation. School Milk: Fat Content Has Declined Dramatically since the Early 1990s. 2008.

8. Patterson J, Saidel M. The Removal of Flavored Milk in Schools Results in a Reduction in Total Milk Purchases in All Grades, K-12. *J Am Diet Assoc.* 2009; 109,(9): A97.

Adapted from: "Top Five Reasons to Raise Your Hand for Flavored Milk." (2010) National Dairy Council.

Common Core Greade-Specific Standards

Figure 4L

CCSS: Opinion/Argument Standards

Anchor Standard	Grade-Specific Details
#1 **Write Opinion/ Argument Pieces** *(H/SS, S, TS: write arguments focused on discipline-specific content)*	• **4 - 5:** Write opinion pieces on topics or texts, supporting a point of view with reasons and information. • **6 - 8:** Write arguments to support claims with clear reasons and relevant evidence. • **9 - 12:** Write arguments to support claims in an analysis of substantive topics or texts, using valid reasoning and relevant and sufficient evidence.

#1a Introductions	• **4 - 5**: Introduce a topic or text clearly, state an opinion, and create an organizational structure in which related ideas are grouped to support the writer's purpose.
	• **6**: Introduce claim(s) and organize the reasons and evidence clearly.
	• **7**: Introduce claim(s), acknowledge alternate or opposing claims, and organize the reasons and evidence logically.
	• **8**: Introduce claim(s), acknowledge and distinguish the claim(s) from alternate or opposing claims, and organize the reasons and evidence logically.
	• **9 - 10**: Introduce precise claim(s), distinguish the claim(s) from alternate or opposing claims, and create an organization that establishes clear relationships among claim(s), counterclaims, reasons, and evidence.
	• **11 - 12**: Introduce precise, knowledgeable claim(s), establish the significance of the claim(s), distinguish the claim(s) from alternate or opposing claims, and create an organization that logically sequences claim(s), counterclaims, reasons, and evidence.
#1b Support/Develop Claims/	• **4**: Provide reasons that are supported by facts and details.
	• **5**: Provide logically ordered reasons that are supported by facts and details.
	• **6 - 8**: Support claim(s) with clear reasons and relevant evidence, using credible sources and demonstrating an understanding of the topic or text.
	• **9 - 10**: Develop claim(s) and counterclaims fairly, supplying evidence for each while pointing out the strengths and limitations of both in a manner that anticipates the audience's knowledge level and concerns.
	• **11 - 12**: Develop claim(s) and counterclaims fairly and thoroughly, supplying the most relevant evidence for each while pointing out the strengths and limitations of both in a manner that anticipates the audience's knowledge level, concerns, values, and possible biases.
#1c Linking Words/ Transitions	• **4**: Link opinion and reasons using words and phrases (e.g., for instance, in order to, in addition).
	• **5**: Link opinion and reasons using words, phrases, and clauses (e.g., consequently, specifically).
	• **6**: Use words, phrases, and clauses to clarify the relationships among claim(s) and reasons.
	• **7 - 8**: Use words, phrases, and clauses to create cohesion and clarify the relationships among claim(s), reasons, and evidence.
	• **9 - 10**: Use words, phrases, and clauses to link the major sections of the text, create cohesion, and clarify the relationships between claim(s) and reasons, between reasons and evidence, and between claim(s) and counterclaims.
	• **11 - 12**: Use words, phrases, and clauses as well as varied syntax to link the major sections of the text, create cohesion, and clarify the relationships between claim(s) and reasons, between reasons and evidence, and between claim(s) and counterclaims.

#1d **Formal Style**	• **6 - 8:** Establish and maintain a formal style. • **9 - 12:** Establish and maintain a formal style and objective tone while attending to the norms and conventions of the discipline in which they are writing.
# 1d (4 – 5) **# 1e (6 – 10)** **Conclusions**	• **4 - 5:** Provide a concluding statement or section related to the opinion presented. • **6:** Provide a concluding statement or section that follows from the argument presented. • **7 - 12:** Provide a concluding statement or section that follows from and supports the argument presented.

Figure 4M

CCSS: Informational Standards

Anchor Standard	Grade-Specific Details
#2 **Write Informative/** **Explanatory Text** *(H/SS,S,TS: Write informative/explanatory texts, including the narration of historical events, scientific procedures/ experiments, or technical processes)*	• **4 - 5:** Write informative/explanatory texts to examine a topic and convey ideas and information clearly. • **6 - 8:** Write informative/explanatory texts to examine a topic and convey ideas, concepts, and information through the selection, organization, and analysis of relevant content. • **9 - 12:** Write informative/explanatory texts to examine and convey complex ideas, concepts, and information clearly and accurately through the effective selection, organization, and analysis of content.
#2a **Introductions/** **Organization**	• **4:** Introduce a topic clearly and group related information in paragraphs and sections; include formatting (e.g., headings), illustrations, and multimedia when useful to aiding comprehension. • **5:** Introduce a topic clearly, provide a general observation and focus, and group related information logically; include formatting (e.g., headings), illustrations, and multimedia when useful to aiding comprehension. • **6:** Introduce a topic; organize ideas, concepts, and information, using strategies such as definition, classification, comparison/contrast, and cause/effect; include formatting (e.g., headings), graphics (e.g., charts, tables), and multimedia when useful to aiding comprehension. • **7:** Introduce a topic clearly, previewing what is to follow; organize ideas, concepts, and information, using strategies such as definition, classification, comparison/contrast, and cause/effect; include formatting (e.g., headings), graphics (e.g., charts, tables), and multimedia when useful to aiding comprehension. • **8:** Introduce a topic clearly, previewing what is to follow; organize ideas, concepts, and information into broader categories; include formatting (e.g., headings), graphics (e.g., charts, tables), and multimedia when useful to aiding comprehension.

	• **9 - 10:** Introduce a topic; organize complex ideas, concepts, and information to make important connections and distinctions; include formatting (e.g., headings), graphics (e.g., figures, tables), and multimedia when useful to aiding comprehension.
	• **11 - 12:** Introduce a topic; organize complex ideas, concepts, and information so that each new element builds on that which precedes it to create a unified whole; include formatting (e.g., headings), graphics (e.g., features, tables), and multimedia when useful to aiding comprehension.
#2b **Develop the Topic**	• **4 - 5:** Develop the topic with facts, definitions, concrete details, quotations, or other information and examples related to the topic. • **6 - 7:** Develop the topic with relevant facts, definitions, concrete details, quotations, or other information and examples. • **8:** Develop the topic with relevant, well-chosen facts, definitions, concrete details, quotations, or other information and examples. • **9 - 10:** Develop the topic with well-chosen, relevant, and sufficient facts, extended definitions, concrete details, quotations, or other information and examples appropriate to the audience's knowledge of the topic. • **11 - 12:** Develop the topic thoroughly by selecting the most significant and relevant facts, extended definitions, concrete details, quotations, or other information and examples appropriate to the audience's knowledge of the topic.
#2c **Linking Words/** **Transitions**	• **4:** Link ideas within categories of information using words and phrases (e.g., another, for example, also, because). • **5:** Link ideas within and across categories of information using words, phrases, and clauses (e.g., in contrast, especially). • **6:** Use appropriate transitions to clarify the relationships among ideas and concepts. • **7 - 8:** Use appropriate and varied transitions to create cohesion and clarify the relationships among ideas and concepts. • **9 - 10:** Use appropriate and varied transitions to link the major sections of the text, create cohesion, and clarify the relationships among complex ideas and concepts. • **11 - 12:** Use appropriate and varied transitions and syntax to link the major sections of the text, create cohesion, and clarify the relationships among complex ideas and concepts.
#2d **Precise Language**	• **4 - 8:** Use precise language and domain-specific vocabulary to inform about or explain the topic. • **9 - 10:** Use precise language and domain-specific vocabulary to manage the complexity of the topic. • **11 - 12:** Use precise language, domain-specific vocabulary, and techniques such as metaphor, simile, and analogy to manage the complexity of the topic.

#2e **Formal Style**	• **6 - 8:** Establish and maintain a formal style. • **9 - 12:** Establish and maintain a formal style and objective tone while attending to the norms and conventions of the discipline in which they are writing.
# 2 e (4 – 5) **# 2 f (6 – 10)** **Conclusions**	• **4 - 6:** Provide a concluding statement or section related to the information or explanation presented. • **7 - 8:** Provide a concluding statement or section that follows from and supports the information or explanation presented. • **9 - 12:** Provide a concluding statement or section that follows from and supports the information or explanation presented (e.g., articulating implications or the significance of the topic).

Figure 4N

CCSS: Narrative Standards

Standard 3 details are found only in the ELA Literacy Standards. The CCSS provide this note about narrative writing in History/Social Studies, Science, and Technical Subjects 6–12:

> *"Students' narrative skills continue to grow in these grades. The Standards require that students be able to incorporate narrative elements effectively into arguments and informative/ explanatory texts. In history/social studies, students must be able to incorporate narrative accounts into their analyses of individuals or events of historical import. In science and technical subjects, students must be able to write precise enough descriptions of the step-by-step procedures they use in their investigations or technical work that others can replicate them and (possibly) reach the same results."*

Anchor Standard	Grade-Specific Details
#3 **Write Narratives**	• **4 - 5:** Write narratives to develop real or imagined experiences or events using effective technique, descriptive details, and clear event sequences. • **6 - 8:** Write narratives to develop real or imagined experiences or events using effective technique, relevant descriptive details, and well-structured event sequences. • **9 - 12:** Write narratives to develop real or imagined experiences or events using effective technique, well-chosen details, and well-structured event sequences.
#3a **Orient the Reader** **(Introduction)**	• **4 - 5:** Orient the reader by establishing a situation and introducing a narrator and/or characters; organize an event sequence that unfolds naturally. • **6:** Engage and orient the reader by establishing a context and introducing a narrator and/or characters; organize an event sequence that unfolds naturally and logically. • **7 - 8:** Engage and orient the reader by establishing a context and point of view and introducing a narrator and/or characters; organize an event sequence that unfolds naturally and logically. • **9 - 10:** Engage and orient the reader by setting out a problem, situation, or observation, establishing one or multiple point(s) of view, and introducing a narrator and/or characters; create a smooth progression of experiences or events.

	• **11 - 12:** Engage and orient the reader by setting out a problem, situation, or observation and its significance, establishing one or multiple point(s) of view, and introducing a narrator and/or characters; create a smooth progression of experiences or events.
#3b **Use Narrative Techniques to Develop the Piece**	• **4:** Use dialogue and description to develop experiences and events or show the responses of characters to situations. • **5:** Use narrative techniques, such as dialogue, description, and pacing, to develop experiences and events or show the responses of characters to situations. • **6-8:** Use narrative techniques, such as dialogue, pacing, description, and reflection, to develop experiences, events, and/or characters. • **9 - 12:** Use narrative techniques, such as dialogue, pacing, description, reflection, and multiple plot lines, to develop experiences, events, and/or characters.
#3c **Transition Words**	• **4:** Use a variety of transitional words and phrases to manage the sequence of events. • **5:** Use a variety of transitional words, phrases, and clauses to manage the sequence of events. • **6 - 7:** Use a variety of transition words, phrases, and clauses to convey sequence and signal shifts from one time frame or setting to another. • **8:** Use a variety of transition words, phrases, and clauses to convey sequence, signal shifts from one time frame or setting to another, and show the relationships among experiences and events. • **9 - 10:** Use a variety of techniques to sequence events so that they build on one another to create a coherent whole. • **11 - 12:** Use a variety of techniques to sequence events so that they build on one another to create a coherent whole, and build toward a particular tone and outcome (e.g., a sense of mystery, suspense, growth, or resolution).
#3d **Use Precise Words**	• **4 - 5:** Use concrete words and phrases and sensory details to convey experiences and events precisely. • **6:** Use precise words and phrases, relevant descriptive details, and sensory language to convey experiences and events. • **7 - 8:** Use precise words and phrases, relevant descriptive details, and sensory language to capture the action and convey experiences and events. • **9 - 12:** Use precise words and phrases, telling details, and sensory language to convey a vivid picture of the experiences, events, setting, and/or characters.
# 3e **Conclusions**	• **4 - 6:** Provide a conclusion that follows from the narrated experiences or events. • **7 - 8:** Provide a conclusion that follows from and reflects on the narrated experiences or events. • **9 - 12:** Provide a conclusion that follows from and reflects on what is experienced, observed, or resolved over the course of the narrative.

Chapter 5: Writing From Sources

The Common Core State Standards (CCSS) strongly emphasize the importance of students' ability to write from sources, using evidence from print and digital material in their own writing. Rather than having students write solely from knowledge or experience, encourage students to analyze and synthesize information from sources in order to answer questions and writing prompts (Achieve the Core, 2013). Several reading and writing standards indicate clear expectations that students combine reading comprehension and writing strategies.

Short or Long Research Projects?

CCSS writing standards #7, #8, and #9 are all associated with the same broader strand, *Research to Build and Present Knowledge*. For grades 3-8, anchor standard #7 begins as follows: "Conduct short research projects..." For grades 9-12, it begins, "Conduct short as well as more sustained research projects ..." See Figure 5E at the end of the chapter for grade-level details for each of these three writing standards, along with the specific standards associated with reading and writing from sources.

Consider the CCSS use of the word *short* as noted above. Although longer research reports are expected in high school, students should gradually acquire, in *all* grades, the reading and writing skills necessary to produce even a short research report.

Having students regularly complete short writing tasks from sources will ultimately grow their skills more effectively than having them write one or two longer research reports, even in high school. Each time a student completes a short research project, he or she has an opportunity to practice a host of subskills, such as searching for sources, reading and gathering information from sources, taking notes, organizing notes into a writing plan, writing a draft, revising, and editing.

Common Core Connection

Writing Standard #7: Conduct short as well as more sustained research projects based on focused questions, demonstrating understanding of the subject under investigation.

Writing Standard #8: Gather relevant information from multiple print and digital sources, assess the credibility and accuracy of each source, and integrate the information while avoiding plagiarism.

Writing Standard #9: Draw evidence from literary or informational texts to support analysis, reflection, and research.

Reading Standard #1: Read closely to determine what the text says explicitly and make logical inferences from it; cite specific text evidence when writing or speaking to support conclusions drawn from the text.

Reading Standard #2: Determine central ideas of themes of a text and analyze their development; summarize the key supporting ideas and details.

About Sources

Background Knowledge

For an informational writing piece, students need background knowledge about a topic in order to provide information to the reader. For an argument piece, students need background knowledge in order to provide evidence to support a claim. One obvious way to acquire background knowledge is through content instruction – students learn about a topic from the teacher, in discussion, and in classroom activities.

Another way to acquire background knowledge is through print or digital sources selected specifically for a writing assignment. Teachers can provide the sources, or students can search for sources collaboratively or independently. When assigning a research project, determine whether students have sufficient background knowledge to complete the task; if not, provide sources.

Providing Sources

Not surprisingly, most teachers identify time to be the strongest challenge they face in devoting significant time to student writing in content classrooms. Having students conduct their own search for sources only seems to exacerbate this problem. Because students simply do not have the time or ability to find quality sources, we recommend that teachers provide sources for informational and argument writing assignments – at least initially. In so doing, teachers should explain how the sources were selected and why they are credible and accurate. Providing sources to students offers the following benefits:

- You can be sure the sources are credible and accurate.
- You can teach students about credible sources by analyzing and evaluating the sources you provide.
- It saves time!
- Knowing the sources' content will help you determine if students used the them appropriately.
- Familiarizing support staff with the sources enables them to provide assistance and develop scaffolds for struggling learners.

Use resources in your school to help find appropriate print and digital sources. Consult with your school librarian or media specialist about websites and online resources that are credible and appropriate for use with students. We have also listed some useful websites for sources in the resources section at the back of the book.

As with explicit instruction, the Graduate Release of Responsibility Model is useful to build students' skills and comfort with source searches. Gradually, students should be "released" to find their own sources.

Tracking Sources

As students are expected to gather information from multiple sources, they must learn to track the sources. Figure 5A is a template for students to gather the necessary information about their sources. Students complete a template for each source, assigning a code letter or number to the source (identified in the box in the top left corner). The code is then used to track sources as students take notes and begin writing a draft. Software programs are also useful guides for students in tracking their sources – see Zotero (zotero.org), Mendeley (mendeley.com), EasyBib (easybib. com), and Bibme (bibme.org).

Figure 5A

Template for Collecting Source Information

CODE LETTER OR NUMBER	**Type of source:** *book, article, video, internet site, interview or discussion* other:
	Title:
	Author:
© **Date:**	
Publisher:	
Internet URL:	
Brief Description:	**Pages:**

This template is available in document format at the Keys to Literacy website:
http://www.keystoliteracy.com/resources/worksheets/

Citing Sources

The CCSS expect that students will gradually learn source citations skills. For example, in grades 4-5, students are required to simply provide a *list of sources;* in grade 6, they must provide basic *bibliographic* source information. Beginning in grade 7, they must begin to follow a *standard format for citation.* The CCSS do not require specific citation formats (e.g., *APA, MLA, Chicago Style*); however, for consistency, schools should adopt a standard format to be accepted by all teachers. For more resources about formal citation formats, please refer to the back of the book.

Students in grades 7 and up may need explicit instruction for citing a source within the text of a writing piece. One way to do this is with a *parenthetical citation,* for example:

- (Smith)
- (Smith, 2010)
- (Smith, p. 263)

Another way is to use footnotes or end notes, which simply entails placing a number in the text that refers to a source listed at the bottom of the page or end of the text.

Students can also weave a reference to a source directly into the text. Consider providing sample language as a scaffold, such as:

- according to _____
- _____ says/explains/writes/describes/notes
- _____ research conducted by _____ shows that
- one expert, _____, says/commented that

Writing An Informational or Argument Piece From Sources

The THINK and PLAN stages of the writing process are crucial for informational and argument writing. These are the stages where students gather information and generate ideas. Figure 5B is a *Set of Steps* for writing an informational or argument piece that incorporates the four stages of the writing process. The remainder of this chapter addresses each step in detail.

Figure 5B

Information or Argument Writing: Set of Steps

Set of Steps	Writing Process Stages
1. Review the assignment requirements.	THINK
2. Identify print or digital sources.	
3. Gather information from sources and take two-column notes.	
4. Organize notes into a writing plan.	PLAN
5. Write a draft.	WRITE
6. Revise and edit the draft.	REVISE

Step 1. Review the assignment requirements.

Before students can begin a writing assignment, they must know the requirements: type of writing, approximate length, content and text structure requirements, source requirements, and due dates. In Chapter 9, we provide a planning guide to set detailed goals for a student writing task. The more specific the requirements, the more likely students will produce a piece that meets teacher expectations. Therefore, the very first step is to review the assignment's requirements. Then, students should continue to refer to them as they gather information from sources, take notes, write a draft, and revise their writing.

Activity

Practice Writing Assignment

Directions: *Review the sample Writing Assignment Guide provided by the trainer. Answer these questions:*

1. What is the audience and purpose of this assignment?

_____

_____

2. What type of writing should be used?

_____

_____

3. What is the form and the length of this assignment?

_____

_____

4. Are sources provided?

_____

_____

5. What are the content and text requirements?

_____

_____

Step 2. Identify print or digital sources.

The second step is for students to determine the sources they will use and gather the necessary information about these sources for proper citation later in the writing process.

Earlier in this chapter, we recommended that teachers identify and provide sources (both print and digital) for students to use in informational or argument writing. As students move into upper grades, they require opportunities to practice identifying their own sources, including determining the credibility and accuracy of these sources.

Once a source is identified, the student should review it to get a sense of its content and how it is organized. For any source that will be used, the student should complete a *Template for Collecting Source Information* (see Figure 5A).

Step 3. Gather information from sources and take two-column notes.

Graham and Harris (2007) point out that information can be gathered from reading, video, discussion with peers or teachers, the Internet, or experiences. Common Core writing standard #8 emphasizes the importance of gathering and integrating relevant information from multiple print and electronic sources. However, this assumes that students have the foundational skills necessary to effectively identify information, including:

- basic decoding and fluency skills in order to read sources
- sufficient vocabulary knowledge
- comprehension skills:
  - identifying and stating main ideas
  - identifying relevant details
  - analyzing and evaluating concepts
  - highlighting, marking, and annotating text
  - making inferences

Some students need supplemental instruction and guided practice to develop these basic reading and comprehension skills at a grade-appropriate level in order to successfully complete classroom writing assignments.

Two-Column Format

Students must save the information gathered from sources in order to remember and organize the content when writing the first draft. Adapted from Walter Pauk's *Cornell System* for taking notes (Sedita, 1989; Pauk, 1997), two-column notes is a format used in other Keys to Literacy programs (*The Key Comprehension Routine, The Key Vocabulary Routine, The ANSWER Key Routine*). See Figure 5C.

Here are some suggestions about taking two-column notes:
- Notes can be taken from any text or non-text source.
- Writing notes during the THINK stage can help students discover and think through what they want to convey in their writing.
- Students should track sources as they take notes.

Consider scaffolding a set of notes by providing the main idea topics in the left column of the notes.

Figure 5C

Two-Column Notes

How to Set Up Two-Column Notes

- Draw a vertical line down the length of the page and a horizontal line intersecting it at the top to form a "T" shape

- The vertical line is approximately one third of the way across the page from the left border

- The topic is written across the top of the notes

- Big ideas are listed in the left column (left 1/3 of the page)

- Supporting details are listed in the right column (right 2/3 of the page)

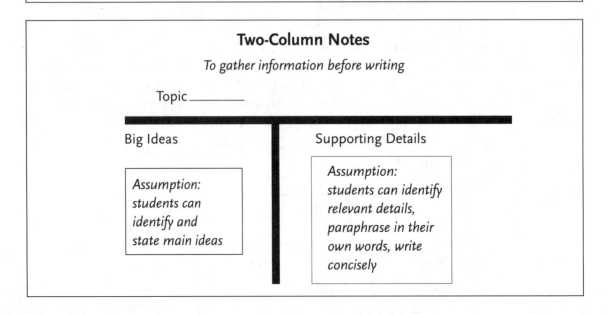

Two-Column Notes

To gather information before writing

Topic _____

Big Ideas

Assumption: students can identify and state main ideas

Supporting Details

Assumption: students can identify relevant details, paraphrase in their own words, write concisely

Effective note takers...	
Do	**Don't**
• Abbreviate • Use symbols • Change verbs • Change word order • Combine ideas by paraphrasing • Quote direct phrases • Track sources • Leave extra space	• Copy word for word • Write in complete sentences • Change proper nouns • Change specific academic vocabulary (e.g., *polygon, bacteria, executive branch*) • Change dates

Note Taking Skills

Teachers may assume that students have the foundational skills necessary to take good notes, which include the following:

- paraphrasing

- writing concisely

- following a consistent note taking format

- abbreviating

- using quotes when copying text

- tracking sources

Some of your students may need supplemental instruction and guided practice to develop these skills at a grade-appropriate level.

Paraphrasing to Avoid Plagiarism

Plagiarism is the use of another person's word or ideas without including the proper credit and citation. It is possible that students may set themselves up for plagiarism at two stages of writing: (1) when they take notes, and (2) when they turn the notes into a draft (Roth, 1999). If students paraphrase in their own words at these stages, it will help them avoid plagiarism significantly. Teachers should encourage students to start paraphrasing during the note taking stage rather than "cut and paste" directly from sources into notes.

Paraphrasing is restating information in different words. When we paraphrase, we maintain the original meaning, but we express it in our own words. Paraphrasing is an active learning strategy that helps us place information into long-term memory as we move from simple to complex levels of thinking. In combination, the following techniques enable students to rephrase information from a source in their own words (Sedita, 1989, pp 67-68):

- Use semantic paraphrasing: Replace vocabulary words and phrases used in the source with accurate synonyms using words of your own or with support from a thesaurus.

- Use syntactic paraphrasing: Change the structure of sentences used in the source by combining simple sentences, breaking longer sentences into shorter sentences, and changing the word order.

- Understand what you are paraphrasing: Carefully read several sentences or paragraphs from a text source until you are sure you understand the main ideas and key details, then write them as concisely as possible in your own words.

- Explain difficult concepts and abstract ideas: Use your own words and phrases to explain difficult concepts presented in the source.

Simply asking students to restate something in their own words is not sufficient instruction for many. In addition to the use of think aloud and modeling paraphrasing techniques, teachers should make students aware that a paraphrase may be longer or shorter than the source text. Consider having students paraphrase as a quick write activity.

Because notes are informal, another way to avoid plagiarism is for students to abbreviate, use visual symbols, and write in concise phrases rather than full sentences when taking notes. This, combined with paraphrasing, makes it less likely that students will copy directly from a source when writing their first drafts.

To learn more about plagiarism and how to support students in avoiding it, consider the following resources.

1. Statement on Best Practices (www.wpacouncil.org)

2. What is plagiarism? (www.plagiarism.org)

Activity

Practice Writing Assignment – Identify Information

_e trainer models marking the text sources to gather information. Keep in mind the WAG requirements. Then answer the questions.

1. Was there a difference in the focus of information for each of the sources?

_____

_____

_____

2. Are the graphics in the sources helpful? Explain:

_____

_____

_____

Activity

Practice Writing Assignment – Take Two-column Notes

<u>*Directions*</u>*: Follow along as the trainer models note taking. Add detail notes in the right column of the notes below. Note that the teacher can scaffold notes by providing the main idea topics. Then answer the questions.*

Topic: _____

main idea/topic 1:	
_____ _____ _____ _____ _____ _____	

main idea/topic 2:

_____

_____

_____

_____

_____

_____

main idea/topic 3:

_____

_____

_____

_____

_____

_____

---

1. Why did the trainer place the source code letters in the notes?

_____

_____

_____

2. Were there any graphics from the sources that might be incorporated into the writing piece?

_____

_____

_____

Step 4. Organize notes into a writing plan.

Keys to Literacy's *top-down topic web* is a useful scaffold that can be used after students gather information and take notes. In Chapter 4, you learned how a topic web can be used to provide a visual representation of writing structure. Details related to the requirements for a writing assignment can be integrated into a topic web for use as a pre-writing planning tool. Teachers can add requirements related to the introduction, conclusion, and body of a writing piece to a topic web as a scaffold prior to writing a first draft. Eventually, students learn how to generate their own topic webs that include requirements from a writing assignment. In Chapter 7 you will learn how to develop topic webs as a pre-writing scaffold.

Step 5. Write a draft.

Introduction

As discussed in Chapter 4, the purpose of an introduction is to inform the reader about the writing topic. Remember, there is no prescribed length for an introduction – it can be as short as one sentence or as long as multiple paragraphs. Students can include any of the following components in an introduction for an informational or argument piece:

- nonfiction lead
- statement of the claim (position) for argument writing
- preview of the central ideas in an informational piece or the major reasons supporting the claim in an argument piece
- background information related to the topic
- thesis statement

Activity

Practice Writing Assignment - Introduction

Directions: Use the space below to write an introduction for the writing piece. Be sure to include a lead and introduction of the topic.

Lead:

_____

_____

_____

_____

_____

_____

_____

_____

Topic:

_____

_____

_____

_____

_____

_____

_____

_____

_____

Body

In most writing, the body is where students develop ideas and information into sentences and paragraphs. Students must determine the organizational structure they will use to present information (i.e., topics, subtopics, main ideas) and argument components (i.e., reasons, evidence, counterclaim, rebuttal). They also need to decide if they will include text-formatting features such as headings or graphics. Note that the CCSS emphasize organization beginning in grade 4.

Sentence and Paragraph Writing Skills

As noted in Chapter 4, students who generally struggle with writing sometimes do not have sufficient *sentence* writing skills. These students need explicit instruction in this basic skill, perhaps as supplemental instruction delivered by an intervention specialist. Although specific instruction on sentence writing is not the focus of *Keys to Content Writing* professional development, Chapter 3 provides suggestions for practice with sentence combining as a quick write activity. Sentence combining is an effective strategy for building sentence writing skills (Graham & Perin, 2007; Saddler, 2012).

As we also discussed in Chapter 4, an informational paragraph is typically organized around *one main idea,* supported by *details.* For most argument writing, the main idea of a paragraph typically presents a *reason* that supports the claim, and the *evidence* is presented as the details. A *topic sentence* is used to state the main idea or reason. There may also be a counterclaim paragraph and a rebuttal paragraph in an argument piece. Younger students are taught that the topic sentence should be the first sentence of a paragraph, but they soon discover that a topic sentence may be placed at the beginning, middle, or end of a paragraph. In fact, many paragraphs do not include a topic sentence – the main idea is *implied* and the reader must *infer* the main idea from the detail sentences.

If appropriate, paragraphs in an informational or argument piece may be grouped into logical sections, and headings are used to convey the subtopic of each section. If the piece is short, sections may not be necessary, and the body will simply be structured in paragraphs.

To review, consider the following terms we've discussed related to sentence and paragraph structure:

- **section:** portion of text with related paragraphs about the same topic or subtopic

- **paragraph:** collection of related sentences that develop a key/main idea; indicated by a new line or indentation

- **main idea:** key concept or main point of a paragraph; may be stated or implied

- **topic sentence:** sentence which contains the main idea

- **detail sentences:** sentences that support and explain the main idea by providing relevant facts, examples, definitions, comparisons, etc.

Using Notes to Write Paragraphs: The Left Column

One source for determining paragraph main ideas is two-column notes. Note first that the topic or subtopic of a writing piece is written across the top of the notes, essentially as a title. The left column contains the words, phrases, and ideas that can be used to write topic sentences that represent paragraph main ideas.

As with all explicit strategy instruction, some students may need scaffolds to achieve comfort and mastery. For students who struggle to write topic sentences, consider providing topic sentences based on these main idea topics in the left column.

Using Notes to Write Sentences: The Right Column

The information in the right column of notes is used to develop the detail sentences of paragraphs. Strong comprehension skills are required for students to analyze and evaluate information in the right column, determine which information will be used, and decide the best order to present the information. If information has been gathered from multiple sources, the student must also be able to integrate and synthesize the information. In addition, a student must think critically to make decisions about which information from the notes to include, the order in which to present it, and how to integrate all of the information in writing the draft. This is a complex task!

Figure 5D illustrates the use of two-column notes in generating sentences and paragraphs for body paragraphs. As you review these examples, note the following:

- The topic sentences are in the left column.
- The numbers indicate the order of presentation.
- The strike-through indicates information that will not be included.
- The arrows indicate integrated information.
- Transitions are underlined in the paragraphs.

Figure 5D

Using Notes to Write Paragraphs

First Section of Notes	
What are 3D printers?	1 • "The Cube: own personal mini-factory" **(A)**
	4 • Different from traditional way of making things **(B)**
TS. **There is a new product for 3D printing available to the public.**	2 • 3D printing also called additive manufacturing **(B)**
	3 • $2.2 billion of 3D printers sold across the world **(B)**

First Body Paragraph

There is a new product for 3D printing available to the public. <u>For example</u>, "The Cube" is a 3D printer that allows you to have "your own personal mini-factory". **(A)** <u>Another</u> name for 3D printing is "additive manufacturing". **(B)** There is a growing market for 3D printing. <u>That is why</u> 3D printers had $2.2 billion dollars in sales across the world last year. **(B)** Printing in 3D is different form the traditional way of making things. **(B)**

Second Section of Notes

How 3D printers work.

TS: **A 3D printer creates objects differently from traditional printers.**

1 • how it works **(A)**
   1. melts plastic from cartridge
3   2. builds layers to create item
5 • download directions to make things **(A)**
2 • different way to make things – builds an object from bottom up **(B)**
3 • very thin layers of material are added on top of each other **(B)**
4 • process is guided by computers **(B)**
1 • 3D printers use different processes, most use powdered plastic **(B)**
• has 2 major parts: **(B)**
   1. "build box" – contains finely ground material
   2. "printing head" – has heat source that melts powder, or jets that spray binder glue over powder.

Second Body Paragraph

A 3D printer creates objects differently from traditional printers. They use different processes and materials, but most use powered plastic. **(A,B)** 3D printers are different from 2 dimensional printers <u>because</u> they build an object from the bottom up. **(B)** They spray very thin layers of the building material on top of each other, <u>like</u> layers in a cake. **(A,B)** <u>Also</u>, the process of 3D printing is guided by computers. **(B)** Directions for making things are downloaded electronically to the 3D printer. **(A)**

Using Transitions

Recall the information about transitions from Chapter 4. Students with grade-level or higher literacy skills tend to incorporate transition words and phrases independently. However, students with weak literacy skills or those with limited English language proficiency often need explicit instruction in transitions. They also benefit from access to a list of common transitions, either as a handout or posted in the classroom. (See Chapter 4 for Keys to Literacy's template.)

Activity

Using Transitions

Directions: *Review the body section from this sample writing piece about 3D printers. Identify places where transitions would be helpful. Use transitions to start sentences or to combine sentences.*

There is a new product for 3D printing available for the public. "The Cube" is a 3D printer that allows you to have your own personal mini-factory. Another name for 3D printing is additive manufacturing. There is a growing market for 3D printing. Last year's world-wide market had $2.2 billion dollars in sales. Printing in 3D is different from the traditional way of making things.

A 3D printer creates objects differently from traditional printers. They use a variety of processes and materials. They use powder or melted plastic from a cartridge. 3D printers are different. They build an object from the bottom up. They pile razor-thin layers of the building material on top of each other, like layers in a cake. 3D printers use computer guided technology. Model plans are downloaded electronically to the printer and provide directions for making objects.

3D printers can make all kinds of things. Basic 3D printers can make inanimate, plastic items. Advanced 3D printers are making very innovative things. A bionic ear that can send and receive sound has been made. A digital model of King Richard III's head was made that shows just what he looked like. Shoes and a dress made of nylon mesh have been made. Replicas of mastodon bones have been made. A 3D printer has made meat from animal cells and material such as amino acids.

Conclusion

Again, referring back to Chapter 4, recall that the purpose of a conclusion is to bring closure to a text, and it seeks to achieve three main goals:

- Rephrase the main topic or claim.
- Summarize key main ideas or reasons.
- Leave the reader with a sense of closure, interesting final impression, or call to action.

Activity

Practice Writing Assignment – Conclusion

<u>*Directions*</u>*: Use the space below to write a conclusion for the writing piece.*

_____

_____

_____

_____

_____

_____

_____

_____

_____

_____

_____

_____

_____

_____

_____

Step 6. Revise and edit the draft.

In Chapter 2, we discussed the importance of opportunities for students to revise their writing. While it is not necessary for every writing task to be revised so it is ready for publication, students should learn to review and revise formal writing assignments for content as well as edit them for possible errors with spelling, punctuation and capitalization, and grammar. You will learn more about feedback and revision in Chapter 9.

Figure 5E

Common Core: Writing From Sources
Writing Standards

Anchor Standard	Grade-Specific Details
# 7 **Conduct Research Projects**	• **4:** Conduct short research projects that build knowledge through investigation of different aspects of a topic. • **5:** Conduct short research projects that use several sources to build knowledge through investigation of different aspects of a topic. • **6:** Conduct short research projects to answer a question, drawing on several sources and refocusing the inquiry when appropriate. • **7:** Conduct short research projects to answer a question, drawing on several sources and generating additional related, focused questions for further research and investigation. • **8:** Conduct short research projects to answer a question (including a self-generated question), drawing on several sources and generating additional related, focused questions that allow for multiple avenues of exploration. • **9 - 12:** Conduct short as well as more sustained research projects to answer a question (including a self-generated question) or solve a problem; narrow or broaden the inquiry when appropriate; synthesize multiple sources on the subject, demonstrating understanding of the subject under investigation.
#8 **Gather Relevant Information**	• **4:** Recall relevant information from experiences or gather relevant information from print and digital sources; take notes and categorize information, and provide a list of sources. • **5:** Recall relevant information from experiences or gather relevant information from print and digital sources; summarize or paraphrase information in notes and finished work, and provide a list of sources. • **6-8:** Gather relevant information from multiple print and digital sources, using search terms effectively; assess the credibility and accuracy of each source; and quote or paraphrase the data and conclusions of others while avoiding plagiarism and following a standard format for citation. • **9 - 10:** Gather relevant information from multiple authoritative print and digital sources, using advanced searches effectively; assess the usefulness of each source in answering the research question; integrate information into the text selectively to maintain the flow of ideas, avoiding plagiarism and following a standard format for citation. • **11-12:** Gather relevant information from multiple authoritative print and digital sources, using advanced searches effectively; assess the strengths and limitations of each source in terms of task, purpose, and audience; integrate information into the text selectively to maintain the flow of ideas, avoiding plagiarism and overreliance on any one source and following a standard format for citation.

#9 Draw Evidence From Text	• **4 – 12:** Draw evidence from literary or informational texts to support analysis, reflection, and research.

Reading Standards

Anchor Standard	Grade-Specific Details
#1 Read Closely, Cite Evidence When Writing	• **4:** Refer to details and examples in a text when explaining what the text says explicitly and when drawing inferences from the text. • **5:** Quote accurately from a text when explaining what the text says explicitly and when drawing inferences from the text. • **6:** Cite textual evidence to support analysis of what the text says explicitly as well as inferences drawn from the text. • **7:** Cite several pieces of textual evidence to support analysis of what the text says explicitly as well as inferences drawn from the text. • **8:** Cite the textual evidence that most strongly supports an analysis of what the text says explicitly as well as inferences drawn from the text. • **9-10:** Cite strong and thorough textual evidence to support analysis of what the text says explicitly as well as inferences drawn from the text. • **11-12:** Cite strong and thorough textual evidence to support analysis of what the text says explicitly as well as inferences drawn from the text, including determining where the text leaves matters uncertain.
#2 Determine Central Ideas, Summarize	• **4:** Determine the main idea of a text and explain how it is supported by key details; summarize the text. • **5:** Determine two or more main ideas of a text and explain how they are supported by key details; summarize the text. • **6:** Determine the central idea of a text and how it is conveyed through particular details; provide a summary of the text distinct from personal opinions or judgments. • **7:** Determine two or more central ideas in a text and analyze their development over the course of the text; provide an objective summary of the text. • **8:** Determine a central idea of a text and analyze its development over the course of the text, including its relationship to supporting ideas; provide an objective summary of the text. • **9 - 10:** Determine a central idea of a text and analyze its development over the course of the text, including how it emerges and is shaped and refined by specific details; provide an objective summary of the text. • **11-12:** Determine two or more central ideas of a text and analyze their development over the course of the text, including how they interact and build on one another to provide a complex analysis; provide an objective summary of the text.

Chapter 6: Writing Models and Mentor Text

Use Writing Models

Most people learn to write by *emulating* others, just as we learn other new skills such as playing a sport or a musical instrument. Writing models, also known as *mentor text,* are used to demonstrate strong writing for students so they can imitate style, language, and structure in their own writing. Mentor models also show authors' use of writing techniques, also called *writing moves.*

Study of models, or opportunities for students to read, analyze, and emulate the critical elements, patterns, and forms of the writing process, is one of the eleven effective instructional practices identified in the *Writing Next* report (Graham & Perin, 2007). Portalupi and Fletcher (2001) explain that students need to "apprentice themselves" to good nonfiction writers as they learn to write their own informational or argument texts. When students emulate a model piece of writing, they imitate the structure, style and language, and techniques that are either general or specific to a certain type of writing.

Of course, emulating a writer's text is not the same as copying text. Teachers unfamiliar with the use of mentor text sometimes express concern that students will simply copy the language from a sample text verbatim. However, if you take the time to analyze sample text for a specific writing technique, give students time to talk and think about the technique, and then provide guided practice for students to try the technique in their own writing, you will find that students can create their own, original text.

Activity

When have you emulated a piece of writing?

<u>Directions</u>: In the space below, describe a recent scenario in your personal or professional life when you imitated the structure, style, or language of a "mentor text."

_____

_____

_____

_____

_____

_____

_____

_____

_____

What Can Be a Writing Model?

While published mentor text is typically used to study models of good writing, any well-written text, including students' writing samples, may be used as model writing.

Samples of mentor text can come from books, articles, classroom textbooks, literature, newspapers, magazines, or websites and blogs. Mentor text may be used broadly to teach students the difference between argument, informational, and narrative text. It can also be used more specifically to teach students specific writing techniques, such as how to write an introduction, use transitions words, or write longer, complex sentences. Depending on the instructional goal for sharing the text with students, the length of a mentor text may vary, from just a few sentences to a whole book.

Consider the following sources for mentor text:

- **Your classroom:** The first place to look is in your classroom! What textbooks, chapter books, or other content reading material are you already using that provides good examples of the writing techniques you want your students to learn?

- **Start a collection:** Be on the lookout for samples of text that you think will be useful, and start a collection for future use. If you prefer not to keep hard copies and you have access to a computer, consider storing them locally on a hard drive or in "the cloud" – with a web-based file sharing or storage platform.

- **Use mentor text resources:** Many books and websites suggest specific books and other reading material that are especially useful as mentor texts. See our suggestions at the end of the book.

Again, writing models can even be student writing. In Chapter 4, you analyzed student writing samples, focusing on how the students wrote introductions and conclusions and how they organized main ideas in the body. Save copies of your students' writing to share as mentor samples! Further suggestions for finding student writing samples are provided at the end of the book.

Identify a Focus for Selecting Mentor Text

While mentor text may be used to provide students with general guidance in a type or form of writing, model text is more typically used to highlight a specific writing skill or writing technique. Therefore, the best way to identify samples of text is to first determine your goal for using it. To do so, review your students' writing, and identify writing skills and techniques that are common weaknesses. Figure 6A suggests some focus areas. Consider providing multiple examples of mentor text that show how different authors use the specific technique you have chosen for a focus.

Figure 6A

Focus Areas for Using Mentor Text

Element	*Specific Focus Suggestions*
general; all types of writing	• writing introductions • writing leads • writing conclusions • incorporating transition words and phrases • organizing the body • development and explanation of ideas • using relevant details and rich descriptions • word choice and incorporating content-related vocabulary • creating a voice (i.e., a distinct personality, style, or point of view of a piece of writing) • writing in first, second, or third person • using capitalization and punctuation • expanding sentences
text features	• writing titles • incorporating graphics, charts, maps and other visuals • generating headings and subheadings
informational and argument writing	• using specific patterns of organization (i.e., description/explanation, sequence/chronology, compare and contrast, cause and effect, problem and solution) • using examples • using quotes and dialogue • using anecdotes • stating a claim • explaining how evidence supports a reason • explaining how a reason supports a claim
narrative writing	• story line: beginning, middle, end strategies • plot sequence, including techniques such as flashback, foreshadow, backstory • creating, developing, describing characters • use of dialogue • developing, describing settings • use of simile, metaphor, personification, alliteration, imagery • writing a personal narrative • writing a biography or autobiography

Activity

Practice With Sample Mentor Text

<u>Directions</u>: *Review the samples of mentor text provided by the trainer, keeping in mind the writing focus identified by the trainer. Answer the questions provided by the trainer, then answer the question below.*

Was it helpful to see more than one example? Explain.

_____

_____

_____

_____

_____

_____

_____

_____

_____

Analyzing Mentor Text

When we analyze a writing sample, we *dissect* the text; we seek to determine what the author did to make his/her *writing craft* effective so we can emulate that craft.

Because many students simply do not know what to look for in a mentor text, they need explicit instruction in analyzing text. Start by using *think aloud* to model writing analysis. Thinking aloud is essentially "eavesdropping on someone's thinking." During a think aloud, teachers verbalize their thoughts and actions as they analyze writing. This may include reading aloud portions of text and then stopping to pose questions about how and why the author chose to use certain words, sentence structure, or specific writing techniques.

The following instructional routine explicitly analyzes model text:

1. Identify 1-2 elements of focus.
2. Read the mentor text aloud.
   - excerpts or the full text
   - ask students to follow along silently
3. Using think aloud, share how you analyze a particular element in the mentor text.
4. Provide time and opportunities for students to discuss and contribute during the think aloud.
5. Invite students to collaborate with a peer to practice the technique.

Use Student Samples at All Stages of the Writing Process

In addition to using final and/or published versions as mentor text, consider showing students samples of writing at earlier stages of the writing process. For example:

- Notes that were taken from sources during the THINK stage of the writing process

- Top-down topic webs or other graphic organizers used at the PLAN stage

- First drafts, complete with revision and editing notes, from the REVISE stage

Student samples of notes, organizers, rough drafts, and revisions are good sources for these models. In fact, some students relate better to writing by their fellow students than published mentor text. To use student writing samples effectively, consider the following guidelines:

- First, determine the focus for analyzing the student samples. This will help you choose the samples.

- Provide 2 or more samples of text written by *different* students about the *same* topic. This will show students that there are multiple ways to express the same topic.

- Typically, choose student samples that are well-written. However, you can also use non-exemplary student writing to show students that writers do not end up with a perfect text on the first draft. When sharing these kinds of samples, ask students for suggestions to improve the writing.

The best source for student samples is your classroom and school. Start a collection of samples from content writing assignments, and collaborate with colleagues to share samples. Be sure to remove student names or other references that might identify the student writer before you share a sample.

Chapter 7: Explicit Instruction and Scaffolds

What is Scaffolding?

Scaffolding is a type of assistance offered by a teacher or a peer to support learning (Benson, 1997; Lange, 2002; Lipscomb et al., 2004). A hallmark of differentiated instruction, scaffolding enables teachers to accommodate individual student learning needs. Instructional scaffolds for writing include:

- Explicit instruction and detailed explanation for the application of a writing strategy or skill
- Breaking a writing task into smaller, more manageable parts
- Using think aloud to verbalize the thinking process as the teacher models use of a writing skill
- Prompts, tips, questions, or cue cards
- Templates, graphic organizers, checklists, or activity guides
- Opportunities for students to work collaboratively at the THINK, PLAN, WRITE, and REVISE stages of the writing process

By scaffolding, the teacher helps a student master a task or concept that the student is initially unable to grasp independently, offering assistance with only those skills that are beyond the student's ability. With the help of scaffolds, the student eventually achieves the instructional task or goal. The amount of scaffolding is gradually released as the student becomes more independent with the use of the strategy or skill. Pearson and Gallagher (1983) labeled this method the *Gradual Release of Responsibility* model. This model is also known as an *I, We, You* approach to teaching. See Figure 7A.

All students benefit from scaffolds, but they are especially critical for helping students who struggle with literacy skills

Figure 7A

Gradual Release of Responsibility

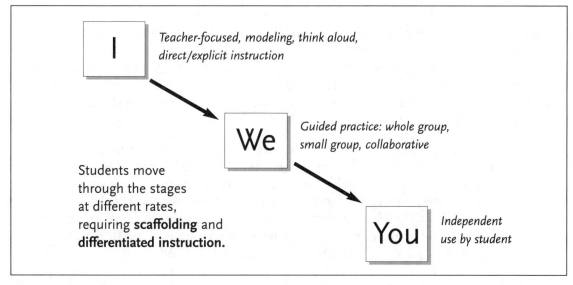

I — Teacher-focused, modeling, think aloud, direct/explicit instruction

We — Guided practice: whole group, small group, collaborative

You — Independent use by student

Students move through the stages at different rates, requiring **scaffolding** and **differentiated instruction.**

Keys to Literacy Scaffolds

Scaffolds may support every stage of the writing process. During training for *Keys to Content Writing*, teachers learn to incorporate the specific scaffolds listed in Figure 7B. We will return to examples of scaffolds later in this chapter.

Figure 7B

Keys to Literacy Scaffolds

Writing Process Stage	Scaffold
All Stages	• think aloud • set of steps • mentor models • opportunities for writing collaboration
THINK	• annotated text • two-column notes
PLAN	• top-down topic web
WRITE	• writing templates • word lists: bridging and transition words/phrases
REVISE	• Keys to Literacy checklists and rubrics

Differentiating Instruction

First introduced in Chapter 1, *differentiated instruction* refers to a teacher's determination about which students require scaffolds as they learn writing skills and the ensuing decisions about the length of support required based on the differences in learning strengths, weaknesses, and general needs. Some students may not require any scaffolds at all; others may need a few scaffolds for a brief period; still others may need more scaffolding for longer periods of time.

As noted in Chapter 1, the Common Core State Standards (CCSS) identify benchmark writing skills for students to acquire by the time they complete each grade. They do not, however, identify *how* teachers should teach these skills. Most classrooms have students with a range of literacy skills, and they also do not specify or differentiate between what or how teachers should teach students with advanced writing skills and those who struggle to write, as clearly indicated in the introduction to the CCSS:

> "The Standards do not define the intervention methods or materials necessary to support students who are well below or well above grade-level expectations. No set of grade-specific standards can fully reflect the great variety in abilities, needs, learning rates, and achievement levels of students in any given classroom... The Standards should also be read as allowing for the widest possible range of students to participate fully from the outset and as permitting appropriate accommodations to ensure maximum participation of students with special needs." (p. 9)

Explicit Instruction is a Scaffold

As you learned in Chapter 2, research finds that explicit instruction of writing strategies can have a dramatic effect on the quality of students' writing, especially for struggling writers. Explicit instruction that incorporates modeling and think aloud is a hallmark of the *I, We, You* model. *Writing Next* (Graham & Perin, 2007) identifies the explicit instruction of writing strategies as the most effective instructional practice of the eleven elements it identifies:

> "Strategy instruction involves explicitly and systematically teaching steps necessary for planning, revising, and editing text." (p. 15)

If students are not able to apply writing strategies appropriate to their grade level, they will need explicit instruction. Consider the following general suggestions for explicit instruction:

- Provide a clear explanation for *why* and *how* to use a strategy.
- Use *think aloud* to model a strategy's use.
- Follow a *Gradual Release of Responsibility* approach:
  - Provide significant support when introducing a new strategy *(I do it)*.
  - Allow sufficient opportunities for guided practice with a strategy, including collaboratively *(We do it)*.
  - Differentiate release of responsibility for independent use of a strategy based on individual student need *(You do it)*.

Figure 7C identifies writing strategies in *Keys to Content Writing* that may require explicit instruction at each stage of the writing process.

Figure 7C

Explicit Instruction of Writing Strategies

General Writing Strategies	How to: • analyze and emulate model text • recognize the differences and similarities among information, argument, and narrative text • follow the stages in the writing process • collaborate with peers to THINK, PLAN, WRITE, REVISE
THINK/PLAN	How to: • identify the audience and purpose • brainstorm and narrow down a topic • gather information from sources into two-column notes • paraphrase • integrate information from multiple sources • track sources • generate and use a top-down topic web as an organizer before writing

	How to:
WRITE/DRAFT	• use a top-down topic web, set of steps, or writing template to write a draft • turn two-column notes into sentences and paragraphs • write introductions and conclusions • use transition words and phrases to make connections among sentences and paragraphs • use proper capitalization and punctuation
REVISE	• review and revise a written draft for content • cite sources • proofread and use editing conventions (spelling, capitalization, punctuation)

Activity

Explicit Instruction

<u>*Directions*</u>: *List writing-related strategies you teach explicitly.*

_____

_____

_____

_____

_____

_____

_____

_____

_____

More About Keys to Literacy Scaffolds

Two-Column Notes

In Chapter 5, we discussed the use of two-column notes to support thinking and planning for writing as well as gathering information from sources before writing. The instructional goal as students move from elementary to secondary grades should be to create independent note takers. Initially, as students learn to take notes, teachers usually have to provide significant scaffolds; again, these scaffolds are gradually released at different rates based on individual student need.

Consider the following scaffolds for two-column notes:

1. Using think aloud, model gathering information from sources.

2. Provide explicit instruction and guided practice for note taking sub-skills, such as paraphrasing, writing concisely, and abbreviating.

3. Using think aloud, model the transfer of notes into sentences and paragraphs for a first draft.

4. Provide some or all of the main ideas in the left column of notes.

5. Provide some of the details in the right column of notes.

6. Distribute a writing template with a section for two-column notes.

7. Create opportunities for students to work collaboratively with peers to practice taking notes.

8. After students finish taking their own notes, have them compare with a set of model notes.

Top-Down Topic Webs

Research supports the use of graphic organizers to represent relationships between ideas in text (National Reading Panel, 2000; Klingner & Vaughn, 2004; Graham & Perrin, 2007). In Chapter 4, we discussed using a top-down topic web as a graphic organizer to deconstruct text, incorporating writing component cards to create visual top-down topic webs that include introductions, conclusions, and body development of sample text.

Similarly, research also supports the use of a graphic organizer as a pre-writing planning tool. Graham and Harris (2007) note that:

> "creating a written plan in advance of writing can be especially advantageous because it provides an external memory, where ideas can be stored without the risk of losing them... planning in advance can reduce the need to plan while writing, freeing needed resources to engage in other processes that demand attention, such as turning ideas into well-crafted sentences." (p. 120)

Numerous graphic organizers are available for use as pre-writing planning tools. Keys to Literacy has adopted the *top-down topic web* as a foundational graphic organizer for *The Key Comprehension Routine* and *Keys to Content Writing* because these topic webs are useful in several ways to support both reading and writing:

- To **aid comprehension**
  Example: *topic web for each day of Keys to Content Writing professional development*

- To provide a **visual representation** of basic writing structures
  Example: *topic webs used to visually represent informational and argument writing in Chapter 4*

- To be a **planning scaffold** before students write
  Example: *Figure 7D*

When used as a planning tool before writing, a top-down topic web is a scaffold that reminds students to include introductions and conclusions and to organize the body of a writing piece. For additional scaffolding, a top-down topic web may also incorporate content and text structure requirements for a specific writing assignment.

Figure 7D provides sample top-down topic webs that would have been effective scaffolds to the student who wrote the sample Grade 8 informational text, *Cross-Country Skis: What Makes Them Go Fast,* in Chapter 4. The first web provides minimal scaffolding – students are simply reminded to include an introduction and conclusion and that the body should contain 2-4 sections, with 2-4 paragraphs per section. The second topic web provides significantly more scaffolding, including: specific requirements for the introduction and conclusion; suggestion that students organize the body into three sections (i.e., camber and flex, structure, wax); and shapes for each section, reminding students to include paragraphs with main ideas and supporting details. This web also suggests two paragraph main ideas for each section.

Additional examples of top-down topic webs as pre-writing scaffolds are provided in Chapter 9.

Figure 7D

Examples of Top-Down Topic Webs as Scaffolds

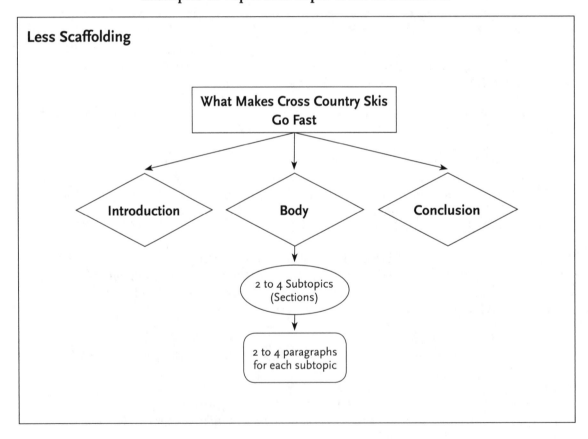

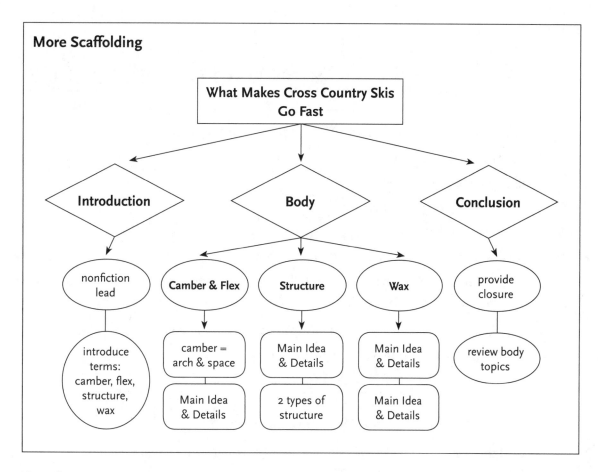

Sets of Steps

As we have already discussed, writing requires the implementation of multiple processes. Some of these processes are general (e.g., how to take two-column notes) and some are specific to content writing tasks (e.g., how to write a science lab report). Like many processes we follow in our daily lives, the writing process is simply a series of steps or tasks; breaking it down into a series of steps supports application of the process by making it more manageable.

Students vary in the degree of explicit instruction they need to learn and apply the steps of the writing process. Until they are able to use a process independently, many students benefit from a visual reminder in the form of a set of steps. The goal of this particular scaffold is to gradually release the need to consult the list as students internalize the process. See Figure 7E for some example sets of steps. You can use these examples with your students, but we encourage you to develop your own sets of steps that are tailored to writing tasks you assign.

Figure 7E

Examples of *Sets of Steps*

How to Collect Information From a Source

1. Pre-read the text and identify the information that is relevant to your topic.
2. Highlight relevant information.
   - Use one color for main ideas.
   - Use another color for supporting details.
3. Carry over the information into two-column notes.
   - Main ideas go in the left column, details in the right.
   - Paraphrase in your own words.
   - Use quotation marks around text you copy word for word.
4. Be sure to note the name of the source and page numbers.

How to Write a Summary

1. Read the material and identify the main ideas. Distinguish the main ideas from the details.
2. Write the main ideas in phrase form.
3. Begin the summary with an introductory statement.
4. Turn the main ideas into sentences, occasionally including details when it is necessary to convey the main idea.
5. Combine sentences into one or more paragraphs.
6. Use transition words to connect the sentences and the paragraphs.
7. Proofread the summary for punctuation, spelling, sentence structure, and content.

How to Write an Information Piece

1. Review the assignment requirements.

2. Identify print or digital sources.

3. Gather information from sources into two-column notes.

4. Organize notes into a writing plan.
   - chunk information and identify sub-topics
   - determine overall structure of the piece
     - introduction and conclusion decisions
     - paragraph and section decisions
   - develop a topic web to reflect writing plan

5. Write a draft.
   - write an introduction
   - write the body
   - write a conclusion
   - include transitions
   - add citations

6. Revise and edit the draft.

How to Write an Argument Piece

1. Identify the topic and review the sources.

2. Identify your claim.

3. Gather evidence from sources that supports your claim. Use two-column notes.

4. Review the evidence to generate reasons that support your claim.

5. If required, generate a counterclaim and take notes of ideas for a rebuttal.

6. Organize notes into a writing plan.
   - determine the order of the reasons you will present
   - if required, determine where you will present the counterclaim and rebuttal
   - include an introduction and conclusion in the plan
   - develop a topic web to reflect the writing plan

7. Write a draft.
   - write an introduction
   - write the body
     - write a paragraph for each reason that includes supporting evidence
     - write a paragraph that states the counter-claim and presents a rebuttal
   - write a conclusion
   - include transitions
   - add citations

8. Revise and edit the draft.

Writing a Research Report: Grades 4 - 5

1. What is your topic?
   - Get help from your teacher to pick your topic.
   - Make sure your topic is not too big.

2. Identify sources and collect information.
   - What do you already know about the topic?
   - Is there someone you can talk to who knows something about the topic?
   - Ask your teacher to help you find print and digital sources about the topic.
   - Read the print source(s) and/or watch the video(s) to find information about your topic.
   - Use two-column notes to write down important information.
     - Write main ideas in the left column, details in the right column.

3. Use a top-down topic web to plan the order of the main ideas about your topic.

4. Write a rough draft.
   - Start with an introductory sentence or paragraph that tells your topic and says one or two things about the topic.
   - Follow the order of topics on your topic web.
   - Use the information from your two-column notes to write sentences and paragraphs.
     - Write a paragraph for every main idea in the left column.
     - Start each paragraph with a topic sentence that states the main idea.
     - Use the details from the right column to write your supporting sentences.
   - If your report is more than 6 paragraphs, group the paragraphs into sections and write a heading for each section.
   - Use transition words and phrases.
   - End with a concluding sentence or paragraph that restates your topic and says something about the information in your report.

5. Review the draft
   - Follow a checklist to review your draft.
   - Be sure your ideas make sense, are complete, and are organized.
   - Check your draft for spelling, capitalization, and punctuation.
   - Ask someone else to review the draft.

6. Write a final draft
   - Fix your draft.
   - Add a list of your sources.

Writing a Research Report: Grades 6 - 12

1. Create a time line for your project.
   - Use a calendar to mark deadlines.
   - Carefully plan how much time you will need to complete each step.

2. Choose your topic.
   - Learn something about the topic to help narrow it down.
       - Read something short or talk to someone familiar with the topic.
   - Be sure there is enough information available to support your topic.
   - Write a draft title and introduction that includes the topic and purpose of your report.

3. Identify sources and collect information.
   - Locate print and digital sources, identify experts to interview.
   - Skim the texts and preview videos to find relevant information.
   - Take two-column notes.
       - Write main ideas in the left column, details in the right column.
       - Use quotation marks to track direct quotes.
       - Keep track of sources and page numbers.

4. Plan the overall organization of your report using a top-down topic web.
   - Organize the information from the notes into major topics and sub-topics.
   - Decide on the best order to present the topics.
   - Use the top-down topic web to show the plan for writing the report.

5. Write a rough draft.
   - Following the order of topics and sub-topics on your topic web, write sentences and paragraphs about the information from your notes.
   - Follow good paragraph structure as you write about the information.
       - Include a topic sentence that states the main idea.
       - Be sure all the sentences support the main idea.
   - Group the paragraphs into sections and add section headings.
   - Use transition words and phrases to make connections between sentences and among paragraphs.
   - Continue to track your sources.
   - Revise the draft title and introduction.
   - Add a conclusion

6. Review the draft.
   - Review for content.
   - Review for mechanics.

- Use a checklist as a reminder of what to review.
- Ask someone else to review the draft.

7. Write a final draft.
   - Make changes based on your review and feedback from others.
   - Develop a bibliography to formally cite sources.

How to Write An Overview of a News Article

1. Start with an introduction that includes this information: article, title, author, publication date.

2. Write 1 to 3 sentences about each of the following:

   - *Who or what is the article about?*

   - *What did the who/what do, OR what happened to the who/what?*

   - *When?*

   - *Where?*

   - *How?*

   - *Why?*

3. Conclude with a personal reaction to the article or make a connection to another news article you recently read.

4. Use transition words or phrases.

Writing Templates

For even more scaffolded support than a set of steps, a writing template provides space and support for students to draft introductions, bodies, and conclusions; a template may also include space to take notes for the body, for which it may be additionally helpful to provide a list of suggested transition words and phrases. See Figure 7F for examples of writing templates, and additional examples are provided in Chapter 9. Again, you can use these writing templates with your students, but we encourage you to develop your own templates that are tailored to writing tasks you assign. For students with especially weak writing skills, consider accepting a completed writing template as a rough draft of a writing assignment.

Some students who struggle to write sentences and paragraphs may also benefit from paragraph templates. A paragraph template provides space for students to write a topic and concluding sentence, along with space and sentence prompts or starters for the supporting sentences. See Figure 7G for templates for each of the five most common patterns of organization: cause and effect, problem and solution, sequence/chronology, description/explanation, compare and contrast.

Figure 7F

Examples of *Writing Templates*

Summary Template

1. List the main ideas in phrase form.

_____

_____

_____

_____

_____

2. Write an introductory sentence that states the topic of the summary.

_____

_____

_____

3. Turn the main ideas into sentences using your own words. You can combine some of the main ideas into one sentence.

_____

_____

_____

_____

_____

_____

_____

_____

_____

_____

4. Add transition words from the list below.
   first, next, finally, before, after, during, later, also, another, in addition, in conclusion, to sum up, similarly, however, on the contrary, most important, for example, as a result, therefore

5. Proofread and edit your summary.

Information Writing Template

1. Write the introduction.

State the topic: _____

_____

List some of the ideas presented in the body: _____

_____

_____

2. Write the body of the piece.

Paragraph 1

Topic Sentence: _____

Supporting sentences: _____

_____

_____

_____

Paragraph 2

Topic Sentence: _____

Supporting sentences: _____

_____

_____

_____

3. Write the conclusion.

Restate the topic: _____

_____

Refer to the information presented: _____

_____

_____

_____

4. Use transition words and phrases.
> *also, another, as a result, because, besides, finally, first, for example*
> *in addition, in conclusion, most importantly, such as, that is why, to sum up*

Opinion Writing Template

1. Introduce your claim (the position you are taking).

State your claim: (do not start with "I think...") _____
_____
_____
_____

2. Determine the reasons and evidence to support your claim.

Reason	Evidence (examples, facts, statistics, expert opinion)
1.	
2.	
3.	

3. Provide a conclusion that restates your claim.

Restate your claim:
_____
_____
_____

Summarize your reasons:
_____
_____
_____

4. Include transitions:

also, for example, in fact, likewise, most important, although, because

Friendly Opinion Letter Template

Return address line 1
Return address line 2
Date (Month & Day, Year)

Dear (Name)

Introductory statement (state claim) _____

_____

_____

_____

_____

_____

Body paragraph 1 (reason 1 & evidence) _____

_____

_____

_____

_____

_____

Body paragraph 2 (reason 2 & evidence) _____

_____

_____

_____

_____

_____

Concluding statement (restate claim, summarize reasons) _____

_____

_____

_____

_____

Closing (Sincerely),

Signature

Argument Writing Template

1. Introduce your claim (the position you are taking).

State the claim: _____
_____
_____
_____

State the alternate or opposing claim: _____
_____
_____
_____

2. Present the reasons and evidence to support your claim.
(you will use the evidence to explain how each reason supports your claim.)

Reason	Evidence (examples, facts, statistics, expert opinion)
1.	
2.	
3.	
4.	

3. Give a counter-claim and a rebuttal.

Counterclaim	Rebuttal

4. Provide a conclusion.

Restate the claim: _____

_____

_____

_____

Summarize your reasons: _____

_____

_____

_____

Include Transitions.

above all, also, although, another, because, by comparison, first, for example, for instance, for that reason, furthermore, however, in addition, in conclusion, in contrast, in fact, in short, to sum up, lastly, likewise, most important, second, similarly, that is why, therefore, to illustrate, unlike, without a doubt

Composition: Analysis of a Speech

Use this template for the THINK, PLAN, and WRITE stages

Introductory Statement
- Include information about the speaker, title of the speech, audience, and occasion for the speech.
- Include at least one overall statement about the speech.

_____

_____

_____

_____

_____

Body of the Composition
- List points you want to make to respond to each question.
- You will use the lists to generate paragraphs for each box.
- Be sure to include a topic sentence for each paragraph.

Body Paragraph 1

What is the main message of the speech?

Body Paragraph 2

How do you think the audience and the setting are related to the speech?

Body Paragraph 3

Describe any persuasive language and techniques used in the speech.

Body Paragraph 4

Why was this speech appropriate for the time and place it was delivered?

Conclusion of the Composition

- List points you want to make to respond to the concluding question.
- You will use this list to generate the first part of your concluding paragraph.
- Write at least one personal reaction you have to the speech.

Is this speech relevant today?

Use Transition Words

Include at least 4 transition words/phrases in the composition. Choose from the list or use your own.

another, as a result, before, compared to, during, eventually, finally, for example, for instance, in addition, in the meantime, most important, similarly, that is why, without a doubt

Figure 7G

Paragraph Templates

Cause and Effect

Topic sentence: _____

_____

_____

Details:

    (cause) _____

    Because of this _____

    The effect was _____

    Another effect was _____

Concluding sentence: _____

_____

_____

Common Transitions:

    because of, as a result, caused by, consequently, for that reason, that is why, therefore, thus

---

Problem and Solution

Topic sentence: _____

_____

_____

Details:

    The problem was _____

    Also _____

    The solution was _____

    Another solution was _____

Concluding sentence: _____

_____

_____

Common Transitions:

    the problem is, the question is, a solution is, therefore, if...then

---

Sequence or Chronology

Topic sentence: _____

_____

_____

Details:

     First _____

     Second _____

     Next _____

     Finally _____

Concluding sentence: _____

_____

_____

Common Transitions:
    first, second, initially, before, next, following, after, then, finally, lastly

---

Description or Explanation

Topic sentence: _____

_____

_____

Details:

     One thing _____

     Another _____

     In addition _____

Concluding sentence: _____

_____

_____

Common Transitions:
    for instance, such as, another, in addition, for example, furthermore, also

---

Compare and Contrast

Topic sentence: _____

_____

_____

Compare Details:

One similarity is_____

They both _____

A final way they are the same _____

Contrast Details:

One way they are different_____

Another way they are different _____

A final difference is _____

Concluding sentence: _____

_____

_____

Common Transitions:

by comparison, compared to, in like manner, likewise, similarly, but, however, in contrast, on the contrary, on the other hand, unlike

---

Activity

Scaffolds for Your Students

Answer the following questions:

What percentage of the students you teach would benefit from at least one of the Keys to Literacy scaffolds?

_____

_____

Do you think these scaffolds might "hold back" or impede your advanced writers? Explain.

_____

_____

_____

_____

What percentage of the students you teach will need additional scaffolding?

_____

_____

Chapter 8: Feedback and Revision

It is important to increase the amount of writing going on in your class; however, frequency and amount are not sufficient if not accompanied by writing instruction, including feedback and time to revise. The *feedback* that students receive matters as much as writing instruction itself. Without feedback, students cannot learn exactly how to improve their writing. Students also need time to reflect on this feedback and then improve their drafts through *revision*.

Consider coaching as an analogy for the importance of writing feedback and revision. Before a coach sends players into a game, he or she teaches the fundamental skills through coaching and watching experts (modeling), provides time for players to practice individual skills, and then expects that they apply this learning in actual play. Figure 8A compares the similarities between *learning a sport* and *learning to write*. Note that much more time is spent learning and practicing a sport than is spent actually playing games. The same is true for writing – much more time should be spent on using feedback to practice writing skills than on completing final drafts.

Figure 8A

Learning a Sport	*Learning to Write*
Instruction by the coach about how to play the game.	Instruction by the teacher about how to write.
Learn the fundamentals of the game by watching expert players.	Analyze and emulate mentor text.
Receive feedback from the coach and other players about strengths and weaknesses in playing skills.	Receive feedback from the teacher and peers about strengths and weaknesses in writing skills.
Practice individual skills in isolation to the point of automaticity, through guided practice.	Practice specific writing skills using quick writes and classroom activities.
Practice putting all the skills together during scrimmage games to build fluency as a player.	Write lots of drafts to build fluency as a writer.
Result: game-ready players!	Result: good writers!

Feedback

Feedback allows students to determine whether their writing is clear and conveys the ideas and information they want to communicate. Quite simply, the purpose of feedback is to help students improve their writing. Berne (2009) explains it this way:

"A teacher responds to student work in progress, either orally or in writing. The

student uses that response
- to create another, stronger version of the same paper
- to try a new technique to see what happens
- as one more piece of feedback that he or she may accept or reject."

Research About Effective Feedback

Consider the following guidelines, based on research about effective feedback (Bangert-Downs et al., 1991; Walberg, 1999; Wiggins, 1993; Wiggins, 2012):

- Provide feedback about the final product AND throughout the process.

- Provide user-friendly feedback that is specific, concrete, and manageable. Feedback is not of much value if it is confusing or overwhelming for the student.

- Make the desired outcomes clearer by using criterion-referenced feedback (e.g., checklists, rubrics).

- The sooner, the better: The longer students wait for feedback, the weaker the connection to their effort – and the less likely they are to benefit.

- Provide opportunities for students to give feedback to their peers and to provide their own feedback by monitoring their work against established criteria.

- Make the feedback actionable by providing opportunities for students to revise their writing. In order to learn from feedback, opportunities for application are critical to improvement.

In 2011, Biber, Nekrasova, and Horn conducted a large-scale review of the research on writing feedback, revealing the following major findings:

- All students make gains in writing development in response to feedback. (p.50)

- Less proficient writers demonstrate greater writing improvement in response to feedback than more proficient writers. (p.50)

- Larger gains in writing development result from feedback that is expressed through written comments rather than from locating and/or correcting grammatical errors. (p.50)

- Feedback focused purely on form is less effective than feedback focused on content *and* form. This finding supports the claim that writing tasks and feedback should be meaningful for students, with tasks that focus on the communication of information. (p.41)

Finding Time to Review Student Writing

A common issue that many teachers face is finding the time to review student writing in order to provide feedback or a grade. This saying is often used to sum up this challenge:

"If you have time to grade everything that students write, they are not writing enough!"

Keys to Content Writing includes instructional suggestions and graphic organizers that support several of the following suggestions that Burke (2008) gives for helping teachers handle the "paper load" associated with giving students feedback:

- Instead of correcting everything on a paper, provide simple comments instead, focusing on a few things that students do well and what they can do to improve.

- Use scoring guides (checklists, rubrics) to offer specific feedback in a short amount of time.

- Find opportunities for students to work collaboratively to provide feedback to one another.

- Cull examples from representative papers and provide feedback to the whole class using these papers.

Targeted Feedback

While it is helpful to provide feedback about multiple elements of student writing simultaneously, teachers can also provide targeted feedback to address only one or two elements at a time. In fact, many teachers find they do not have the time to write individual comments about every element in each student's writing, and selecting a few writing skills or techniques for more targeted feedback is a good solution.

Let's return to the coaching analogy. Rather than tell players everything they are "doing wrong," a good coach focuses on one or two skills at a time for targeted improvement. He or she gives feedback about those skills, including suggestions for how to improve. Most importantly, the coach provides opportunities for the players to practice the skill, with guided feedback, until they improve. The practice time targets specific skills (e.g., passing, dribbling) rather than playing a full game.

Targeted feedback for writing works the same way. Teachers target one or two writing skills for feedback (e.g., writing introductions, using transitions) and then provide time to practice *only* those skills. Quick writes are a useful tool for this sort of practice with a specific skill.

Consider offering targeted feedback on the following writing elements and skills:

- Quality of the introduction or conclusion

- Use of transitions

- Use of bridging language to explain how evidence supports reasons and reasons support claims in argument pieces

- Correct and skillfull integration of subject-specific vocabulary

- Organization of the piece and development of ideas

- Consideration of audience and purpose

- Quality of sentence construction

The focus of targeted feedback can be the same for all students in the class, or it can be different for each student based on individual goals for writing improvement.

Criterion-Referenced Feedback: Checklists and Rubrics

As noted above, research finds that criterion-referenced feedback tools, such as checklists and rubrics, make feedback more effective. *Keys to Content Writing* offers checklists and rubrics for informational and argument writing for use with students in grades 4-12. These feedback tools address the skills and text structures in *Keys to Content Writing* professional development, and they are aligned to Common Core State Standards (CCSS). These tools are available at the end of this chapter and online from the Keys to Literacy's website (https://keystoliteracy.com/resources/worksheets/).

Activity

Feedback Tools

<u>Directions</u>: *Review the checklists and rubrics at the end of the chapter. Are they similar to feedback tools you use? Describe the similarities and differences.*

_____

_____

_____

_____

_____

_____

_____

_____

_____

_____

_____

_____

_____

_____

_____

_____

Suggestions for Modifying Feedback Tools

Keys to Content Writing checklists and rubrics are generic and cover a broad range of writing skills. We encourage you to modify these tools by deleting or adding items to align specifically with the writing tasks you assign to students. See Figure 8B for examples. You will see that the line items from the generic checklists have been modified – items have been removed, deleted, or modified. If your school or district develops its own criterion-referenced tools for writing feedback, these *Keys to Content Writing* tools offer valuable guidance.

Figure 8B

Examples of Modified Checklists

Modified Teacher Checklist: Information Writing

Introduction	Excellent	Getting There	Not Yet
Is there a lead that engages the reader?			
Does the introduction identify the topic clearly?			
Does the introduction preview what is to follow?			
Does the introduction include the required background information?			
Development of Ideas			
Are the topics and subtopics presented in a logical, organized way?			
Is there sufficient detail and elaboration?			
Are the ideas and information clear and focused?			
Is evidence from sources integrated effectively?			
Are transitions used to create cohesion?			
Is the style, tone, and language appropriate to the audience, task, and purpose?			
Content			
Is content requirement one met (i.e., idenfity 3 renewable resources and 3 non-renewable resources)?			
Is content requirement two met (i.e., include the pros and cons of each resource)?			
Is content requirement three met (i.e., include the 4 focus vocabulary terms)?			
Does the writing demonstrate understanding of content?			
Is the information accurate and relevant?			
Conclusion			
Does the conclusion summarize the types of resources?			
Does the conclusion create closure to the piece?			
Sources			
Was the information from the three sources properly cited using MLA format?			

Conventions	Yes	No
Is there a systematic pattern of spelling or punctuation errors?		

Keys to Writing © 2011 www.keystoliteracy.com

Modified Teacher Checklist: Information Writing

Introduction	Excellent	Getting There	Not Yet
Does the introduction identify the topic of the lab report?			
Does the introduction state the hypothesis of the experiment?			
Development of Ideas			
Are the steps of the experiment presented in a logical, organized way?			
Is there sufficient detail and elaboration?			
Are the ideas and information clear and focused?			
Are transitions used to create cohesion?			
Content			
Content requirement: list all materials used in the experiment.			
Content requirement: include a description of possible modifications to the experiment that might produce different results.			
Is the content explained sufficiently?			
Does the writing demonstrate understanding of the experimental process?			
Does the piece include precise language and subject-specific vocabulary?			
Conclusion			
Does the conclusion make it clear if the hypothesis was confirmed?			
Does the conclusion create closure to the piece?			
Sources			
N.A.			

Conventions	Yes	No
Is there a systematic pattern of errors?		

Keys to Writing © 2011 www.keystoliteracy.com

Modified Teacher Checklist: Opinion

Introduction	Excellent	Getting There	Not Yet
Does the introduction identify claim (position)?			
Does the introduction preview at least one reason supporting the claim?			
Development of Ideas			
Is the claim supported with logical reasons?			
Are the reasons and evidence presented in an organized way?			
Is the reason explained using evidence?			
Are there at least 2 transition words used?			
Is there a formal style and an objective tone established and maintained throughout the piece?			
Content			
Is this content requirement met: include at least 2 reasons			
Is this content requirement met: include at least 1 piece of evidence for each reason that is a fact or statistic.			
Is the content explained sufficiently?			
Does the writing demonstrate understanding of the content?			
Does the piece include challenging vocabulary?			
Conclusion			
Does the conclusion restate the claim?			
Does the conclusion bring closure to the piece?			
Sources			
Were the sources for the facts and statistics listed at the end of the piece in a bibliography?			

Conventions	Yes	No
Are there any capitalization or punctuation mistakes?		
Are there any spelling mistakes?		
Are the sentences grammatically correct?		

Keys to Writing © 2011 www.keystoliteracy.com

Modified Teacher Checklist: Argument Writing

Introduction	Excellent	Getting There	Not Yet
Does the introduction identify claim?			
Does the introduction include background information about the authors of the sources?			
Does the introduction preview what is to follow with clear organization?			
Development of Ideas			
Is the claim supported with logical reasons and relevant evidence?			
Are the reasons and evidence presented in an organized way?			
Is evidence from sources integrated effectively?			
Is the counter-claim presented clearly?			
Is the rebuttal supported with logical reasons and evidence?			
Are at least 4 transitions used to link and to create cohesion among claim(s), reasons, and evidence?			
Is precise language (words, phrases, and clauses) used to clarify the relationships among claims, reasons, and evidence?			
Is there a formal style and an objective tone established and maintained throughout the piece?			
Content			
Content Requirement: include at least 3 reasons.			
Content Requirement: include at least pieces of evidence for each reason.			
Content Requirement: present some of the evidence using a visual (i.e., chart, graph, etc.)			
Are the reasons and evidence clear and focused?			
Is the content explained sufficiently?			
Does the writing demonstrate understanding of the content?			
Is the information presented accurate and relevant?			

Conclusion			
Does the conclusion highlight and support the claim?			
Does the concluding statement or section follow from and support the argument presented?			
Does the conclusion bring closure to the piece?			
Sources			
Requirement: find and use at least 3 credible sources			
Was the information from sources properly cited in text?			
Were the sources properly cited in the reference list?			

Conventions	Yes	No
Is there a systematic pattern of errors?		

Keys to Writing © 2011 www.keystoliteracy.com

Peer and Self-Feedback

A key research finding about effective feedback is that students' writing skills improve when they have opportunities to receive and give feedback to their peers (Trupiano, 2006). The feedback must be *specific,* and it is most effective when students use criterion-referenced tools. The research also sheds additional light on peer feedback, including the following:

- When students are paired for peer editing, they share both positive ("what works") feedback about a set of notes or a draft, as well as constructive feedback ("needs work"). Students in the same class make especially good peer editors because they are familiar with the parameters of an assignment and face the same tasks and concerns. (Murray, 2004)

- Multiple studies show that both the student writer and peer reviewer benefit from peer feedback (Trupiano, 2006). When they evaluate another person's writing, students become adept at identifying writing strengths and weaknesses, which in turn allows them to better revise their own writing. By receiving comments and suggestions from peers, students also become more critical of their own work.

- Peer revising is most effective when combined with instruction on evaluation criteria or revising strategies. Without this instruction, students may be reluctant to criticize each other or may be unable to provide feedback because they lack strong evaluation and revision skills (MacArther, 2007).

Figure 8C identifies some of the advantages and common pitfalls of providing students with opportunities to give peer feedback.

Figure 8C

Peer Feedback: Advantages and Common Pitfalls

advantages of peer feedback	*pitfalls of peer feedback*
• Allows for more quick, direct, timely feedback than the teacher can provide • Flexible: can be done in class, outside class, online; spoken or written • Expands a sense of audience	• Poor planning by the teacher • Too few or too many guidelines • No strategy modeling; unclear expectations • Student reluctance to participate because of prior negative experiences with peer feedback or they are not convinced of its value

Keys to Content Writing provides a checklist designed to be a tool for peer feedback or self-feedback. See Figure 8D. This template is also available on Keys to Literacy's website (https://keystoliteracy.com/resources/worksheets/). Note that the checklist encourages *active feedback,* i.e., underlining, annotations, providing suggestions for improvement.

Figure 8D

Self or Peer Feedback Checklist

What I like about this writing piece:

_____

_____

_____

_____

_____

_____

	Yes	No
Is there a good introduction?		
When you read the piece out loud, does it sound good to you?		*Underline any parts that are confusing.*
Are the ideas in the writing clear?		*Put a ? mark next to spots that are not clear and make suggestions.*
Is the piece organized?	*Provide a specific, positive comment about how the piece was organized.*	*Put the letter O in places that are disorganized and make suggestions.*
Is there enough information?		*Write INFO in spots that need more and make suggestions.*
Is there enough interesting and varied vocabulary?	*Put a * star in places where rich language was used.*	*Put the letter V with suggested vocabulary in places where the word choice could be improved.*
Were transitions used to make connections?	*Circle transition words or phrases that were used effectively.*	*Put the letter T in places where a transition would be helpful.*
Is there a good conclusion?		
Other		

Additional comments or Suggestions:

_____

_____

_____

_____

This template is available in document format at the Keys to Literacy website:
http://www.keystoliteracy.com/resources/worksheets/

Revision

Revision is a sequence of changes to writing in which ideas, words, phrases, and sentences are added, deleted, moved, or changed. Revision supports critical thinking skills as students analyze and evaluate a piece of writing, whether it is their own or a peer's. MacArthur (2007) identifies two specific reasons why revision is important:

- Revision is an important aspect of the composing process that is used extensively by good writers.

- Revision provides an opportunity for students to not only improve the quality of a particular composition, but this improvement also continues in their future writing.

Revision is a difficult process to teach. Students frequently do not know how to improve their writing and often simply do not want to take the necessary time to do so. Students also mistakenly assume that revision simply entails editing for mechanical errors, such as spelling and grammar.

Students need to hear a consistent message from all teachers that revising their writing is an important step toward becoming a better writer. Shelbie Witte (2013) relates this importance to other life skills:

> "We live in a world of revision. Whether it be the ways in which we approach our lives, alter a recipe, accessorize an outfit, or modify our golf swings, our world evolves because of the revision that happens within it. Our writing, too, evolves as we consider ways to add prose, remove words from our poetry, reorganize our arguments in analyses, and substitute better words for almost-right words." (p. 33)

The REVISE Stage of the Writing Process

In Chapter 2, we introduced the *Keys to Content Writing* model for the writing process. The last stage, REVISE, includes both revision for content (i.e., editing) and revision for mechanics conventions (i.e., proofreading). *Keys to Content Writing* recommends that students focus the first round of revision on content and organization, focusing less initially on correcting mechanical errors.

Shelbie Witte (2013, p. 34) also suggests that "teachers need to help students realize that revising is not about just fixing grammatical and surface errors, but also refers to the strength of an argument and overall structure of a piece, including content." Witte points out that student writing suffers when teachers or peers focus their feedback on just grammatical or sentence errors:

> "A focus on grammatical errors or a concern for correct form over the development of content and ideas can quickly cut off the excitement of composing. On the other hand, teacher feedback on idea development and content can effectively help students improve content."

When students focus revision on the *content* of their writing, they clarify and reshape their writing to effectively communicate their points. Therefore, content teachers who are using *writing to learn* should focus the revision process more on the content of writing and clarity of presentation than on more basic proofreading for conventions. This does not mean, however, that spelling, punctuation, and grammar conventions are unimportant and should be ignored in the revision process.

Provide Opportunities for Revision

Without the opportunity to revise writing based on feedback from peers or the teacher, students cannot learn how to improve their writing. It is therefore essential that teachers devote homework and/or class time for students to rewrite at least portions of their writing. Every piece of writing does not need to be completely rewritten; especially if time is limited, teachers may choose to have students narrow their focus on rewriting just sections of an assignment.

Once again, let's use the coaching analogy. If a coach simply tells his or her players that they are not applying a skill correctly and does not give them the necessary time to revise and practice *correct* use of the skill, their overall skills will not improve. Without a chance to make corrections, players will likely keep making the same mistakes.

The same is true for writing. If students do not have an opportunity to correct their writing through revision, writing skills will not improve.

Teacher Checklist: Information Writing

Introduction	Excellent	Getting There	Not Yet
Is there a lead that engages the reader?			
Does the introduction identify the topic clearly?			
Does the introduction preview what is to follow?			
Development of Ideas			
Are the topics and subtopics presented in a logical, organized way?			
Is there sufficient detail and elaboration?			
Are the ideas and information clear and focused?			
Is evidence from sources integrated effectively?			
Is the rebuttal supported with logical reasons and evidence?			
Are transitions used to create cohesion?			
Is the style, tone, and language appropriate to the audience, task, and purpose?			
Content			
Are the content requirements met?			
Is the content explained sufficiently?			
Does the writing demonstrate understanding of content?			
Is the information accurate and relevant?			
Does the piece include precise language and subject-specific vocabulary?			
Conclusion			
Does the conclusion highlight and support the key points?			
Does the conclusion create closure to the piece?			

Sources			
If sources were used, were they credible?			
Was the information properly cited?			

Conventions	Yes	No
Is there a systematic pattern of errors?		
Are there any capitalization or punctuation mistakes?		
Are there any spelling mistakes?		
Are the sentences grammatically correct?		

What I like about this writing piece:

_____
_____
_____
_____
_____
_____
_____
_____

Additional comments or suggestions:

_____
_____
_____
_____
_____
_____
_____
_____

Teacher Checklist: Opinion/Argument Writing

Introduction	Excellent	Getting There	Not Yet
Is there a lead that engages the reader?			
Does the introduction identify the claim?			
Does the introduction acknowledge alternate or opposing claims?			
Does the introduction preview what is to follow with clear organization?			
Development of Ideas			
Is claim supported with logical reasons and relevant evidence?			
Are the reasons and evidence presented in an organized way?			
Is evidence from sources integrated effectively?			
Is the counter-claim presented clearly?			
Is the rebuttal supported with logical reasons and evidence?			
Are transitions used to link and to create cohesion among claim(s), reasons, and evidence?			
Is precise language (words, phrases, and clauses) used to clarify the relationships among claims, reasons, and evidence?			
Is there a formal style and an objective tone established and maintained throughout the piece?			
Content			
Are the content requirements met?			
Are the reasons and evidence clear and focused?			
Is the content explained sufficiently?			
Does the writing demonstrate understanding of content?			
Is the information presented accurate and relevant?			
Does the piece include precise and subject-specific vocabulary?			
Conclusion			
Does the conclusion highlight and support the claim?			
Does the concluding statement or section follow from and support the argument presented?			
Does the conclusion bring closure to the piece?			

Sources			
If sources were used, were they credible?			
Was the information properly cited?			

Conventions	Yes	No
Is there a systematic pattern of errors?		
Are there any capitalization or punctuation mistakes?		
Are there any spelling mistakes?		
Are the sentences grammatically correct?		

What I like about this writing piece:

_____

_____

_____

_____

_____

_____

_____

_____

Additional comments or suggestions:

_____

_____

_____

_____

_____

_____

_____

_____

_____

_____

Comprehensive Rubric: Informational Writing

	4	3	2	1
Introduction	Begins with a lead that engages reader; effectively introduces topic; ideas organized and previewed.	Lead is present; topic and related information are introduced adequately.	Lead is missing or confusing; introduction is weak (lacking clear focus); ideas not clearly focused around topic.	No lead; topic not defined or confusing.
Content	Writing demonstrates thorough understanding of content.	Writing demonstrates sufficient understanding of content.	Writing demonstrates minimal understanding of the content.	Writing demonstrates misunderstandings about the content.
Requirements	Content requirements exceeded.	Content requirements met adequately.	Some content requirements met.	Content requirements were not met.
Examined & Explained	Content is examined and sufficiently explained; information is accurate and relevant; comprehensive evidence from sources is integrated effectively.	Content is explained; most information is accurate and relevant; evidence from sources is present.	Content has been mentioned, but not thoroughly explained; evidence from sources is vague or not integrated well; questionable credibility/accuracy of sources.	Content is absent from paper; evidence from sources is minimal, absent, or incorrect; question of credibility/ accuracy of sources.
Vocabulary	Precise language and subject-specific vocabulary is used accurately & effectively.	Precise language and subject-specific vocabulary is used consistently & accurately.	Subject-specific vocabulary is sometimes used accurately.	Subject-specific vocabulary is misused or not present.
Development of ideas *Organization*	Logical organization of ideas; clear and focused; sufficient and relevant detail.	Adequate organization; more detail or clarity needed to develop and extend ideas.	Underdeveloped ideas; redundancy or repetitious paraphrasing; may be formulaic.	Disorganized; details irrelevant or missing; writing may be related to topic but lacks focus.
Transitions	Appropriate and varied transitions are used throughout to clarify relationships among ideas.	Adequate use of transitions.	Inconsistent use of transitions.	Minimal, if any, transitions are used.
Conclusion	Conclusion effectively creates closure to the piece, highlights and supports the key points.	Conclusion adequately supports key points.	Conclusion is present, but lacks clear connection to information presented.	Conclusion is missing or not clearly connected to information presented.
Style	Style, tone, and language well suited to audience, task, purpose; consistent throughout the piece.	Style, tone, and language appropriate for the audience, task and purpose.	Style, tone or language may not be appropriate to the audience, task or purpose at times.	Style, tone or task not appropriate to audience, task or purpose.
Other				

©2011 www.keystoliteracy.com

This template is available in document format at the Keys to Literacy website:
http://www.keystoliteracy.com/resources/worksheets/

Comprehensive Rubric: Argument Writing

	4	3	2	1
Introduction	Begins with a lead that engages reader; effectively introduces topic; introduces the claim; reasons previewed.	Lead is present; topic and statement of claim introduced adequately.	Lead is missing or confusing; introduction is weak (lacking clear focus); claim is unclear.	No lead; topic not defined or confusing; claim not stated.
Content	Writing demonstrates thorough understanding of content.	Writing demonstrates sufficient understanding of content.	Writing demonstrates minimal understanding of the content.	Writing demonstrates content misunderstanding.
Requirements	Content requirements exceeded.	Content requirements met adequately.	Some content requirements met.	Content requirements were not met.
Examined & Explained	Content is examined and sufficiently explained; information is accurate and relevant; comprehensive evidence from sources is integrated effectively.	Content is explained; most information is accurate and relevant; evidence from sources is present.	Content has been mentioned, but not thoroughly explained; evidence from sources is vague or not integrated well; questionable credibility/accuracy of sources.	Content is absent from paper; evidence from sources is minimal, absent, or incorrect; question of credibility/ accuracy of sources.
Vocabulary	Precise language and subject-specific vocabulary is used accurately & effectively.	Precise language and subject-specific vocabulary is used consistently & accurately.	Subject-specific vocabulary is sometimes used accurately.	Subject-specific vocabulary is misused or not present.
Development of ideas *Organization*	Claim is supported with logical reasons; evidence supporting reasons is effective and presented in an organized way; rebuttal to counter-claim is clear and reasoned; ideas are clear and focused; sufficient and relevant detail.	Claim is supported with reasons; evidence is provided that explains reasons; a rebuttal to counter-claim is provided; more detail or clarity needed to develop and extend ideas.	Underdeveloped reasons and supporting evidence; redundancy or repetitious paraphrasing; rebuttal to counter-claim may be missing or unclear.	Disorganized; reasons and evidence are irrelevant or missing; writing may be related to topic but lacks focus.
Transitions	Appropriate and varied transitions are used throughout to clarify relationships among ideas.	Adequate use of transitions.	Inconsistent use of transitions.	Minimal, if any, transitions are used.
Conclusion	Conclusion effectively creates closure to the piece, highlights and supports the claim.	Conclusion adequately supports the claim.	Conclusion is present, but lacks clear connection to claim presented.	Conclusion is missing or not clearly connected to the claim.
Style	Style, tone, and language well suited to audience, task, purpose; consistent throughout the piece.	Style, tone, and language appropriate for the audience, task and purpose.	Style, tone or language may not be appropriate to the audience, task or purpose at times.	Style, tone or task not appropriate to audience, task or purpose.
Other				

©2011 www.keystoliteracy.com

This template is available in document format at the Keys to Literacy website:
http://www.keystoliteracy.com/resources/worksheets/

Chapter 9: Writing Assignment Guide (WAG)

The *Writing Assignment Guide* (WAG) is designed to help teachers plan formal writing assignments. Teachers can share the WAG with students to clearly communicate the requirements of a writing assignment, supports the teacher will provide, and opportunities they will have for feedback, revision, and collaboration.

As discussed in Chapter 2, extensive research identifies the most effective practices for teaching and using writing (Graham & Perin, 2007; Graham & Hebert, 2010; Graham et al., 2012), including setting product goals, identifying authentic audiences, teaching the stages of the writing process, writing about content, teaching text structure, using writing models, providing scaffolds for students who struggle to write, providing opportunities for students to collaborate, and providing opportunities for students to receive feedback and revise writing.

The *Writing Assignment Guide* is organized around six planning components that incorporate the instructional practices listed above. See Figure 9A for more detail about each component. Numbers of related *Writing Next* findings are included in the left column.

Figure 9A

WAG Planning Components

Set Writing Goals (Writing Next #4)	Identify and clarify the writing task: set specific product goals that include characteristics of the finished product. This includes identifying the audience and purpose, providing guidelines about length, the type of writing to be used (e.g., narrative, informational, argument), suggested form, and requirements for the finished product.
	Goal-setting can be the basis for grading writing assignments.
Show Models (Writing Next #10)	Provide students opportunities to read, analyze, and emulate models of good writing.
	Show models of every step in the writing process.
Provide Scaffolds (Writing Next #1, 11)	Provide supports for completing a writing task such as steps to follow, top-down topic webs, two-column notes, or writing templates.
Provide Opportunities for Collaboration (Writing Next #3)	Provide opportunities for students to work with peers or the teacher to plan, draft, revise, and edit their writing. Collaboration engages students more in the writing process because writing is a social activity that is best practiced in a community.

Provide Feedback (Writing Next #3)	The feedback students receive matters as much as the writing instruction they receive. Without feedback, students won't learn how to improve their writing. • Students need to know if their writing is accurate and conveying the message. • Feedback can be from the teacher, peers, or the student himself. • Feedback should be more than marking mechanical errors on final drafts. Teachers should: • provide feedback throughout the writing process. • focus on the content of the writing first, mechanics later. • provide feedback that is descriptive, specific, and based on the individual needs of the student; use feedback checklists or rubrics.
Provide Opportunities for Revision (Writing Next #9)	Students need time to reflect on self-assessment and feedback from others, and then improve their drafts through revision. Students need explicit instruction for how to incorporate feedback to revise writing. Not every writing task has to be revised to the point of *publication ready*, but students need to have some opportunities to revise based on feedback.

The WAG Planning Template

The graphic organizer in Figure 9B is a blank copy of a WAG template. This template is also available at the Keys to Literacy website (https://keystoliteracy.com/resources/worksheets/).

Figure 9B

Keys to Content Writing
Writing Assignment Guide

Writing Assignment:
Unit of Study/Content Connection: Learning Outcomes related to standards:

Set Goals for the Writing Assignment	Type of writing: __ informational __ argument __ narrative __ combo Audience: Purpose: Length & Form: Due dates: Content and Text Structure Requirements : • _____ • _____ • _____ • _____ • _____ Requirements for sources: • _____ • _____
Models	Look at these examples:
Scaffolds	Use these supports:

Feedback Process	Feedback from your peers: Feedback from the teacher:
Opportunities for Revision	
Opportunities for Collaboration	At the THINK and PLAN stage: At the WRITE Stage: At the REVISE Stage:

Classroom Examples

Samples of WAGs generated by other teachers will be helpful in determining how best to use a WAG to plan a writing assignment for your students. In Appendix A, you will find classroom examples of WAGs for writing assignments across multiple grades and subjects; there are also examples of scaffolds for these WAGs. Use these model WAGs as you develop your own WAG, for a writing assignment for your students, over the remainder of this chapter.

WAG Planning Questions

The guiding questions in Figure 9C will help you complete each section of the WAG. Refer to these questions as you develop a WAG for your own writing assignment.

Figure 9C

Writing Assignment Planning Questions

Part 1: Set Goals for the Writing Assignment	
Unit of Study, Content Connection	• What content topic are you currently covering? • What are your goals and related content standards? • What are your literacy skill goals and related literacy standards?
Type of Writing	• Which of the following types of writing would be best for the assignment: *argument, informational, narrative,* or a *combination?*
Audience	• Does the writing assignment lend itself to an authentic audience (in addition to the teacher and student peers)? • Consider these options: *members of the community, organizations or their members, businesses and corporations, politicians, younger or older students, family members, peers, blogs, student publications* • Who will actually read the writing piece?
Purpose	• What do you want the writing piece to do as it relates to the topic? • What is the reason for communicating with the audience through this piece? • What should the writing accomplish?
Length	• Suggest a range in number of words, sentences, paragraphs, or pages. • Consider: *content requirements, text structure requirements, number of sources, amount of content information, form (i.e., letter, essay, brochure, etc.).*
Form	• Identify a form for the assignment. Consider these options: *brochure, pamphlet, blog entry, journal entry, article, web page, letter, speech, poster, essay, composition, advertisement, research report, literary analysis essay.*
Due Dates	• Determine if the assignment lends itself to due dates associated with the stages of the writing process. • Consider setting a due date for each stage. For example: THINK: _____ Due: _____ PLAN: _____ Due: _____ WRITE: _____ Due: _____ REVISE: _____ Due: _____

Content and Text Structure Requirements	• Content Requirements
	   – Which content information must students address, including related vocabulary?
	   – How will you assess the content?
	• Text Structure Requirements
	   – What are the specific requirements for the introduction, conclusion, transitions, and/or body?
	   – How will you assess the structure?

Source Requirements	• Should students refer to the reading material or electronic sources you have been using for this topic? • How many sources must students use? • Which additional sources can you provide? • Do you expect students to find their own sources? • How should students cite sources?

Part 2: Show Models

• Will students be analyzing other students' writing samples?

• Will you create a sample model?

• Is there published mentor text available for use as a model (e.g., newspaper article, book, website)?

• What is the focus of the model analysis? Consider these options: *how to write an introduction, conclusion, nonfiction lead; use of transitions; formal or informal style of writing; use of precise or academic vocabulary; sentence elaboration; paragraph structure; logical and organized development of body; structure of a specific type or form of writing.*

Part 3: Provide Scaffolds

• Is there a scaffold you will provide and require <u>all</u> students to use?

• Is there a scaffold that you will provide only to struggling writers?

• Does a scaffold already exist to support this assignment, or will you need to create or modify one?

• Consider these options: *two-column notes, top-down topic webs, set of steps or directions, annotated sources, writing template, checklist, list of questions, student collaboration guidelines*

Part 4: Feedback Process

- Who will provide feedback – peer and/or teacher?
- Will the feedback be in person or in writing?
- When will the feedback occur?
- What are the feedback areas of focus?
- Will you use a feedback checklist? If so, is there one available, or will you need to create one?

Part 5: Opportunities for Revision

- Will students have time to incorporate feedback to revise their writing?
- Will the revision target specific areas?
- When and how will this revision happen?
- Does the assignment lend itself to a final draft?

Part 6: Opportunities for Collaboration

- Does the assignment lend itself to peer collaboration at the THINK, PLAN, WRITE, or REVISE stage of the writing process? If so, which?
- Will students collaborate with partners or small groups?
- How will you best assign partners or small groups – homogeneous or heterogeneous? Will you assign the pairs/groups, or will students choose?
- What expectations will you set for behavior, process, goals, and final product?
- How will you communicate these expectations (e.g., handout, classroom poster)?

Activity

Advantages of Using a WAG

Directions: Review the sample writing assignments. Jot down some notes about what might be problematic for students and how using a WAG might address those problems.

Example 1:
Select an animal of your choice. Write a paper, 1-2 typed pages in length (double-spaced) that addresses the following items: description, unusual characteristics, habitat, feeding patterns, life span, gestation period, caring for newborns, prey and predators, and any current challenges to its continued existence. The paper is due in one week.

_____

_____

_____

_____

_____

Example 2:

Select a mathematician from the list below. Research your mathematician. Write a biography, 1-2 typed pages in length, including why this mathematician is famous in the math world. Due Friday.

_____

_____

_____

_____

_____

Example 3:

Research the state you've been assigned. Write a report, 2-3 pages in length, that tells important information about that state. You can include things such as flora and fauna of the state, the economics of the state, or any other aspects of the state you find interesting.

_____

_____

_____

_____

_____

_____

_____

Source for classroom writing assignment examples: Fred Wolff

WAG: Set Goals for the Writing Assignment

Writing Next (Graham & Perin, 2007) indicates that *setting product goals* is the fourth most effective practice of the eleven most effective instructional elements to improve student writing:

> "Setting product goals involves assigning students specific, reachable goals for the writing they are to complete. It includes identifying the purpose of the assignment as well as characteristics of the final product... Specific goals include (a) adding more ideas to a paper when revising, or establishing a goal to write a specific kind of paper and (b) assigning goals for specific structural elements in a composition." (p. 17)

As you can see, *Set Goals* is among the first sections of the WAG, which describes the writing assignment and identifies the related content and literacy standards. It also presents specific goals for the assignment, including type and form of writing, length, due dates, and requirements for content, text structure, and use of sources. In the coming pages, you will have an opportunity to practice developing the *Set Goals* section of the WAG for your writing assignment.

Activity

Do you use a formal planning guide to develop writing assignments for your students? If so, does your guide share any components with the Keys to Content Writing *WAG?*

_____

_____

_____

_____

_____

_____

_____

_____

_____

_____

_____

_____

The Assignment

The first section of the WAG is for a simple description of the writing assignment. You can fill in this part of the WAG at any point during the planning process, but be prepared to make modifications as you make decisions about other elements of the WAG plan; you can even finalize this section last, if necessary. Figure 9D shows examples of assignments from the informational and argument WAG examples in Appendix A.

Figure 9D

Examples of Assignments: Informational

Grade 4: Develop a brochure that explains important school policies.

Grade 7: Develop a web page that explains how the recent drought in the Horn of Africa has impacted the people and the economy of that region.

Grades 6-8: Summarize the lifestyle choices and early detection screening tests that play an important role in preventing the progression of heart disease.

High School: Write an informational article about how a violin is made, including a history of violin construction.

High School: Write an informational pamphlet for voters about the various types of renewable and nonrenewable energy sources.

Examples of Assignments: Argument

Grade 4: Write a letter to our school principal that convinces her to continue to have two recess periods a day for the K-3 students at our school.

Grade 6: Write and submit an argument essay about the promise of geothermal energy as an alternative to fossil fuels.

Grade 7: Write an argument in support of continued funding for NASA's $17 billion budget to be published as an editorial in a national newspaper.

Grade 8: You will write an essay in which you take a position on the following question, and support your claim using teacher-provided primary source documents: Did feudalism and the Roman Catholic Church effectively provide security for the people of medieval Europe and create a more stable society? If so, how? If not, what were their failings?

Grade 9: Write a literary analysis that presents evidence for why the book or movie version of "The Boy in the Striped Pajamas" is better.

Grade 10: Write an editorial for our city newspaper that supports passage of a proposed bond levy to fund the building of new facilities at the high school.

Activity

You Do It

<u>*Directions*</u>*: Use the modified WAG at the end of this chapter. Think about a content writing assignment you might assign to your students, and make some notes below. Draft an assignment description in the WAG's first section. Finalize the assignment after you complete the rest of the WAG.*

Notes about the assignment:

_____

_____

_____

_____

_____

_____

_____

_____

_____

_____

_____

_____

_____

<u>*Unit of Study and Content Connection*</u>

The next WAG section connects the writing assignment to a unit of study; it is also where you identify related content and literacy standards. Figure 9E shows examples of content connections and standards from the informational and argument WAG examples in Appendix A.

Figure 9E

Examples of Unit of Study/Content Connections: Informational

Grade 4:
- ELA class — writing
- Literacy standard — use sources to accurately and reliably write an effective informational piece

Grade 7:
- Social studies — Africa
- Social Studies standard — explain how drought and desertification affect parts of Africa
- Literacy standard — use sources to accurately and reliably write an effective informational piece

Grades 6-8:
- Health — disease prevention and control
- Health standards — identify ways individuals can reduce the risk of factors related to chronic disease, describe the importance of early detection in preventing the progression of a disease
- Literacy standards — write an informative text that conveys ideas and information clearly; summarize key ideas from a text

High School:
- English — comparative study of historical fiction
- Literacy standards — CCSS#W8: Write informative texts to examine a topic and convey ideas and information clearly. CCSS #W2: Gather information from multiple print and digital sources, assess the credibility and accuracy of each source, and integrate the information while avoiding plagiarism. CCSS #R2: Read closely to determine what the text says and make logical inferences from it; practice citing specific textual evidence when writing.

High School:
- Science — energy resources in the Earth's system
- Earth Science — recognize, describe, and compare renewable energy sources
- Literacy standards — use sources to accurately and reliably write an effective informational piece

---

Examples of Unit of Study/Content Connections: Argument

Grade 4:
- ELA — Letter writing
- Literacy standards — opinion writing including evidence and examples based on sources and first-hand experience

Grade 6:
- Science — Standard #2.1: energy resources in the Earth system
- Literacy standards — W#1: Argument writing

Grade 7:
- Science — Astronomy standards of the Massachusetts Curriculum Frameworks related to the solar system
- Literacy standards — argument writing; gathering information from multiple sources

Grade 8:
- Social Studies — WH #1.7: Describe the major economic, social, and political developments that took place in medieval Europe.

Grade 9:
- History — WH #1.26: background, course, and consequence of the Holocaust
- Literacy standards — Reading #7: analyze the representation of a subject in two different artistic mediums; Writing #1: argument writing

Grade 10:
- History/Civics — USG #3.12: use a variety of sources, including newspapers, to identify current state and local legislative issues and examine the influence on the legislative process of political parties, interest groups, grass roots organizations, lobbyists, public opinion, the news media, and individual voters; USG #5.9: together with other students, identify a significant public policy issue in the community, gather information about that issue, fairly evaluate the various points of view and competing interests
- Literacy standard — Writing #1: Argument writing

Activity

Your Thoughts

Why do you think a WAG begins with the identification of a unit of study, content connections, and related literacy standards?

_____

_____

_____

_____

_____

_____

_____

_____

_____

Activity

You Do It

Use the modified WAG at the end of this chapter. Complete the unit of study/content connection section of the WAG, considering the following planning questions:
- *What content topic are you currently covering?*
- *What are your goals and the related content standards?*
- *What are your literacy skill goals and the related literacy standards?*

Notes about unit of study/content connection:

_____

_____

_____

_____

_____

_____

_____

_____

_____

Type of Writing

One of the first things teachers should determine is which type of writing best suits the writing assignment. Remember, the basic writing types are as follows:

- **Informational:** if the main goal of the writing piece is to inform or explain
- **Argument:** if the main goal is to convince
- **Narrative:** if the main goal is to tell a story or present a series of events

However, you may determine that a combination of writing types is best for the assignment.

Activity

You Do It

Use the modified WAG at the end of this chapter. Complete the type of writing section as you consider:

- *Which of the following types of writing would be best for the assignment: argument, informational, narrative, or a combination?*

Notes about type of writing:

_____

_____

_____

_____

_____

_____

_____

_____

_____

_____

_____

Audience

The audience and purpose elements of the WAG are aligned with CCSS writing standard #4. The audience is an individual or group to whom the writing is addressed, although it must not always be a *real* audience who will *actually* read it. Audience awareness influences decisions throughout the writing process about (*McKensie & Tompkins, 1984*):

- tone (i.e. objective, critical, apathetic, sincere, skeptical, etc.)

- language and word choice, style, or voice
- which information and how much detail to include
- how to arrange the information

Common Core Connection

Writing Standard #4:
Produce clear and coherent writing in which the development, organization, and style are appropriate to task, purpose, and audience.

Many students assume that the only audience for their writing is their teachers. However, the more *authentic* the audience is, the more engaged students will be. Not all of students' classroom writing will have an authentic audience, but teachers should try to create authentic audiences whenever possible – and, equally important, make sure that students are aware of this audience. Anne Rodier of the National Writing Project (2000) discusses authentic audiences as follows:

> "Students have to believe that what they have to say is important enough to bother writing. They have to experience writing for real audiences before they will know that writing can bring them power."

The prolific American writer, John Steinbeck also offers some advice about audience:

> "I have found that sometimes it helps to pick out one person — a real person you know, or an imagined person and write to that one."

First, you must determine if your writing assignment lends itself to an authentic audience (in addition to the teacher and student peers). If it does, create an audience. See Figure 9F for some suggestions to help you identify authentic audiences for writing assignments. Figure 9G lists authentic audiences from the informational and argument classroom WAG examples in Appendix A.

Figure 9F

Consider These Authentic Audiences

- Members of the community
- Organizations or their members
- Businesses & corporations
- Politicians
- Younger or older students
- Family members
- Peers
- Blogs (guest postings)
- Publications friendly to tweens & teens

Figure 9G

Authentic Audience Examples: Informational

Grade 4: Students who are new to our school and who do not know important policies and expectations.

Grade 7: Potential online donors who we want to contribute to our fundraising efforts related to the recent drought in Africa.

Grades 6-8: A family member or family friend who you think needs to learn how to prevent heart disease.

High School: Your information article will be included in the concert program brochure for the spring high school band concert that features a guest professional violinist. The audience for your piece will be all of the concert attendees.

High School: Senior citizens at the Maryann Morse Assisted Living facility – they are voters with limited access to computers trying to make an informed decision about ballot questions related to proposed energy projects in our area.

Authentic Audience Examples: Argument

Grade 4: Principal of our school

Grade 6: College students judging essays submitted to The Harvard University Center for the Environment.

Grade 7: The general public who read the editorial section of the newspaper.

Grade 9: Editors of the student magazine published by the National Council for Social Studies.

Grade 10: Voters from our community who read the local newspaper and who will be voting on a proposed bond levy.

Activity

You Do It

Use the modified WAG at the end of this chapter. Complete the audience section of the WAG, considering the following planning questions:

- *Does the writing assignment lend itself to an authentic audience (in addition to the teacher and student peers)?*
- *Consider these options: members of the community, organizations or their members, businesses and corporations, politicians, younger or older students, family members, peers, blogs, student publications*
- *Who will actually read the writing piece?*

Notes about audience:

_____

_____

_____

_____

_____

_____

_____

_____

_____

_____

Purpose

The purpose is closely connected to the audience. It is what you seek to accomplish in the writing with the audience in mind. The purpose typically is to express ideas, inform, explore a topic, or persuade, so the statement of purpose often begins with a verb. Figure 9H lists examples of purpose from the informational and argument classroom WAG examples in Appendix A.

Figure 9H

Purpose Examples: Informational

Grade 4: to inform new students so that they will be successful in following procedures

Grade 7: to provide sufficient explanation to make an informed decision about donating

Grades 6-8: to explain to the reader what he or she can do to prevent heart disease

High School: to inform readers about what goes into the making of a violin, including the history of violin making

High School: to inform senior citizen voters about the various energy resources so they can make an informed decision on voting day

---

Purpose Examples: Argument

Grade 4: to convince the principal that having two recess periods a day for K-3 is an important part of a well-balanced school day

Grade 6: to write a convincing argument for why geothermal energy is a worthwhile investment to replace fossil fuels

Grade 7: to write a convincing argument for why the government should continue to fund NASA in their budget

Grade 8: to convince the reader that your position is the most logical one to take

Grade 9: to convince readers that the book or movie provides better historical fiction about the Holocaust

Grade 10: to convince voters to vote in support of the bond levy

---

Activity

You Do It

Use the modified WAG at the end of this chapter. Complete the purpose section of the WAG. Consider the following planning questions:

- *What do you want the writing piece to do as it relates to the topic?*
- *What is the reason for communicating with the audience through this piece?*
- *What should the writing accomplish?*

Notes about purpose:

_____

_____

_____

_____

_____

_____

_____

_____

_____

_____

<u>*Content and Text Structure Requirements*</u>

This part of the WAG should provide specific details about what is expected in terms of content information, including vocabulary, and text structures (requirements for the introduction, conclusion, transitions, and body development). Requirements for content and text structures may often be combined into requirement statements listed on a WAG under *introduction, body,* and *conclusion* categories. As you saw in Chapter 7, the teacher and/or students can also develop a top-down topic web to provide a visual representation of the content and text structure requirements. Later in this chapter, you will have an opportunity to generate a top-down topic web that reflects the requirements in your WAG.

Well-developed content and text structure requirements clearly outline expectations for success. These requirements also provide a springboard to generate checklists or rubrics for providing feedback, evaluating writing, and grading. The more specific the requirements, the clearer the expectations for a final product will be. Figure 9I lists examples of content and text structure requirements from the informational and argument classroom WAG examples in Appendix A.

You may find it helpful to use *backward design* (Wiggins & McTighe, 2005) to determine your requirements. As its name suggests, this process starts with identifying the desired outcome for a writing assignment, and then works backwards to develop the requirements.

Figure 9I

Examples of Content and Text Structure Requirements: Informational

Grade 4:
- Visibly appealing cover with a title and picture of our school
- Inside first panel: introduction listing the policies to be explained
- 2 inside panels: paragraphs explaining the policies about school absences, being late to school, and being in the building after school
- At least 1 picture or diagram on the inside of the brochure
- End back panel: conclusion that summarizes the topic and sub-topics in the brochure
- Middle back panel: information about the source and the pages used

Grade 7:
- Introduction that includes a description of the regional location & brief timeline of events leading to the drought
- Body that includes an explanation of the severe food crisis that resulted & the threat to economic development
- Conclusion that explains how our fundraising dollars will be used
- Include this specific vocabulary: drought, desertification, famine, economy
- Include at least 3 transitions

Grades 6-8:

- An introductory statement that introduces the topic of the summary.
- In the body, identify at least 3 lifestyle choices and at least 2 screening tests.
- In the body, explain how at least 1 lifestyle choice helps to prevent heart disease.
- Use at least 2 transitions in each paragraph, and 1 transition to connect 2 body paragraphs.

High School:

- Introduction that presents the topic, background information about the uniqueness of the violin, and a reference to early violin making.
- Body that includes the history and changes in violin making to the present.
- Include in the body details about the making of a violin that come from the related movie and book (see source requirements).
- Conclusion that includes a connection between the making of a violin and a violinist.
- Include these topic-specific vocabulary words: fingerboard, soundpost, bridge, luthier, mortise, varnish.
- Use at least 3 transitions within paragraphs and at least 2 transitions to connect paragraphs.

High School:

- Include visually appealing cover with a title.
- Introduction should introduce the overall topic and clarify the differences between renewable and nonrenewable energy resources.
- Body: provide an explanatory paragraph for each renewable energy resource (solar, wind, water) including the pros and cons of each.
- Body: provide an explanatory paragraph for each nonrenewable energy source (fossil fuels, nuclear) including the pros and cons of each.
- Conclusion: include an explanation of why energy solutions are needed (growing population, accessibility issues).
- Use 2-4 photos with appropriate credit given.

Examples of Content and Text Structure Requirements: Argument

Grade 4:

- An introduction that states your claim (K-3 students need two recess periods a day.)
- Two supporting reasons that support your claim, include at least one reason that is presented in the sources, for the second reason, you may consider yourself an "expert" if you have firsthand experience about recess in grades K-3.

- Include at least one piece of evidence to support each reason, Hints: (1) evidence might include examples, facts, statistics, expert's opinions, (2) do NOT make up your own facts or statistics.
- A conclusion that restates your claim and urges the principal to take action.

Grade 6:

- Introduction that starts with a catchy lead, identifies the problem with energy from fossil fuels, and states a positive claim about geothermal energy.
- Body development that includes at least two reasons supporting geothermal energy, including evidence to support each reason.
- Body development that includes one counter-claim argument and your rebuttal
- Conclusion that supports the argument presented.

Grade 7:

- Introduction that includes the current NASA budget figure, general positive impacts/discoveries from NASA, and a positive claim about funding NASA.
- Body development that includes at least two reasons supporting the funding of NASA including evidence to support each reason.
- Body development that includes one counter-claim argument and your rebuttal.
- Conclusion that supports the argument presented.

Grade 8:

- Introduction
  - Background info on topic (Early Middle Ages, Feudalism, Medieval Catholic Church)
  - States claim
  - Previews reasons
- Body
  - Presents arguments and evidence
  - Presents at least one counter-claim
  - Provides evidence-based rebuttal to counter-claim
- Conclusion
  - Reviews claim & supporting evidence
  - Effectively connects topic & claim to larger scope of history (contextualizes)

Grade 9:

- Introduction that provides brief background knowledge about the setting, characters, and plot summary, state your claim and at least 2 literary components you compared in the movie and book that led to your position.
- Body paragraphs that present each literary component and provide specific details, including quotes or descriptions of scenes, from the book and the movie as evidence to support your position.

- Include a counter-claim that presents one area in which the opposite choice of the book or movie could make a case that it was better.
- Include transitions that connect sentences and paragraphs.
- Include a conclusion that restates your position and reviews your major reasons supporting that position.

Grade 10:
- Introduction that includes a description of the new facilities and repairs that will be covered by the bond levy, also be sure to state your position clearly in the introduction.
- Body paragraphs that present at least three reasons to support your claim, including detailed evidence.
- Body paragraphs that present at least one counter-claim and a rebuttal to that counter-claim.
- Include transitions that connect sentences and paragraphs.
- Include a conclusion that restates your position and includes summary comments designed to convince voters to pass the bond levy.

Activity

You Do It

Use the modified WAG at the end of this chapter. Complete the content and text structure section of the WAG, considering the following planning questions:

- *Content Requirements*
  - *Which content information must students address, including related vocabulary?*
  - *How will you assess the content?*
- *Text Structure Requirements*
  - *What are the specific requirements for the introduction, conclusion, transitions, and/or body?*
  - *How will you assess the structure?*

Notes about content and text structure:

_____

_____

_____

_____

_____

_____

_____

_____

_____

_____

Source Requirements

This part of the WAG is where the teacher provides information about the sources to be used, how many to use, and requirements for citation. Figure 9J lists examples of source requirements from the informational and argument classroom WAG examples in Appendix A.

Figure 9J

Examples of Source Requirements: Informational

Grade 4:
- Use our school's student handbook. You can also interview a teacher or the principal.
- Include page numbers from the handbook on the back panel.
- Include the name of the teacher or principal if some of your information came from an interview.

Grade 7:
- Use information from at least 2 of the 3 sources provided by the teacher.
- Give credit to sources within the writing (ex: according to...).

Grades 6-8:
- Use Chapter 6 of the textbook.

High School:
- Use information from at least 2 of the 3 informational sources provided by the teacher. Cite sources within the text of your piece as well as in a formal references section at the end.
- Include details about the making of a violin that come from reading the book *The Keeper of Secrets* and watching the movie *The Red Violin*. Be sure to note that these details are based on historical fiction.

High School:
- Include information from at least two of the three sources provided in class.
- Cite sources using MLA style.

Examples of Source Requirements: Argument

Grade 4:
- Think of at least one reason from each of these sources:
  - NPR (National Public Radio) podcast (about dip in obesity rates of young school children due to activity during school)
  - TIME for Kids article (doctors say kids need recess during school)

Grade 6:
- Use evidence from at least 1 source provided by the teacher.
- Reference the source in the essay.

Grade 7:
- Use evidence from at least three of the sources provided by the teacher. (See list of resources)
- Reference the source in the essay.

Grade 8:
(use a minimum of 3 of the following):
- Gregory of Tours (539-594): The Conversion of Clovis
- Annals of Xanten, 845-853
- Feudal Capitularies — 9th century
- Fulbert of Chartres: On Feudal Obligations, 1020
- "The Peasant's Cares" (poem)
- Gregory VII: Dictatus Papae, 1090
- Letter: To Pope Gregory VII from HRE Henry IV, 1076
- William of St. Thierry: *Life of Saint Bernard,* 1140 c.
- Constitutions of Clarendon, 1164
- Edward Grim: The Murder of Thomas Becket

Grade 9:
- Include specific quotes from the book.
- Use quotation marks and cite page numbers for book quotes within the text.

Grade 10:
- Use evidence from the recent speech given by the Superintendent to the School Committee.
- Include reasons and evidence based on your observation and personal experience as a student in the high school.

Activity

You Do It

Use the modified WAG at the end of this chapter. Complete the source requirements section of the WAG, considering the following planning questions:

- *Should students use any of the reading material or electronic sources you have been using for this content topic?*
- *How many sources should they use?*
- *What additional sources can you provide?*
- *Do you expect students to find their own sources?*
- *How should they cite sources?*

Notes about source requirements:

_____

_____

_____

_____

_____

_____

_____

_____

_____

_____

Length and Form

It is helpful to provide students with guidelines about your expectations for the finished length of the final draft, preferably by suggesting a *range* in the number of words, sentences, paragraphs, or pages. Providing a range gives students enough guidance about what is expected while simultaneously allowing them some flexibility. For example, some students might only need six paragraphs for the body of a writing piece, while others may need nine paragraphs to "get the job done."

Determine the range of length based on the writing type, the form of the writing piece, and the content and text requirements, because these decisions will affect the length most directly. Avoid picking an arbitrary number of words, paragraphs, or pages.

The writing *form* is the layout students are to use. Teachers should identify a form that will accommodate the writing type as well as content and text requirements. In order to make your writing assignments more authentic and engaging for students, try to use a variety of forms. Writing forms are not limited to one type of writing. Many forms, such as a blog entry, a letter, or a speech, may be used for argument, informational, or narrative writing. Figure 9K lists writing forms that may be elicited from students on PARCC (Partnership for Assessment of Readiness for College and Career) assessments. Figure 9L lists examples of length and form from the informational and argument classroom WAG examples in Appendix A.

Figure 9K

PARCC List of Writing Forms

In grades 3-5 students may be asked to produce:	• Adventure stories • Autobiography • Biography • Book reviews • Brochures • Character Sketches • Descriptions • Diaries • Encyclopedia or Wiki entries • Endings • Essays • Explanations • Fables • Fantasy stories • Fiction • How-to-do-it articles	• Humorous stories • Legends • Letters • Magazine articles • Myths • News articles • Pamphlets • Persuasive letters • Reports • Reviews • Scenes (from a play) • Short stories • Science articles • Science fiction stories • Sequels • Speeches
In addition to those forms listed for grades 3-5, students in grade 6-8 may be asked to produce:	• Anecdotes • Apologies • Complaints • Editorials • Interviews	
In addition to those forms listed for grades 3-8, students in grades 9-11 may be asked to produce:	• Satires • Spoofs • Testimonials	

Source: Partnership for Assessment of Readiness for College and Career. Writing Forms.
Retrieved from: www.parcconline.org/samples/english-language-artsliteracy/writing-forms

Figure 9L

Examples of Length/Form: Informational

Grade 4: 6 panel brochure

Grade 7: 3 to 6 paragraphs, web page

Grades 6-8: 3/4 to 1 page, summary

High School: 1 to 2 pages, article

High School: 2 pages, pamphlet

Examples of Length/Form: Argument

Grade 4: 3/4 to 1 page, letter

Grade 6: between 400 and 600 words, argument essay

Grade 7: 1 to 1 and 1/2 pages, single spaced, typed, newspaper editorial

Grade 8: 3-5 pages, essay

Grade 9: 2 to 3 pages, typed, sized 10 font, one-inch margins, literary analysis

Grade 10: 1 to 2 pages, typed, size 10 font, one-inch margins, newspaper editorial

---

Activity

You Do It

Use the modified WAG at the end of this chapter. Complete the length and form section of the WAG, considering the following:

- *Identify a form for the assignment. Consider these options: brochure, pamphlet, blog entry, journal entry, article, web page, letter, speech, poster, essay, composition, advertisement, research report, literary analysis.*

Notes about length and form:

_____

_____

_____

_____

_____

_____

_____

_____

_____

_____

_____

Due Dates

Some writing lends itself to a series of due dates that correspond to the stages in the writing process, for example:

- THINK stage: submit annotated or highlighted sources, two-column notes, list of ideas for a writing piece

- PLAN stage: submit a top-down topic web or other type of planning graphic organizer

- WRITE stage: submit a first draft of part or all of the assignment; complete a completed writing template

- REVISE stage: submit a completed peer or student feedback checklist; a revision of part or all of the assignment that incorporates feedback; a final version of the writing piece

When teachers expect students to turn in tasks at the THINK, PLAN, and WRITE stages of the writing process, they convey that the process is as important as the finished product. Teacher feedback to students about THINK and PLAN tasks also provides an opportunity to improve the information from sources and plan before writing. Consider grading these separate tasks as well, rather than only grading the final draft; this will reinforce the value of each writing stage.

Figure 9M lists examples of due dates from the informational and argument classroom WAG examples in Appendix A.

Figure 9M

Examples of Due Dates: Informational

Grade 4: Draft of wording to go into the brochure: due on Thursday (pencil version); final copy of brochure with pen and colored markers: due a week later

Grade 7: THINK: notes due Wednesday; WRITE: draft is due to a peer on Thursday; final version due Tuesday

Grades 6-8: Completed notes due on Friday; draft is due to a peer on Tuesday; final version due Thursday; share with the family member or friend and ask them to initial it by next Tuesday

High School: Draft is due to a peer on Wednesday; final version due Friday

High School: Draft is due to peer #1 on Wed. and peer #2 on Fri.; final version due Wednesday, May 15th

---

> **Examples of Due Dates: Argument**
>
> **Grade 4:** First draft due Wednesday; second draft: next Monday
>
> **Grade 6:** Information from sources due January 15; first draft due January 20; final draft due January 28
>
> **Grade 7:** Research/note taking: 2 days; first draft: 3 days (including class time and homework); peer editing: 1 day; final copy: 2 days
>
> **Grade 9:** Notes due on April 12; first draft due on April 20; final draft due on May 1

Activity

You Do It

> *Use the modified WAG at the end of this chapter. Complete the due dates section of the WAG, considering the following:*
>
> - *Determine if the assignment lends itself to due dates associated with the stages of the writing process.*
> - *Consider setting a due date for a task at each stage.*
>
> Notes about due dates:
>
> _____
>
> _____
>
> _____
>
> _____
>
> _____
>
> _____
>
> _____
>
> _____
>
> _____
>
> _____
>
> _____
>
> _____

WAG: Feedback Process, Opportunities for Revision

In Chapter 8, we discussed the importance of opportunities for students to receive feedback and make revisions based on that feedback, and we introduced the *Keys to Content Writing* feedback checklists and rubrics. The feedback section of the WAG is where teachers determine when and how feedback will be provided about student writing, including notes, pre-writing plans, and first drafts. Both the teacher and student peers may deliver feedback. The revision section of the WAG is where teachers determine the type of revision required for the writing assignment.

Figure 9N lists examples of feedback and revision sections from the informational and argument classroom WAG examples in Appendix A.

Figure 9N

Feedback and Revision Examples: Informational

Grade 4:
- <u>Feedback from peers</u>: you will get to share your draft wording with two partners on Thursday to get their suggestions for how to improve the wording.
- <u>Feedback from teacher</u>: I will also give you feedback on your draft wording.
- <u>Revision</u>: you will revise your draft wording for homework over the weekend after you get feedback from your partners and me.

Grade 7:
- <u>Feedback from peers</u>: you will give and receive feedback from a partner using the Peer Feedback Checklist.
- <u>Feedback from teacher</u>: I will give you suggestions for revision based on the personal writing goals we identified for this month.
- <u>Revision</u>: you will complete a final draft that will be posted on my class webpage.

Grades 6-8:
- <u>Feedback from peers</u>: your peer will give you feedback on your draft, including if you included all of the major lifestyle choices and screening tests.
- <u>Feedback from teacher</u>: I will give you suggestions for revision on Friday.
- <u>Revision</u>: you will write a final draft based on the feedback from your peer and me before you share it with the family member or friend.

High School:
- <u>Feedback from peers</u>: you and your peer will use the peer checklist to provide feedback to each other.
- <u>Feedback from the teacher</u>: I will give you feedback on the draft you turn in to me.
- <u>Revision</u>: your final article should be ready to submit to the music teacher for consideration in the concert program.

High School:
- <u>Feedback from peers</u>: you will get feedback from two peers for your two drafts.
- <u>Feedback from teacher</u>: I will give you feedback that you will use to create the final pamphlet with pictures.
- <u>Revision</u>: You will make final revisions to the text before adding the pictures to create the pamphlet. We will send the pamphlets to the seniors.

Feedback and Revision Examples: Argument

Grade 4:
- <u>Feedback from peers</u>: you will receive feedback from your first partner as you read the sources and take notes. You will receive feedback from a different partner when you share your first draft.
- <u>Feedback from teacher</u>: I will give you feedback about your writing template and your first draft. I will also give you feedback with a grade for your final draft.
- <u>Revision</u>: you will have time in class to use the feedback from a partner and the teacher to write a final draft.

Grade 6:
- <u>Feedback from peers</u>: you will receive feedback from 2 peers for the reasons and evidence you write in your notes. They will also give you feedback on your first draft.
- <u>Feedback from teacher</u>: I will give you feedback on your final draft.
- <u>Revision</u>: you are required to type a copy that you will submit for the contest after feedback from the teacher.

Grade 7:
- <u>Feedback from peers</u>: in class peer review for claim, counter-claim, and rebuttal to counter claim. (Structured with rubric and checklist — Example: circle claim, highlight counter-claim, etc.)
- <u>Feedback from teacher</u>: in class editing/feedback.
- <u>Revision</u>: in class after peer editing and at home during revision process.

Grade 8:
- <u>Feedback from peers</u>: you will complete peer editing upon completion of your first draft.
- <u>Feedback from teacher</u>: Teacher will provide checklist based on rubric. Peers will be strategically chosen for effective feedback.

Grade 9:
- <u>Feedback from peers</u>: You will share a first draft with a peer who will use the Peer Feedback Checklist.
- <u>Feedback from teacher</u>: Your history teacher will give you feedback on your first draft. Your English teacher will give you feedback on your final draft.
- <u>Revision</u>: you are required to write a first and final draft.

Grade 10:
- <u>Feedback from peers</u>: you will share a first draft with a peer who will use the Peer Feedback Checklist.
- <u>Feedback from teacher</u>: I will give you feedback on your final draft.
- <u>Revision</u>: you are required to write a first and final draft.

Activity

Create a Feedback Checklist

<u>*Part 1*</u>: *Use the* Keys to Content Writing *informational or argument feedback checklist. Modify it to suit your writing assignment by considering these sections of your WAG: content and text structure requirements, source requirements, length and form, due dates.*

<u>*Part 2*</u>: *How might you assign grading points to each item?*

_____

_____

_____

_____

_____

_____

<u>*Part 3*</u>: *What opportunities for feedback and revision will you provide for this writing assignment? Consider the following planning questions:*

- *Who will provide feedback – peer or teacher?*
- *Will the feedback be in person or in writing?*
- *When will the feedback occur?*
- *What are the target feedback areas?*
- *Should you use a feedback checklist? If so, is there one available, or will you need to create one?*
- *Will there be an opportunity for students to revise their work based on feedback?*
- *Will the revision target specific areas?*
- *When and how will this revision happen?*
- *Does the assignment lend itself to a final draft?*

Notes about feedback and revision:

_____

_____

_____

_____

_____

_____

_____

_____

_____

_____

209

WAG: Models

In Chapter 6, you learned that using models of writing, including mentor text, is a highly effective practice for improving student writing. The models section of the WAG is the place where teachers identify the mentor text or student samples they will provide to assist with the writing assignment. It is essential to determine a focus for the analysis of model text. Consider these options for focus areas:

> *how to write an introduction, conclusion, nonfiction lead; use of transitions; formal or informal style of writing; use of precise or academic vocabulary; sentence elaboration; paragraph structure; logical and organized development of a body; structure of a specific type or form of writing*

Activity

You Do It

Describe the models you will provide for your writing assignment. Consider the following planning questions:

- *Will students be analyzing other students' writing samples?*
- *Will you create a "sample" model?*
- *Is there published mentor text that can be used as a model (e.g., newspaper article, book, web page)?*
- *What is the focus of the model analysis?*

Notes about models:

_____

_____

_____

_____

_____

_____

_____

_____

_____

_____

_____

WAG: Scaffolds

In Chapter 7, we discussed the differentiation of instruction through the explicit teaching of writing strategies and the use of scaffolds, such as annotated text sources, two-column notes, top-down topic webs, sets of steps, writing templates, and word lists. The scaffolds section of the WAG is where teachers identify the scaffolds they will provide for all or some of the students.

Activity

Create a Top-Down Topic Web

<u>Directions</u>: *Review the content and text structure requirements you developed for your writing assignment. Then generate a top-down topic web to use with students as a pre-writing plan for your writing assignment. Consider the following:*

- *Start your topic web by placing shapes for "introduction," "body," and "conclusion" at the top of the page.*
- *Make sure to include the writing assignment's major requirements in the topic web.*
- *How might you add additional detail to the topic web to support students who struggle with writing?*

Activity

You Do It

Describe the scaffolds you might provide at the THINK, PLAN, WRITE, and REVISE stages of the writing assignment. Consider the following planning questions:

- *Is there a scaffold you will provide and require <u>all</u> students to use?*
- *Is there a scaffold that you will provide only to struggling writers?*
- *Is there a scaffold that already exists to support this assignment, or will you need to create or modify a scaffold?*
- *Consider these options: two-column notes, top-down topic webs, set of steps or directions, annotated sources, writing template, checklist, list of questions, student collaboration guidelines*

Notes about scaffolds:

_____

_____

_____

_____

_____

_____

_____

_____

_____

_____

_____

_____

_____

_____

WAG: Opportunities for Collaboration

In Chapter 2, we discussed how student collaboration at every stage of the writing process can significantly improve writing skills. The collaboration section of the WAG is where teachers identify the opportunities they will provide for students to collaborate on a writing assignment. This section provides space to list collaborative opportunities at the THINK and PLAN stage, the WRITE stage, and the REVISE stage.

Figure 90 lists examples of feedback and revision sections from the informational and argument classroom WAG examples in Appendix A.

Figure 90

Opportunities for Collaboration: Informational

Grade 4:
- At the THINK and PLAN stage: You will have some time in class with 2 partners to discuss the information in the student handbook before you start to write your draft wording.
- At the WRITE stage: You will collaborate with 2 partners before you write your final copy of the brochure

Grade 7:
- At the THINK and PLAN stage: You will have an opportunity to share your notes with a partner.
- At the REVISE stage: You will share your draft with a partner.

Grades 6-8:
- At the WRITE stage: You will show your draft to a student partner.
- At the REVISE stage: You will show your finished summary to a family member or family friend.

High School:
- At the REVISE stage: You will share your draft with a peer.

High School:
- At the THINK and PLAN stage: You can work with a partner to take notes.
- At the REVISE stage: You will share your first draft with peer #1. After you revise the first draft, you will share your second draft with peer #2

Opportunities for Collaboration: Argument

Grade 4:
- At the THINK and PLAN stage: You will work with a partner to read the sources and find evidence to support your claim. You will also work with this partner to complete the writing template.
- At the REVISE Stage: You will share your draft letter with a different partner who will give you feedback about the content and conventions.

Grade 6:
- At the THINK and PLAN stage: You will collaborate with 2 peers after the gather notes stage.
- At the WRITE Stage: You will collaborate with 2 peers to receive feedback on your rough draft.

Grade 7:
- At the THINK and PLAN stage: Discuss reasons for and against funding NASA during research and review of sources.
- At the WRITE Stage: Students can collaborate on taking notes with main ideas and details.
- At the REVISE Stage: Students will share and peer edit their arguments.

Grade 8:
- At the THINK and PLAN stage: You will collaborate with a partner(s) during the reading, interpretation, summarizing, and evaluating of documents for this assignment.
- At the WRITE Stage: You will draft your essay independently
- At the REVISE Stage: You will revise using a teacher-provided checklist with peer input and support. You will complete re-writes, edits, and revisions independently.

Grade 9:
- At the THINK and PLAN stage: You will participate in a whole class discussion during English class to brainstorm and identify literary components to consider for the comparison of the book and movie. You will also participate in a small group discussion during History class with students who have chosen the same position as you.
- At the REVISE Stage: You will receive feedback from a peer that you can use to revise your draft into a final piece.

Grade 10:
- At the THINK and PLAN stage: You will participate in a whole class discussion and brainstorm to identify reasons to support the claim and counter-claims.
- At the REVISE Stage: You will receive feedback from a peer that you can use to revise your draft into a final piece.

Activity

You Do It

Describe the opportunities for collaboration you will provide for your writing assignment. Consider the following planning questions:
- *Does the assignment lend itself to peer collaboration at the THINK, PLAN, WRITE, or REVISE stage of the writing process?*
- *Will peer collaboration be with partners or in small groups?*
- *How will you best assign partners or small groups (homogeneous or heterogeneous, assigned by teacher or student choice)?*
- *What expectations will you set for behavior, process, goals, and final product?*
- *How can you communicate these expectations (e.g., handout, classroom poster)?*

Notes about collaboration:

_____

_____

_____

_____

_____

_____

_____

_____

_____

_____

_____

_____

_____

Sharing WAGs With Students

The WAG is a tool to help teachers plan formal writing assignments. The sections of the WAG are designed to encourage teachers to incorporate best writing instruction practices, such as setting specific goals, providing models and scaffolds, planning for feedback and revision, and planning opportunities for collaboration.

However, the information in a WAG is also helpful for students. Once you complete a WAG, it is important that you share the information about the assignment with students. Some teachers like to call the student version a *SWAG* (Student Writing Assignment Guide).

The format you use to share should be based on the age and skills of your students, which will entail adapting it for its most appropriate use as the following options suggest:

- Share your version of the WAG.

- Modify the WAG by presenting the information in a more student-friendly layout.

- Consider providing several versions of the WAG that include modifications for requirements and scaffolds to differentiate instruction.

See Figure 9P for a blank template that you can use or adapt as a SWAG for your students. Figure 9Q provides several SWAG examples.

Figure 9P

SWAG: Student Writing Guide

Content Topic:

Assignment

Audience and Purpose

Length and Form

Due Dates

Content and Text Structure Requirements

Requirements for Sources

View These Models

Use These Scaffolds

You Will Receive This Feedback

Revision

Opportunities for You to Collaborate

Figure 9Q

SWAG Example #1

Name _____ Date _____ Period _____

Blow up or Blast Off? Funding the U.S. Space Program

Assignment:

Write an argument in support of continued funding for NASA's $17 billion budget to be published in an editorial in a national newspaper.

Unit of Study/Content connection:

Astronomy standards of the Massachusetts CurriculumFrameworks related to the solar system.

Learning Outcomes Related to Standards:

- Compare and contrast objects in the solar system.
- Argument writing.
- Gathering information from multiple sources

Goal/Requirements:

Write an argument in support of funding the NASA budget.

Audience:

The audience for this assignment is the general public reading the newspaper. It includes taxpayers and politicians who may influence funding.

Purpose:

To write a convincing argument for why the government should continue to fund NASA.

Length and Form:

1 to 1-1/2 page single spaced, typed
May be submitted digitally via Google
Docs. Typed printed drafts required
for peer editing in class.

Due Dates:

See checklist.

Content and Text Structure Requirements:

- Introduction that includes the current NASA budget figure, general positive impacts, discoveries from NASA, and a positive claim about funding NASA.
- Body development that includes at least two reasons supporting the funding of NASA including evidence to support each reason.
- Body development that includes one counter-claim argument and your rebuttal.
- Conclusion that supports the argument presented.

Requirements for sources:

- Use evidence from at least three of the sources provided by the teacher. (See list of resources).
- Reference the sources in the essay.

SWAG Example #2

Student Writing Guide

Content Topic: Drought in Africa

Assignment

Develop a web page that explains how the recent drought in the horn of Africa has impacted the people and the economy of that region. This will be an informational writing piece.

Audience and Purpose

The audience for this piece is people who might potentially contribute to an online fundraising effort to support the people affected by the drought.

The purpose is to provide enough information to potential donors so they can make an informed decision about donating.

Length and Form

The form is a web page that is 3 to 6 paragraphs long.

Due Dates

The first draft is due on Thursday to be shared with a peer.

The final version is due on Tuesday.

Content and Text Structure Requirements

- Include in your introduction a description of the regional location and a brief timeline of events leading to the drought.
- Include in the body an explanation of the severe food crisis and the threat to economic development that resulted from the drought.
- Include in your conclusion an explanation of how the fundraising dollars will be used.
- Include these vocabulary terms in the piece: drought, desertification, famine, economy.
- Include at least 3 transitions words/phrases in the piece.

Requirements for Sources

- Use information from at least 2 of the 3 sources provided by me.
- Give credit to sources within the writing. For example, "according to…"

View These Models and Use These Scaffolds

I will show in class 2 examples of United Nations website reports for you to emulate. I will give you a two-column note template for you to use to gather information from the sources. I will also give you a sample web-page writing template that you can use to help you write the first draft.

You Will Receive This Feedback

- You will be assigned a partner. Give and receive feedback for your first drafts using the Peer Feedback Checklist.
- I will also give you feedback on your first draft that will focus on the personal writing goals you have identified for this month.
- Use this feedback before you write your final version.

SWAG Example #3

SWAG *Student Writing Assignment Guide*

Writing Assignment:

- **Task:** write a speech
- **Audience:** your parent or caregiver
- **Purpose:** use your knowledge of climate zones to convince your family to stay in this climate zone or move to another zone

Set Goals for the Writing Assignment	Type of writing: ___ informational _X_opinion/argument ___narrative ___combo Audience: your parent or caregiver Purpose: to convince them to relocate or remain in a particular climate zone

	Length & Form: 5 to 8 paragraphs, speech form **Due dates:** • Rough draft due December 5th • Final draft due December 19th • Speech: recite to parent or caregiver over school break **Content and Text Structure Requirements :** • <u>Provide 2 visuals</u>, one that includes a map of the climate location. • <u>Introductory paragraph</u>: include a non-fiction lead and brief description of your home climate. Include a claim statement that identifies your climate of choice. • <u>First body paragraph</u>: introduce and define climate vs weather. Include a description of precipitation types and amounts in your climate of choice. • <u>Include body paragraph(s)</u> that describe the temperature range of your climate of choice. Include interesting vegetation and animals. • <u>Include body paragraph(s)</u> that describes climate-based activities and hobbies in your climate of choice. • <u>Concluding paragraph</u>: restate your claim and include a fact about your climate that would be appealing to your parent or caregiver. • <u>Include at least 3 transitions</u> phrases in the speech. **Requirements for sources:** Include information from: • Harcourt Science Weekly • AND 1 of these websites: <u>www.brainpop.com</u>, <u>www.weather.com</u>, <u>www.blueplanetbiomes.com</u> Cite your sources within the text of your speech
Feedback Process	**Feedback from your peers:** You will partner with a peer and use the peer checklist before you complete the final draft. **Feedback from the teacher:** I will provide feedback on your final draft . **Feedback from your caregiver at home:** Caregivers will fill out a checklist after you give your speech.
Opportunities for Collaboration	**At the THINK and PLAN stage:** There will be opportunities for turn and talk with other students. **At the REVISE Stage:** You will give and receive feedback from a partner.

SWAG Example #4

★ ★

Name _____ Date _____ Period _____

"And then she did something that made pretending impossible" (128)

Stargirl <u>Narrative</u> Writing Assignment

Assignment:

Write an alternate excerpt from Chapter 24 of Stargirl that develops the conflict in an interesting and original way.

Content Connections:

Novel, *Stargirl* by Jerry Spinelli

Audience:

The audience for this assignment, aside from your teacher and your peers, is Jerry Spinelli. We will be sending our excerpts to him to see what he thinks about our original ideas for alternate ways he could have developed the conflict in this chapter.

Purpose:

To write an interesting, original narrative excerpt that shows an alternate way Jerry Spinelli could have developed Chapter 24 of *Stargirl*.

Length and Form:

1 to 2 pages, double spaced, typed in 12 pt font. Must be submitted via Google Docs. Typed and printed drafts required for peer editing in class (in specified days).

Grading:

This assessment will count as a test grade. A rubric will be provided in class.

Content and Text Structure Requirements: (You MUST include)

   Beginning:

   • a beginning that introduces the setting and the characters that will appear in your excerpt

   Middle:

   • a middle that develops the conflict through characters' actions, words, and thoughts (Leo)
   • includes a clear sequence of events
   • includes character interactions (dialogue)

   End:

   • an end that leaves the reader with a clear sense that the conflict has escalated

Note: We will be following all of the steps in the writing process as we work on this assessment, including THINKING, PLANNING, WRITING, and REVISING. We will be working on peer editing in class and you will be provided with teachers feedback in class and on Google Docs.

★ ★

Activity

You Do It

Describe a SWAG you will use with students for your writing assignment.

_____

_____

_____

_____

_____

_____

_____

_____

_____

_____

_____

_____

_____

_____

_____

_____

Modified WAG for Chapter Activities

Writing Assignment:

Unit of Study/Content Connection:

Learning Outcomes related to standards:

Set Goals for the Writing Assignment	Type of writing: ___ informational ___ argument ___ narrative ___ combo
	Audience:
	Purpose:
	Length & Form
	Due dates:
	Content and Text Structure Requirements :
	Requirement for Sources:

NOTES:

Appendix

Classroom WAG Examples

Writing Assignment:

Develop a brochure that explains important school policies.

Unit of Study/Content Connection:

ELA class – writing

Learning Outcomes related to standards:

Literacy standard: use sources to accurately and reliably
write an effective informational piece.

Set Goals for the Writing Assignment	Type of writing: __X_ informational ___argument ___narrative ___combo Audience: Students who are new to our school and who do not know important policies and expectations. Purpose: To inform new students so that they will be successful in following procedures. Length & Form: Brochure, 6 panels, that includes paragraphs of information. Due dates: • Draft of wording to go into the brochure: due on Thursday (pencil version) • Final copy of brochure with pen and colored markers: due a week later Content and Text Structure Requirements : • Visibly appealing cover with a title and picture of our school • Inside first panel: paragraphs explaining the policies about school absences, being late to school, and being in the building after school. • At least 1 picture or diagram on the inside of the brochure • End back panel: conclusion that summarizes the topic and sub-topics in the brochure • Middle back panel: information about the source and the pages used

	Requirements for sources: • Use our school's student handbook. You can also interview a teacher or the principal. • Include page numbers from the handbook on the back panel. • Include the name of the teacher or principal if some of your information came from an interview.
Models	Look at these examples: • Teacher-created example of what the final brochure should look like. • Sample brochures that the teacher brings to class to see how brochures are organized.
Scaffolds	Use these supports: • Set of steps for how to complete a brochure • Top-down topic web that shows the structure of a brochure • Diagram of the brochure panels
Feedback Process	Feedback from your peers: You will get to share your draft wording with two partners on Thursday to get their suggestions for how to improve the wording. Feedback from the teacher: I will also give you feedback on your draft wording.
Opportunities for Revision	You will revise your draft wording for homework over the weekend after you get feedback from your partners and me.
Opportunities for Collaboration	At the THINK and PLAN stage: You will have some time in class with 2 partners to discuss the information in the student handbook before you start to write your draft wording. At the WRITE Stage: You will collaborate with 2 partners before you write your final copy of the brochure. At the REVISE Stage:

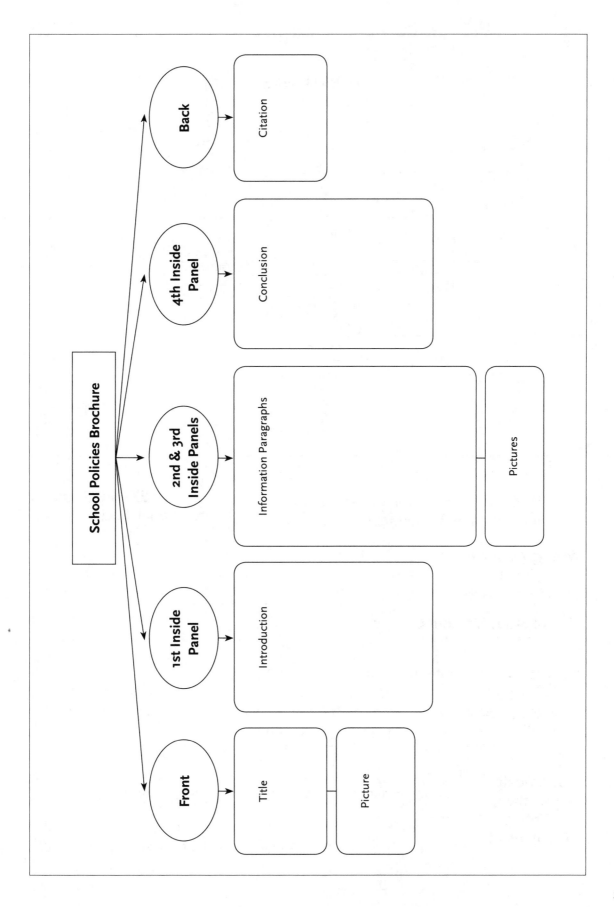

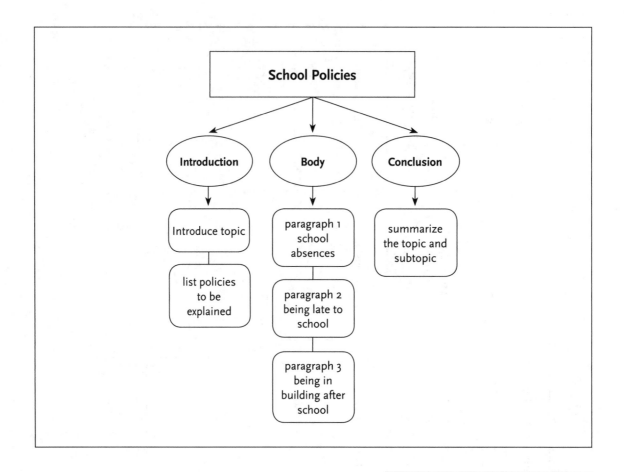

Writing Assignment Guide

Gr. 7 EXAMPLE
Informational, Social Studies

Writing Assignment:

Develop a web page that explains how the recent drought in the Horn of Africa has impacted the people & the economy of that region.

Unit of Study/Content Connection:

Social Studies: Africa (grade 7)

Learning Outcomes related to standards:

Social Studies: Explain how drought & desertification affect parts of Africa

Literacy standards: Use sources to accurately & reliably write an effective informational piece

Set Goals for the Writing Assignment	Type of writing: __X_ informational ___argument ___narrative ___combo Audience: Potential online donors who we want to contribute to our fundraising efforts.

Purpose:
To provide sufficient explanation to make an informed decision about donating.

Length & Form:
3-6 paragraphs; web page

Due dates:
- Draft is due to a peer on Thursday
- Final version due Tuesday

Content and Text Structure Requirements :
- Introduction that includes a description of the regional location & brief timeline of events leading to drought
- Body that includes an explanation of the severe food crisis that resulted & the threat to economic development
- Conclusion that explains how our fundraising dollars will be used
- Include this specific vocabulary: drought, desertification, famine, economy
- Include at least 3 transitions

Requirements for sources:
- Use information from at least 2 of the 3 sources provided by the teacher
- Give credit to sources within the writing (ex: according to…)

Models

Look at these examples:
Model the organization of your piece after the 2 sample United Nations website reports

---

Scaffolds

Use these supports:
- Two-column notes for gathering information
- Web page writing template

Feedback Process

Feedback from your peers:
You will give and receive feedback from a partner using the Peer Feedback Checklist.

Feedback from the teacher:
I will give you suggestions for revision based on the personal writing goals we identified for this month.

Opportunities for Revision	You will complete a final draft that will be posted on my class webpage.
Opportunities for Collaboration	At the THINK and PLAN stage: You will have an opportunity to share your notes with a partner. At the WRITE Stage: At the REVISE Stage: You will share your draft with a partner.

www.keystoliteracy.com

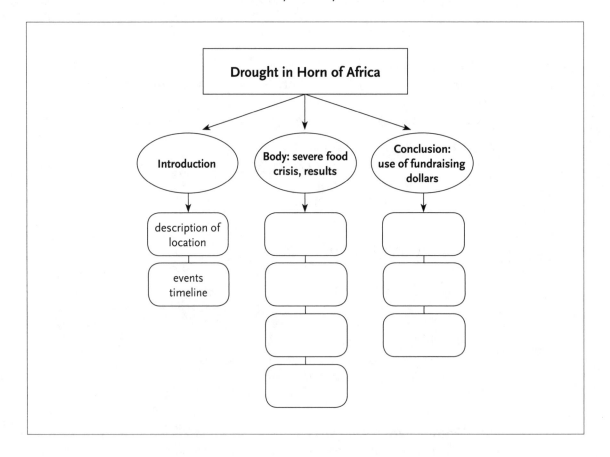

Writing Template

Writing Task:

Develop a web page that explains how the recent drought in the Horn of Africa has impacted the people & the economy of that region.

Introduction: *(introduce topic)*_____

_____

(description of location AND brief timeline of events)

_____

_____

_____

_____

_____

_____

BODY *(explain severe food crisis and resulting threat to economic development; be sure to credit sources in the paragraphs)*

Body Paragraph 1:

  *Topic Sentence:*_____

_____

_____

_____

*Detail Sentences:*_____

_____

_____

_____

_____

_____

_____

_____

_____

Body Paragraph 2:

   *Topic Sentence:*_____

_____

_____

_____

*Detail Sentences:*_____

_____

_____

_____

_____

_____

_____

Body Paragraph 3:

   *Topic Sentence:*_____

_____

_____

_____

*Detail Sentences:*_____

_____

_____

_____

_____

_____

_____

_____

_____

Body Paragraph 4:

*Topic Sentence:*_____

_____

_____

_____

*Detail Sentence:*_____

_____

_____

_____

_____

_____

_____

Conclusion: *(explain how fundraising dollars will be used)*

_____

_____

_____

_____

_____

_____

_____

_____

_____

_____

_____

Use Transitions – Suggestions:

also, another, as a result, because, besides, finally, first, for example, in addition, in conclusion, most importantly, such as, that is why, to sum up

Keys to Content Writing
Writing Assignment Guide

| **Grades 6-8 EXAMPLE**
Summary, Health Class |

Writing Assignment:

Summarize the lifestyle choices & early detection screening tests that play an important role in preventing the progression of heart disease.

Unit of Study/Content Connection:

      Health: Disease Prevention & Control (grades 6-8)

Learning Outcomes related to standards:

Health: Identify ways individuals can reduce risk factors related to chronic diseases; describe the importance of early detection in preventing the progression of a disease

Literacy standards: write an informative text that conveys ideas & information clearly; summarize key ideas & details from a text

---

| **Set Goals for the Writing Assignment** | Type of writing:
__X_ informational ____argument ____narrative ____combo

Audience:
a family member or family friend who you think most needs this information

Purpose:
to explain to the reader what he or she can do to prevent heart disease

Length & Form:
• ¾ page - 1 page; typed

Due dates:
    • Completed notes due on Friday
    • Draft is due to a peer on Tuesday
    • Final version due Thursday
    • Share with a family member or friend; ask them to initial it by next Tuesday

Content and Text Structure Requirements :
    • An introductory statement that introduces the topic of the summary
    • In the body, identify at least 3 lifestyle choices and at least 2 screening tests
    • In the body, explain how at least 1 lifestyle choice helps to prevent heart disease
    • Use at least 2 transitions in each paragraph, and 1 transition to connect the 2 body paragraphs.
    • Include a concluding statement

Requirements for sources:
    • Chapter 6 of the textbook |

Models	Look at these examples: • Student sample summaries from last year
Scaffolds	Use these supports: • Use your two column notes from chapter 6 • Use the topic web to organize your main ideas • Refer to the "how to write a summary" guide
Feedback Process	Feedback from your peers: Your peer will give you feedback on your draft, including if you included all of the major lifestyle choices and screening tests. Feedback from the teacher: I will give you suggestions for revision on Friday.
Opportunities for Revision	You will write a final draft based on the feedback from your peer and me before you share it with the family member or friend.
Opportunities for Collaboration	At the THINK and PLAN stage: At the WRITE Stage: You will show your draft to a student partner. At the REVISE Stage: You will show your finished summary to a family member or family friend.

www.keystoliteracy.com

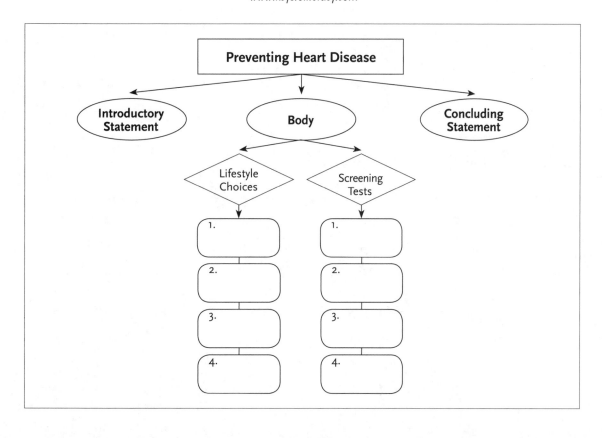

Writing Template

Writing Task:

Summarize the lifestyle choices & early detection screening tests that play an important role in preventing the progression of heart disease.

Introductory Statement *(introduce topic)*: _____

_____

_____

Body Paragraph 1:

*Topic Sentence:*_____

_____

_____

_____

*Detail Sentences (identify at least 3 lifestyle choices and 2 screening tests):*_____

_____

_____

_____

_____

_____

_____

_____

_____

Body Paragraph 2:

*Topic Sentence:*_____

_____

_____

_____

Detail Sentences (explain how at least 1 lifestyle choice helps to prevent heart disease):

_____

_____

_____

_____

_____

_____

_____

_____

_____

Conclusion *(urge the person to take preventative steps):*_____

_____

_____

_____

_____

_____

_____

_____

Use Transitions – Suggestions:

also, another, as a result, because, besides, finally, first, for example, in addition,
in conclusion, most importantly, such as, that is why, to sum up

<table>
<tr><td>*Keys to Content Writing*
Writing Assignment Guide</td><td>**High School EXAMPLE**
Informational, English</td></tr>
</table>

Writing Assignment:

Write an informational article about how a violin is made, including a history of violin construction. The article will be included in our high school band's annual concert program.

Unit of Study/Content Connection:

Comparative Study of Historical Fiction:
"The Red Violin" (movie, 1998); "The Keeper of Secrets" (book, 2011)

Learning Outcomes related to standards:

<u>Writing</u>: CCSS#2 Write informative texts to examine a topic and convey ideas and information clearly.
CCSS #8 Gather relevant information from multiple and print digital sources, assess the credibility and accuracy of each source, and integrate the information while avoiding plagiarism.
<u>Reading</u>: CCSS#2 Read closely to determine what the text says & make logical inferences from it; practice citing specific textual evidence when writing

<table>
<tr>
<td rowspan="8">Set Goals for the Writing Assignment</td>
<td>
Type of writing:
__X_ informational ___argument ___narrative ___combo

Audience:
Your informational article will be included in the concert program brochure for the spring high school band concert that features a guest professional violinist. The audience for your piece will be all of the concert-goers.

Purpose:
To inform readers about what goes into the making of a violin, including a history of violin making.

Length & Form:
• 1-2 pages, article

Due dates:
   • Draft is due to a peer on Wednesday (in class)
   • Final version due Friday

Content and Text Structure Requirements :
   • Introduction that presents the topic, background information about the uniqueness of the violin, and a reference to early violin making.
   • Body that includes the history and changes in violin making to the present.
</td>
</tr>
</table>

	• Include in the body details about the making of a violin that come from the related movie and book (see source requirements). • Conclusion that includes a connection between the making of a violin and a violinist. • Include these topic-specific vocabulary words: fingerboard, soundpost, bridge, luthier, mortise, varnish. • Use at least 3 transitions within paragraphs and at least 2 transitions to connect paragraphs. **Requirements for sources:** • Use information from at least 2 of the 3 informational sources provided by the teacher. Cite sources within the text of your piece as well as in a formal references section at the end. • Include details about the making of a violin that come from reading the book "The Keeper of Secrets" and watching the movie "The Red Violin". Be sure to note that these details are based on historical fiction.
Models	Look at these examples: • Sample articles (provided by the teacher) about the making of other musical instruments.
Scaffolds	Use these supports: • Informational format top-down topic web
Feedback Process	Feedback from your peers: You and your peer will use the peer checklist to provide feedback to each other. Feedback from the teacher: I will give you feedback on the draft you turn in to me.
Opportunities for Revision	Your final article should be ready to submit to the music teacher for consideration in the concert program.
Opportunities for Collaboration	At the THINK and PLAN stage: At the WRITE Stage: At the REVISE Stage: You will share your draft with a peer.

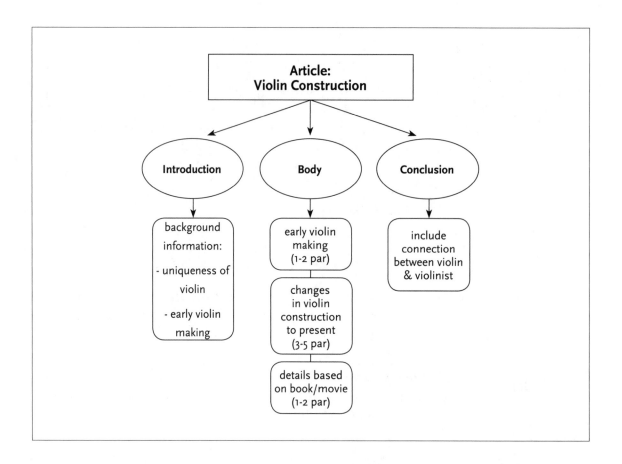

Writing Template

Writing Task: Write an article about how a violin is made, including a history of violin construction.

1. Introduction

Topic _____

_____

Background Information (the uniqueness of the violin, early violin making):

_____

_____

_____

_____

_____

_____

2. Body

Main Idea/Topic	Details
Early violin making	
Changes in violin construction to present	

Details based on
movie & book

3. Conclusion

Create closure: _____

_____

_____

_____

Connection between violin and violinist: _____

_____

_____

_____

Include Transitions

at first, beginning with, eventually, finally, from then on, after that, first, next, another, similarly, in addition, likewise, although, however above all, most important, for example, for instance, consequently, for that reason, therefore, in conclusion, in other words, to sum up

©2012 www.keystoliteracy.com

Keys to Content Writing
Writing Assignment Guide

High School EXAMPLE
Informational, Science

Writing Assignment:
Write an informational pamphlet for voters about the various types of renewable and nonrenewable energy sources.

Unit of Study/Content Connection:
Science: Energy Resources in the Earth System

Learning Outcomes related to standards:
Earth Science: recognize, describe & compare renewable energy resources
Literacy standards: Use sources to accurately & reliably write an effective informational piece

Set Goals for the Writing Assignment	Type of writing: __X_ informational ___argument ___narrative ___combo Audience: The senior citizens at the Maryann Morse Assisted Living facility; they are voters with limited access to computers trying to make an informed decision about ballot questions related to proposed energy projects in our area.

	Purpose: To inform senior citizen voters about the various energy resources so they can make an informed decision on voting day. **Length & Form:** • 2 pages; pamphlet style **Due dates:** • Draft is due to peer #1 on Wed. & peer #2 on Fri. • Final version due Wednesday, May 15th **Content and Text Structure Requirements :** • Include visually appealing cover with a title • Introduction should introduce the overall topic and clarify the differences between renewable & nonrenewable energy resources • Body: provide an explanatory paragraph for each renewable energy resource (solar, wind, water) including the pros & cons of each • Body: provide an explanatory paragraph for each nonrenewable energy source (fossil fuels, nuclear) including the pros & cons of each • Conclusion: include an explanation of why energy solutions are needed (growing population, accessibility issues) • Use 2-4 photos with appropriate credit given. **Requirements for sources:** • Include information from at least two of the three sources provided in class • Cite sources using MLA style
Models	**Look at these examples:** • Model your pamphlet after one of the 3 different examples.
Scaffolds	**Use these supports:** • Use the blank two column notes to gather information • Use the top-down topic web for this project • Refer to the MLA citation guidelines that were given in October
Feedback Process	**Feedback from your peers:** You will get feedback from two peers for your two drafts. **Feedback from the teacher:** I will give you feedback that you will use to create the final pamphlet with pictures.

Opportunities for Revision	You will make final revisions to the text before adding the pictures to create the pamphlet. We will send the pamphlets to the seniors.
Opportunities for Collaboration	At the THINK and PLAN stage: You can work with a partner if you want to take the notes. At the WRITE Stage: At the REVISE Stage: • You will share your first draft with peer #1 • After your revise the first draft, you will share your second draft with peer #2

www.keystoliteracy.com

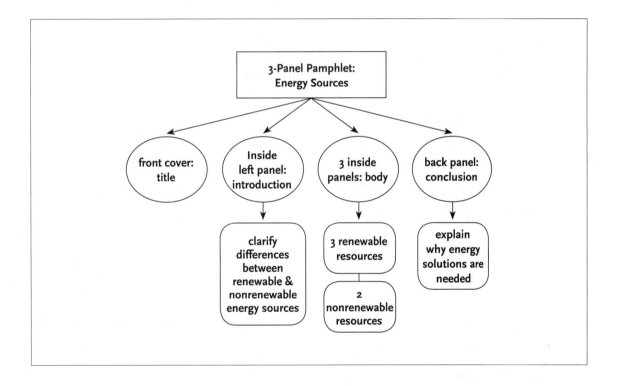

Writing Template

Writing Task:

Write an informational pamphlet for voters about the various types of renewable and nonrenewable energy sources.

Front cover: *(title)* _____

_____

picture(s) _____

_____

Inside left panel – Introduction:

Sentence to introduce topic: _____

_____

_____

Differences between renewable and nonrenewable resources:

1st difference: _____

_____

_____

_____

2nd difference: _____

_____

_____

_____

picture(s) _____

_____

3 Inside panels – Body:

Solar Power – explanation, pros, cons: _____

_____

_____

_____

_____

_____

Wind Power – explanation, pros, cons: _____

_____

_____

_____

_____

_____

Water Power – explanation, pros, cons: _____

_____

_____

_____

_____

_____

Fossil Fuels – explanation, pros, cons: _____

_____

_____

_____

_____

_____

Nuclear Power – explanation, pros, cons: _____

_____

_____

_____

_____

_____

picture(s) _____

_____

_____

Back panel – Conclusion:

*Summary of renewable and nonrenewable resources:*_____

_____

_____

_____

_____

_____

Why we need energy sources – describe growing population and accessibility issues:

_____

_____

_____

_____

_____

*picture(s)*_____

_____

_____

© 2012 www.keystoliteracy.com

Keys to Content Writing
Writing Assignment Guide

Grade 4
ELA Friendly Opinion Letter

Writing Assignment:
Write a letter to our school principal that convinces her to continue to have two recess periods a day for the K-3 students in our school.

Unit of Study/Content Connection:
Letter Writing.

Learning Outcomes related to standards:
Opinion writing including evidence and examples based on sources and first-hand experience.

Set Goals for the Writing Assignment	**Type of writing:** opinion
	
	Audience:
	teacher, school principal
	
	Purpose:
	To convince the principal that having two recess periods a day for K-3 is an important part of a well-balanced school day.
	
	Length & Form:
	• ¾ to 1 page (typed or handwritten)
	• Friendly letter format
	
	Due dates:
	• First draft: this Wednesday
	• Final draft: next Monday
	
	Content and Text Structure Requirements :
	• An introduction that states your claim (k-3 students need two recess periods a day).
	• Two supporting reasons that support your claim. Include at least one reason that is presented in the sources. For the second reason, you may consider yourself an "expert" if you have firsthand experience about recess in grades K-3.
	• Include at least one piece of evidence to support each reason. Hints: (1) evidence might include examples, facts, statistics, expert's opinions; (2) do NOT make up your own facts or statistics.
	• A conclusion that restates your claim and urges the principal to take action.
	
	Requirements for sources:
	• Think of at least one reason from each of these sources:
	   o NPR (National Public Radio) podcast (about dip in obesity rates of young school children due to activity during school)
	   o TIME for Kids article (doctors say kids need recess during school)

Models	**Look at these examples:** • Sample opinion letter from Common Core Appendix A • Samples of friendly letters from our ELA reading and writing text
Scaffolds	**Use these supports:** • Opinion writing template

Feedback Process	Feedback from your peers: • You will receive feedback from your first partner as you read the sources and take notes. • You will receive feedback from a different partner when you share your first draft. Feedback from the teacher: • I will give you feedback about your writing template and your first draft. • I will also give you feedback with a grade for your final draft.
Opportunities for Revision	You will have time in class to use the feedback from a partner and the teacher to write a final draft.
Opportunities for Collaboration	At the THINK and PLAN stage: You will work with a partner to read the sources and find evidence to support your claim. You will also work with this partner to complete the writing template. At the WRITE Stage: At the REVISE Stage: You will share your draft letter with a different partner who will give you feedback about the content and conventions.

www.keystoliteracy.com

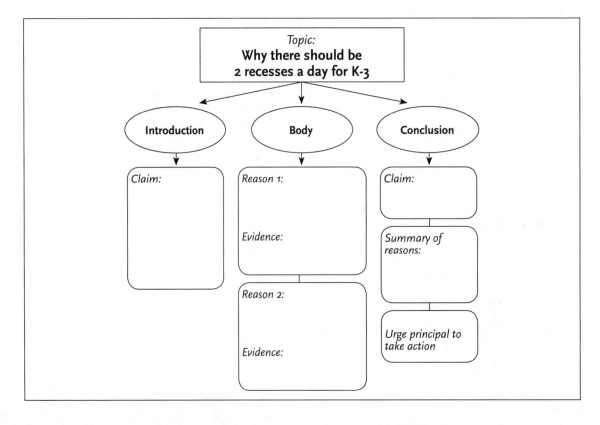

Friendly Opinion Letter Template

Return address line 1
Return address line 2
Date (Month & Day, Year)

Dear (Name)

Introductory statement (state claim) _____

_____

Body paragraph 1 (reason 1 & evidence) _____

_____

_____

_____

_____

_____

_____

_____

Body paragraph 2 (reason 2 & evidence) _____

_____

_____

_____

_____

_____

_____

Concluding statement (restate claim, summarize reasons) _____

_____

_____

_____

_____

_____

_____

Closing (Sincerely),

Signature

Keys to Content Writing **Writing Assignment Guide**	**Grade 5 Example** **Informational, Social Studies**

Writing Assignment:

Create an informational brochure describing a major Pre-Columbian civilization.

Unit of Study/Content Connection: Social Studies - civilizations

Learning Outcomes related to standards:

- History, Geography, Economics #5.2 and #5.4: Identify 3 major Pre-Columbian civilizations that existed in Central and South America and their locations. Describe their political structure, religious practices, technology, and communication. Explain why the Aztec and Inca civilizations declined in the 16th century.
- Writing #2: Write information texts to examine a topic and convey ideas and information clearly.

<table>
<tr>
<td rowspan="2">Set Goals
for the
Writing
Assignment</td>
<td>

Type of writing:
__X_ informational ___argument ___narrative ___combo

Audience:
Fifth grade scholars from a buddy class

Purpose:
Inform buddy scholars about an ancient Mesoamerican culture that impacted the growth of Pre-Columbian civilization. The final presentation of brochures will be showcased for the school community at a Town Hall Meeting.

Length & Form:
    six paneled brochure

Due dates:
- Rough Draft: Due at the end of week 6
- Final Brochure: Due at the end of week 7
- Student Scoring: During week 8
- Town Hall Meeting: October 27, presentation times TBD

Content and Text Structure Requirements :
- Visually appealing cover with a title.
- Include at least one graphic (map, timeline, photograph).
- Introduction should include name, location, and dates of chosen civilization.
- Body should include political structure, religious practices, and use of technology.

</td>
</tr>
</table>

	<ul><li>Body should also include the major cause(s) of the decline of the civilization.</li><li>Include at least 3 of these vocabulary words: agriculture, conqueror, trade, tribue, empire, Conquistador.</li><li>Conclusion should include the relevance and lasting impact of the contributions of the civilization today.</li></ul>**Requirements for sources:**<ul><li>Include a list of sources on the final panel.</li><li>Must use information from Harcourt Horizons textbook, Trueflix and World Book.</li><li>Must use information from at least one of these: <u>Civilizations of the Americans: The Maya</u> by Judith Lechner, <u>A True Book: The Aztec</u> by Andrew Santella, <u>Find Out About the Aztecs and Maya</u> by Fiona Macdonald.</li></ul>
Models	**Look at these examples:** Samples from last year's classes about ancient civilizations in Africa.
Scaffolds	**Use these supports:**<ul><li>topic web with content and text structure requirements</li><li>set of steps for writing an information piece</li><li>set of steps: how to collect information from a source</li><li>paragraph frames</li><li>two-column notes</li></ul>
Feedback Process	**Feedback from your peers:** At the culmination of the project, to determine winners, scholars will be scoring each other's work based on a rubric given by the teacher. **Feedback from the teacher:** Using a checklist, the teacher will provide feedback based on the rough draft. Using a rubric, the teacher will score the final draft to determine the letter grade for the project.
Opportunities for Revision	Based on teacher feedback, students will have time to revise their rough draft before starting their final brochure.
Opportunities for Collaboration	**At the THINK and PLAN stage:** Partner reading, research collaboration **At the REVISE Stage:** Revision with use of peer editing checklist

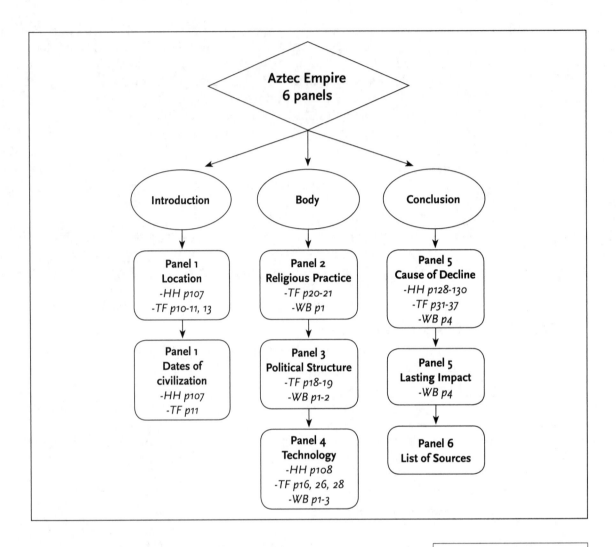

Keys to Content Writing
Writing Assignment Guide

| **Grade 6** |
| **Science** |

Writing Assignment:

Write and submit an argument essay about the promise of geothermal energy as an alternative to fossil fuels.

Unit of Study/Content Connection:

renewable and nonrenewable sources of energy

Learning Outcomes related to standards:

- Science standard #2.1: Energy resources in the Earth system
- Literacy standard W#1: Argument writing

Set Goals for the Writing Assignment	**Type of writing:** ___ informational _X_ argument ___ narrative ___ combo **Audience:** The Harvard University Center for the Environment (HUCE) is sponsoring a middle school argument essay contest on the topic of renewable sources of energy. The winner of the contest will have the essay read aloud at the HUCE annual conference on youth and the environment. The winner will also receive front row seats at the conference for 10 fellow students and a teacher from his/her school. The audience for your piece will be college student judges from HUCE. **Purpose:** To write a convincing argument for why geothermal energy is a worthwhile investment to replace fossil fuels **Length & Form:** Between 400 and 600 words. Argument essay format. Drafts may be handwritten; final copy must be typed. **Due dates:** • Information from sources due January 15 • First draft due January 20 • Final draft due January 28 **Content and Text Structure Requirements :** • Introduction that starts with a catchy lead, identifies the problem with energy from fossil fuels, and states a positive claim about geothermal energy. • Body development that includes at least two reasons supporting geothermal energy, including evidence to support each reason. • Body development that includes one counter-claim argument and your rebuttal. • Conclusion that supports the argument presented. **Requirements for sources:** • Use evidence from at least 1 source provided by the teacher. • Reference the source in the essay.
Models	**Look at these examples:** Samples of contest finalist essays from the past two years.
Scaffolds	**Use these supports:** • Set of Steps • Argument writing template

Feedback Process	**Feedback from your peers:** You will receive feedback from 2 peers for the reasons and evidence you write in your notes. They will also give you feedback on your first draft. **Feedback from the teacher:** I will give you feedback on your final draft.
Opportunities for Revision	You are required to type a copy that you will submit for the contest after feedback from the teacher.
Opportunities for Collaboration	**At the THINK and PLAN stage:** You will collaborate with 2 peers after the gather notes stage. **At the WRITE Stage:** You will collaborate with 2 peers to receive feedback on your rough draft. **At the REVISE Stage:**

www.keystoliteracy.com

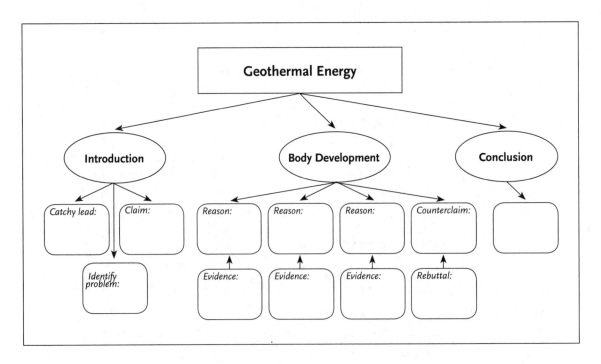

Argument Template

TASK: *Write an argument essay about the promise of geothermal energy as an alternative to fossil fuels. The essay will be submitted to the HUCE essay contest.*

1. INTRODUCTION

Lead:_____

Identify the main problem with energy from fossil fuels: _____

_____

_____

State a positive claim about geothermal energy: _____

_____

_____

2. BODY

Reason 1:_____

_____

_____

_____

Evidence: _____

_____

_____

_____

_____

_____

_____

_____

_____

_____

_____

_____

_____

_____

_____

Reason 2:_____

_____

_____

Evidence:_____

_____

_____

_____

_____

_____

_____

_____

_____

_____

_____

Counterclaim: _____

_____

_____

_____

_____

Rebuttal: _____

_____

_____

_____

_____

_____

_____

_____

3. CONCLUSION

Restate the claim: _____

_____

_____

_____

_____

_____

_____

Summarize your reasons: _____

_____

_____

_____

_____

Include Transitions

above all, also, although, another, because, by comparison, first, for example, for instance, for that reason, furthermore, however, in addition, in conclusion, in contrast, in fact, in short, to sum up, lastly, likewise, most important, second, similarly, that is why, therefore, to illustrate, unlike, without a doubt

Grade 7
Science

Writing Assignment:

Write an argument in support of continued funding for NASA's $17 billion budget to be published in an editorial in a national newspaper.

Unit of Study/Content Connection: Astronomy standards of the Massachusetts Curriculum Frameworks related to the solar system.

Learning Outcomes related to standards:
- Compare and contrast objects in the solar system.
- Argument writing.
- Gathering information from multiple sources

Set Goals for the Writing Assignment	**Type of writing:** ___ informational _X_ argument ___ narrative ___ combo **Audience:** The audience for this assignment is the general public reading the newspaper. It includes taxpayers and politicians who may influence funding. **Purpose:** To write a convincing argument for why the government should continue to fund NASA on their budget. **Length & Form:** 1 to 1 ½ page single spaced, typed. May be submitted digitally via Google Docs. Typed printed drafts required for peer editing in class. **Due dates:** • Research/note taking: 2 days • First draft: 3 days (including class time and homework) • Peer editing: 1 day • Final Copy: 2 days **Content and Text Structure Requirements :** • Introduction that includes the current NASA budget figure, general positive impacts/discoveries from NASA, and a positive claim about funding NASA. • Body development that includes at least two reasons supporting the funding of NASA including evidence to support each reason. • Body development that includes one counter-claim argument and your rebuttal. • Conclusion that supports the argument presented.

	Requirements for sources: • Use evidence from at least three of the sources provided by the teacher. (See list of resources) • Reference the source in the essay.
Models	Look at these examples: • Editorials • Other examples
Scaffolds	Use these supports: • Checklist with steps (due dates and steps) • Argument writing template • Two-column notes template for main idea and details • Transition words and phrases template
Feedback Process	Feedback from your peers: In class, peer review for claim, counter-claim, and rebuttal to counter claim. (Structured with rubric and checklist - Example: circle claim, highlight counter-claim, etc.) Feedback from the teacher: In class editing/feedback.
Opportunities for Revision	In class after peer editing and at home during revision process.
Opportunities for Collaboration	At the THINK and PLAN stage: Discuss reasons for and against funding NASA during research and review of sources. At the WRITE Stage: Students can collaborate on taking notes with main ideas and details. At the REVISE Stage: Students will share and peer edit their arguments.

Developed by Jim Schliefke and Ellen Forman, Grade 7 science teachers, Franklin Public Schools, MA

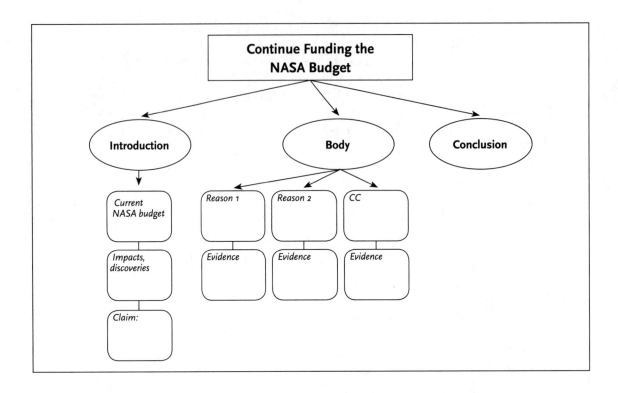

Argument Template

TASK: *Write a newspaper editorial argument in support of funding for NASA's $17 billion budget.*

1. INTRODUCTION

Provide background information

(current NASA budget figure) _____

_____

(general positive impacts/discoveries from NASA) _____

_____

_____

_____

_____

State a positive claim about funding NASA: _____

_____

_____

_____

_____

2. BODY

Reason 1:_____

_____

_____

_____

_____

Evidence:_____

_____

_____

_____

_____

_____

_____

_____

_____

_____

Reason 2:_____

_____

_____

_____

Evidence:_____

_____

_____

_____

_____

_____

_____
_____
_____
_____
_____
_____
_____
_____

Counterclaim: _____

_____
_____
_____
_____
_____

Rebuttal: _____

_____
_____
_____
_____
_____
_____
_____
_____

3. CONCLUSION

Restate the claim: _____

_____
_____

_____

_____

_____

_____

_____

Summarize your reasons: _____

_____

_____

_____

_____

_____

Include Transitions

above all, also, although, another, because, by comparison, first, for example, for instance, for that reason, furthermore, however, in addition, in conclusion, in contrast, in fact, in short, to sum up, lastly, likewise, most important, second, similarly, that is why, therefore, to illustrate, unlike, without a doubt

© 2012 The Key Writing Routine *www.keystoliteracy.com*

Keys to Content Writing
Writing Assignment Guide

| **Grade 8** |
| **Social Studies** |

Writing Assignment:

You will write an essay in which you take a position on the following question, and support your claim using teacher provided primary source documents:

Did feudalism and the Roman Catholic Church effectively provide security for the people of medieval Europe and create a more stable society? If so, how? If not, what were their failings?

Unit of Study/Content Connection:

Learning Outcomes related to standards:

WHI.7 Describe the major economic, social, and political developments that took place in medieval Europe. (H, E)

    A. the growing influence of Christianity and the Catholic Church

    B. the differing orders of medieval society, the development of feudalism, and the development of private property as a distinguishing feature of western civilization

---

Set Goals for the Writing Assignment

Type of writing:

___ informational _X_ argument ___ narrative ___ combo

Audience:
scholarly

Purpose:
To convince the reader that your position is the most logical one to take.

Length & Form:
3-5 pages; essay form

Due dates:
Final draft due December 10

Content and Text Structure Requirements :
- Introduction
  - Background info on topic (Early Middle Ages, Feudalism, Medieval Catholic Church)
  - States claim
  - Previews reasons (blueprint)
- Body
  - Presents arguments and evidence
  - Presents at least one counter-claim
  - Provides evidence-based rebuttal to counter-claim
- Conclusion
  - Reviews claim & supporting evidence
  - Effectively connects topic & claim to larger scope of history (contextualizes)

Requirements for sources:
(use a minimum of 3 of the following):
- Gregory of Tours (539-594): The Conversion of Clovis
- Annals of Xanten, 845-853

	<ul><li>"Feudal Capitularies – 9th century"</li><li>Fulbert of Chartres: On Feudal Obligations, 1020</li><li>"The Peasant's Cares" (poem)</li><li>Gregory VII: Dictatus Papae, 1090</li><li>Letter: To Pope Gregory VII from HRE Henry IV, 1076</li><li>William of St. Thierry: Life of Saint Bernard, 1140 c.</li><li>Constitutions of Clarendon, 1164</li><li>Edward Grim: The Murder of Thomas Becket</li></ul>
Models	Look at these examples:
Scaffolds	Use these supports:<ul><li>Peer feedback checklist</li><li>Rubric</li></ul>
Feedback Process	Feedback from your peers:<ul><li>You will complete peer editing upon completion of your first draft.</li><li>Teacher will provide checklist based on rubric. Peers will be strategically chosen for effective feedback.</li></ul>
Opportunities for Revision	
Opportunities for Collaboration	At the THINK and PLAN stage:<ul><li>You will collaborate with a partner(s) during the reading, interpretation, summarizing, and evaluating of documents for this assignment.</li></ul>At the WRITE Stage:<ul><li>You will draft your essay independently</li></ul>At the REVISE Stage:<ul><li>You will revise using a teacher-provided checklist with peer input and support.</li><li>You will complete re-writes, edits, and revisions independently</li></ul>

Developed by Jonathan Mello, Franklin Public Schools, MA

Feudalism, the Medieval Catholic Church, & European Society
Opinion/Argument Writing Checklist

Introduction	Excellent	Getting There	Not Yet
Does the introduction provide background information on the general topic? If so, bracket it.			
Does the introduction identify claim? If so, highlight and label it.			
Does the introduction acknowledge alternate or opposing claims? If so, star each.			
Does the introduction preview what is to follow with clear organization? If so, circle the preview/blueprint.			
Development of Ideas			
Is claim supported with logical reasons and relevant evidence? If so, label each reason with an "R" in the margin, and each piece of evidence with an "E."			
Are the reasons and evidence presented in an organized way?			
Is evidence from sources integrated effectively? If so, put an "!" where they did so.			
Is the counter-claim presented clearly? If so, label it with "CC" in the margin.			
Is the rebuttal supported with logical reasons and evidence? Identify the rebuttal with "REB" in the margin.			
Are transitions used to link and to create cohesion among claim(s), reasons, and evidence?			
Is there a formal style and an objective tone established and maintained throughout the piece?			
Content			
Are the content requirements met?			
Are the reasons and evidence clear and focused? Place a "?" next to any reasons and evidence that are unclear.			
Is the content explained sufficiently?			
Does the writing demonstrate understanding of content?			
Is the information presented accurate and relevant? Place an "IA" next to any inaccurate statements and an "IR" next to any irrelevant statements.			

Does the piece include precise and subject-specific vocabulary? Highlight all required vocabulary words used in the piece: • manor, fief, noble, pope, bishop, barbarian, Viking, monarch			
Conclusion			
Does the conclusion highlight and support the claim? If so, highlight the claim in the conclusion.			
Does the concluding statement or section follow form and support the argument presented?			
Does the conclusion bring closure to the piece?			

Conventions	Yes	No
Is there a systematic pattern of errors?		
Are there any capitalization or punctuation mistakes? Place three lines under any letter that should be capitalized; place a slash through any letter that is capitalized but shouldn't be.		
Are there any spelling mistakes? Circle misspelled words and write 'SP' above.		
Are the sentences grammatically correct? Underline sentence fragments or run-on sentences and label them "fr" or "r-o" in the margin.		

What I like about this writing piece:

_____

_____

_____

_____

_____

_____

_____

_____

_____

_____

_____

Additional Comments or Suggestions:

_____

_____

_____

_____

_____

_____

_____

_____

_____

_____

_____

| *Keys to Content Writing*
Writing Assignment Guide | **Grade 9 English & History Classes
Combined Assignment** |

Writing Assignment:

Write a literary analysis that presents evidence for why the book or movie version of "The Boy in the Striped Pajamas" is better.

Unit of Study/Content Connection:

World War II and the Holocaust

Learning Outcomes related to standards:

- History standard WHII.26: background, course, and consequences of the Holocaust.
- Reading standard # 7: Analyze the representation of a subject in two different artistic mediums.
- Writing standard W#1: Argument writing

| **Set Goals for the Writing Assignment** | Type of writing:
___ informational _X_ argument ___ narrative ___ combo

Audience:
Our high school subscribes to a student magazine published by the National Council for the Social Studies. They will be publishing |

an edition that focuses on the Holocaust during World War II. The magazine is looking for student articles and reviews of books or movies related to this topic Your piece will be submitted to the magazine. The audience for your piece will be editors for the magazine, and possibly high school students around the county who read the magazine.

Purpose:
To convince readers that the book or movie provides better historical fiction about the Holocaust.

Length & Form:
2 to 3 pages, typed, size 10 font, one-inch margins.

Due dates:
- Notes due on April 12.
- First draft due on April 20.
- Final draft due on May 1.

Content and Text Structure Requirements :
- Introduction that provides brief background knowledge about the setting, characters, and plot summary. State your claim and at least 2 literary components you compared in the movie and book that led to your position.
- Body paragraphs that present each literary component and provide specific details, including quotes or descriptions of scenes, from the book and the movie as evidence to support your position.
- Include a counter-claim that presents one area in which the opposite choice of the book or movie could make a case that it was better.
- Include transitions that connect sentences and paragraphs.
- Include a conclusion that restates your position and reviews your major reasons supporting that position.

Requirements for sources:
- Include specific quotes from the book.
- Use quotation marks and cite page numbers for book quotes within the text.

Models	Look at these examples: Mentor, published samples of book/movie analyses.

Scaffolds	Use these supports:
	  - List of transition words and phrases
	  - Argument top-down topic web

Feedback Process	**Feedback from your peers:** You will share a first draft with a peer who will use the Peer Feedback Checklist. **Feedback from the teacher:** Your history teacher will give you feedback on your first draft. Your English teacher will give you feedback on your final draft.
Opportunities for Revision	You are required to write a first and final draft.
Opportunities for Collaboration	**At the THINK and PLAN stage:** You will participate in a whole class discussion during English class to brainstorm and identify literary components to consider for the comparison of the book and movie. You will also participate in a small group discussion during History class with students who have chosen the same position as you. **At the WRITE Stage:** **At the REVISE Stage:** You will receive feedback from a peer that you can use to revise your draft into a final piece.

www.keystoliteracy.com

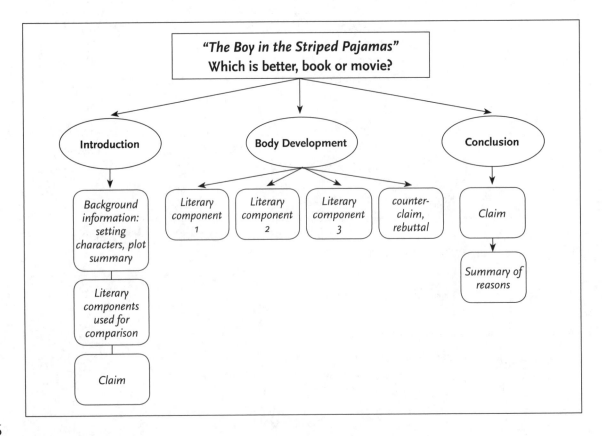

Keys to Content Writing **Writing Assignment Guide**	**Grade 10** **History/Civics**

Writing Assignment:

Write an editorial for our city newspaper that supports passage of a proposed bond levy to fund the building of new facilities at the high school.

Unit of Study/Content Connection:

American Government

Learning Outcomes related to standards:

- USG 3.12: Use a variety of sources, including newspapers, to identify current state and local legislative issues and examine the influence on the legislative process of political parties, interest groups, grass roots organizations, lobbyists, public opinion, the news media, and individual voters.
- USG 5.9: Together with other students, identify a significant public policy issue in the community, gather information about that issue, fairly evaluate the various points of view and competing interests.
- Writing standard W#1: Argument writing

Set Goals for the Writing Assignment	Type of writing: ___ informational _X_ argument ___ narrative ___ combo Audience: Citizens of our city will be voting on the proposed bond levy. The audience for your piece will be voters who read the city newspaper. Purpose: To convince voters to vote in support of the bond levy. Length & Form: 1 to 2 pages, typed, size 10 font, one-inch margins. Due dates: • Notes due on April 12. • First draft due on April 20. • Final draft due on May 1. Content and Text Structure Requirements : • Introduction that includes a description of the new facilities and repairs that will be covered by the bond levy. Also be sure to state your position clearly in the introduction. • Body paragraphs that present at least three reasons to support your claim, including detailed evidence. • Body paragraphs that present at least one counter-claim and a rebuttal to that counter-claim. • Include transitions that connect sentences and paragraphs.

	• Include a conclusion that restates your position and includes summary comments designed to convince voters to pass the bond levy. **Requirements for sources:** • Use evidence from the recent speech given by the Superintendent to the School Committee. • Include reasons and evidence based on your observation and personal experience as a student in the high school.
Models	**Look at these examples:** Sample past editorials related to other ballot questions.
Scaffolds	**Use these supports:** • List of transition words and phrases • Argument top-down topic web
Feedback Process	**Feedback from your peers:** You will share a first draft with a peer who will use the Peer Feedback Checklist. **Feedback from the teacher:** I will give you feedback on your final draft.
Opportunities for Revision	You are required to write a first and final draft.
Opportunities for Collaboration	**At the THINK and PLAN stage:** You will participate in a whole class discussion and brainstorm to identify reasons to support the claim and counter-claims. **At the WRITE Stage:** **At the REVISE Stage:** You will receive feedback from a peer that you can use to revise your draft into a final piece.

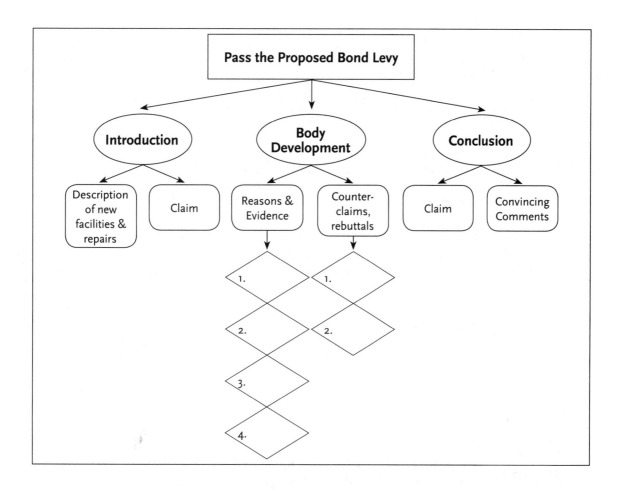

Keys to Content Writing
Writing Assignment Guide

**Grade 6 EXAMPLE
ELA Class**

Writing Assignment:

Write an alternative chapter 13 of <u>The Watsons Go To Birmingham – 1963</u> from Byron's point of view.

Learning Outcomes Related to Literacy Standards:
- RS#2 Literature: determine a theme of a story from details in the text, including how characters in a story or drama respond to challenges.
- RS#6 Literature: Describe how a narrator's or speaker's point of view influences how events are described
- RS #10 Literature: Read and comprehend literature, including stories, dramas, and poetry, independently and proficiently.
- WS #3: Write narratives to develop real or imagined experiences or events using effective technique, descriptive details, and clear event sequences.
- WS #4: Produce clear and coherent writing in which the development and organization are appropriate to task, purpose, and audience.

- WS #5: Develop and strengthen writing as needed by planning, revising, editing, rewriting, or trying a new approach.
- WS #10: Write routinely over extended time frames and shorter time frames for a range of discipline-specific tasks, purposes, and audiences.

Set Goals for the Writing Assignment	**Type of writing:** ___ informational ___argument __X_narrative ___combo **Audience:** Christopher Paul Curtis, author of the book. **Purpose:** To send the chapter to the author to consider writing a new book from Byron's perspective. **Length & Form:** Fictional narrative chapter told from a specific character's point of view, minimum 2 pages. **Due dates:** Rough draft due April 10th Final Draft due May 1 **Content and Text Structure Requirements :** • Create new and appropriate title for the chapter. • Introduction should establish the following narrative elements: Byron's point of view as the narrator, setting, and characters. • Body paragraphs must be at least two or more examples of each of the following literary tools: dialogue, sensory details, transitional words or phrases related to sequence, figurative language. • Body paragraphs must stay true to the events of the chapter; Byron's voice and perspective must accurately reflect his characterization in chapter 13. • Body paragraphs must reflect a logical sequence of events that correspond to the actual events of chapter 13. • Conclusion should follow Byron's experience at the end of chapter 13 and include a reflection of Byron's feelings toward Kenny. **Requirements for sources:** • <u>The Watsons Go to Birmingham – 1963</u>, by Christopher Paul Curtis
Models	**Look at these examples:** • Refer to the teacher's model of chapter 13 written from Joey's point of view.

Scaffolds	Use these supports: • Top-down topic web of the content and text structure requirements • Summary of chapter 13 and summary template • List of transitional words and phrases • Paragraph templates
Feedback Process	Feedback from your peers: Peer sharing will focus on sequence of events, introduction, and conclusion. Feedback from the teacher: The teacher will provide feedback for the rough draft using a checklist.
Opportunities for Revision	Revision will happen at home for homework.
Opportunities for Collaboration	At the THINK and PLAN stage: Student partners will turn and talk to discuss possible differences in Byron's perspective. At the REVISE Stage: Student partners will use peer-editing checklist to provide feedback.

www.keystoliteracy.com

Keys to Content Writing
Writing Assignment Guide

Grade 8 EXAMPLE **ELA Class, Literary Analysis**

Writing Assignment:

In chapter five of "The Outsiders", Ponyboy recites Robert Frost's poem "Nothing Gold Can Stay". Identify a theme that is present in both the poem and the novel. Use evidence from both texts to explain how they are related. Additionally, analyze why S.E. Hinton decided to include the poem in her novel.

Unit of Study/Content Connection: Trimester 2: "The Outsiders"

Learning Outcomes Related to Literacy Standards:
• Writing Standards
  – 2. Write informative/explanatory texts to examine a topic and convey ideas, concepts, and information (2a, b, c, d, e):
  – 8. Quote or paraphrase the data and conclusions of others while avoiding plagiarism and following a standard format of citation
• Language Standards
  – 1.b. Chose among sentence types to signal differing relationships among ideas

Set Goals for the Writing Assignment	Type of writing: __X_ informational ___argument ___narrative ___combo Audience: Peers in class (8th graders who have read the novel and are working on the same assignment) Purpose: to analyze the text and poem in order to explain your interpretation of the meanng, theme, and author's purpose Length & Form: multiple paragraphs (3-6), typed, double spaced, 12 point font, shared on Google Drive Due dates: • brainstorm due: • rough draft due (self revise): • rough draft due (peer revise): • conference with Mrs. Morrison: • final draft due:

	Content and Text Structure Requirements :
	• incorporate this specific vocabulary: theme, author's purpose
	• transitions between ideas
	• introduction that includes:
	  – title and author of novel
	  – title and author of poem
	  – brief explanation of characters, setting, and plot
	  – overview of the poem in the novel
	
	• Body Paragraph(s) that includes
	  – cited textual evidence of the theme of the novel
	    ▪ introduced, stated, explained
	    ▪ analysis of textual evidence (draw conclusions, explain interpretations, analyze significance of words, etc.)
	  – paraphrased evidence of the theme of the poem
	    ▪ introduced, paraphrased, explained
	    ▪ analysis of textual evidence (draw conclusions, explain interpretations, analyze significance of words, etc.)
	
	• Conclusion that includes
	  – a review of the points made in introduction and body paragraphs
	  – an explanation of whether or not the author's purpose for including the poem was achieved in the novel
	  – textual evidence to support statement of author's purpose
	    ▪ introduced, stated, explained
	    ▪ conclude with connection to introduction

Models	Look at these examples: • Models of literary analysis
Scaffolds	Use these supports: • guided questions • brainstorm: use top down web to organize ideas • guided revising checklist • detailed rubric
Feedback Process	Feedback from your peers: • students will brainstorm and write rough drafts with their peers Feedback from the teacher: • students will set up a conference with Mrs. Morrison to ask specific questions and to check the progress of their writing
Opportunities for Revision	• Students will work on revising their writing between rough draft #1 and rough draft #2 • Students will also work during class to self-revise and identify improvements to make to their writing
Opportunities for Collaboration	At the THINK and PLAN stage: • You will work in a collaborative group to determine the common theme, answer guiding questions, and identify textual evidence. At the WRITE Stage: • You will work with your collaborative group to write the first draft At the REVISE Stage:

Glossary
of Terms

Glossary of Terms

Text Structure Terms

body: the part of a writing piece that develops the information and ideas; can contain any number of sections and paragraphs

conclusion: placed at the end of a writing piece, used to sum up the ideas and information presented, creates closure and holds the whole text together by referring back to what has already been said, conclusion goals: rephrase the main topic or claim, summarize the key main ideas or reasons, leave the reader with a sense of closure, interesting final impression, or call to action.

detail sentences: sentences that support and explain the main idea by providing relevant facts, examples, definitions, comparisons, etc.

introduction: placed at the start of a writing piece, introduces an informational or argument writing piece by identifying the overall topic; for argument writing, the claim should always be included; an introduction can range in length from a single sentence to a full page; an introduction may also include the following:

- **lead:** used to catch the interest of the reader at the start of an introduction, sometimes called a hook

- **background knowledge:** basic information related to the topic that is useful to the reader before he/she reads the full piece

- **preview of subtopics:** for informational writing

- **preview of reasons supporting the claim:** for argument writing

- **preview of the counterclaim:** for argument writing

main idea: the key concept or main point being communicated in a paragraph; main ideas can be stated or implied

overall topic: broad, general theme; overall subject of the piece; usually stated in 1-5 words

paragraph: a collection of related sentences that develop a key idea/main idea; indicated by a new line or indentation

section: a chunk of text that includes a number of related paragraphs about the same topic or subtopic

subtopic: topics that are subordinate to the overall topic; students identify subtopics as a way to bring focus to a broader topic

topic sentence: the sentence in which the main idea is stated

transitions: words, phrases, or sentences that connect sentences, paragraphs, or sections; used to clarify relationships, create cohesion, and link ideas

Text-Feature Terms

graphics: visual representations that support text such as charts, diagrams, graphs, figures, tables, photographs

heading or sub-heading: a text feature that previews the subtopics of sections

table of contents, index, glossary: text features that help the reader navigate the text

title: previews the overall topic

Argument Component Terms

claim: the position taken by the writer; what the writer is trying to prove or argue

counterclaim: counterargument; opposing claim; contrasting opinion

evidence: used to support or prove a reason; evidence can include statistics, facts, quotations, examples, definitions, personal experience, experiments, anecdotes, observations, comparisons, expert opinion, interviews, surveys

reason: provided by the writer to support a claim; reasons are supported by evidence

rebuttal: something the writer does to refute or disprove the counterclaim; address the criticism against the claim

Source Terms

accurate: without error; in exact conformity to fact; when you use accurate information you do not make up information

bias: prejudice in favor of one thing or against another; one-sided; lacking a neutral viewpoint

citation: a reference to a source; used to avoid plagiarism

credible: reliable; trustworthy; dependable; when a source is credible it can be counted on to be accurate

plagiarism: taking the words or ideas of someone else and passing them off as your own

relevant: a statement that is related to the matter at hand and appropriate to purpose; when evidence is relevant, it is directly related to your claim and reasons

Other Writing Terms Used in Training

admit/exit ticket: a type of quick write that can be used at the start or end of a class lesson

CCSS: Common Core State Standards

collaborative writing: providing opportunities for students to work with peers or a teacher at any stage of the writing process

conventions: spelling, capitalization, punctuation, use of proper English grammar

disciplinary writing: writing tasks that are unique and specific to subject areas

differentiating instruction: making modifications to a writing task to meet specific needs of individual students; the content, process, and product can be differentiated, including requirements for length, sources, content and text requirements, and amount of scaffolding provided

explicit instruction: an approach to teaching skills or information that is deliberate and structured; includes the use of modeling, think aloud, and scaffolds; explicit instruction avoids making assumptions about student skills or background knowledge

gradual release of responsibility (I, WE, YOU): an instructional approach that teaches students a new skill or information by gradually shifting the responsibility for understanding and application from the teacher to individual students; the amount of explicit instruction and scaffolds that are provided is gradually released as students acquire greater independence

modeling: an instructional practice in which the teacher shows examples and demonstrates application of a skill; a critical element of explicit instruction

mentor models: examples of student or published writing pieces; provided by a teacher and emulated by students

paraphrasing: using one's own words to write information from sources into notes or a writing draft; paraphrasing techniques include replacing source vocabulary with accurate synonyms, changing the sentence pattern, and simplifying complex concepts or abstract ideas

patterns of organization: a set of organizational structures (sometimes referred to as strategies) that can be used to present information; the most common patterns of organization include: cause and effect, problem and solution, sequence or chronology, description or explanation, compare and contrast; certain transition words are used to provide clues to the reader about the pattern being used

quick write: short, informal writing task that is completed in under ten minutes; goal is to help students process, organize, and remember information and ideas; can be used in any subject at any point in a classroom lesson

revision: identifying places in a writing piece that can be improved; revision typically refers to modifications made to ideas, text structure, and choice of vocabulary; editing for conventions is another element of revision

scaffold: an extra support that is provided as students are learning a new skill; it is gradually released as students move towards independent use of the skill; Keys to Literacy scaffolds include think aloud, annotated sources, two-column notes, top-down topic webs, sets of steps, writing templates

scope and sequence: a suggested order of instruction that gradually develops student skills; a scope and sequence usually follows this order: identification and defining, analyze and deconstructing, specific skill practice, writing collaboratively, writing independently

sentence combining: an activity used to develop sentence-writing skills; students combine short sentences into longer, more complex sentences by manipulating, deleting, and adding words

set of steps: a scaffold that is provided to students that lists the steps they should follow to complete a particular writing task or activity

think aloud: an instructional practice in which teachers model their thinking about application of skill by thinking out loud the steps in their thinking

top-down topic web: a graphic organizer that represents ideas in a hierarchical format using alternating shapes, position, and color to emphasize relationships among ideas; used for several purposes: to support comprehension, to illustrate components of a writing piece, as a planning tool before writing

two-column notes: a note-taking format that places main topics or ideas in the left column and supporting details in the right column

WAG (Writing Assignment Guide): a Keys to Literacy planning tool for teachers; used to develop a detailed plan for a student writing assignment that includes the following: setting goals (length, audience and purpose, text and source requirements, due dates, type and form), models to be shared, scaffolds to be provided, opportunities to be provided for collaboration, feedback, and revision; can be shared with students

writing form: the layout of a writing piece; examples include brochures pamphlet, blog entry, journal entry, article, essay, web page, letter, speech, poster, advertisement, etc.

writing models: writing samples that are used to show students what a good piece of writing might look like, or how a particular writing technique might be used; models can be samples of published writing or samples of student writing; students are encouraged to emulate writing models

writing process: the steps (stages) that should be followed when writing; the major stages in the writing process include pre-writing, text production, revising, and editing; Keys to Literacy uses a THINK, PLAN, WRITE, REVISE model to represent the writing process

writing template: a scaffold that is provided to students that includes reminders and space for each part of a writing piece

writing type: used to describe if a piece of writing is informational, argument, narrative, or a combination

Resources and References

Resources

For Finding Student Writing Samples

Achieve the Core
http://www.achievethecore.org/dashboard/300/search/1/1/0/1/2/3/4/5/6/7/8/9/10/11/12
- *A large collection of K-12 student writing samples originally collected by the Vermont Department of Education.*

Common Core, Appendix C
http://www.corestandards.org/assets/Appendix_C.pdf
- *A collection of K-12 student writing samples available from the official Common Core State Standards website.*

Reading & Writing Project, Teachers College – Columbia University
http://readingandwritingproject.org/resources/student-work/student-writing
- *A collection of K-8 student writing samples.*

Write Source
http://www.thewritesource.com/studentmodels/
- *A small collection of K-12 student writing samples.*

For Finding Sources

Boston Debate League
http://www.bostondebate.org/eba/
- *A large collection of lesson plans and sources that can be used to teach evidence-based argumentation. Developed in conjunction with Boston Public Schools, the focus is on upper grades and includes material for all content areas.*

DOGOnews
http://www. dogonews.com
- *A website that offers current events sources and non-fictional content for grades K-5.*

International Debate Education Association
http://idebate.org/
- *Includes a database of hundreds of debate topics that include points for and against each topic and bibliographies of related sources.*

NEWSELA
http://www.newsela.com/
- *An educational website that publishes high-interest news articles daily at five levels of complexity for grades 3-12.*

ProCon.org
http://www.procon.org
- *A website that provides resources for critical thinking without bias. The site researches issues that are controversial and presents sources that represent all sides of an issue.*

Sweet Search
http://www.sweetsearch.com/#
- *A website that searches for sources only from primary sources and credible sites like universities and public repositories. Its database of about 35,000 web sites has been vetted by researchers, librarians, and teachers.*

TRACKSTAR
http://trackstar.4teachers.org/trackstar/
- *A website that provides a place for teachers to collect and store sources, including annotations, for student writing projects. In addition to creating your own "track" of material, you can access numerous other tracks developed by other teachers, including the sources they collected.*

TweenTribune
http://tweentribune.com
- *A website sponsored by the Smithsonian Museum. Offers non-fiction articles.*

About Mentor Text

WritingFix
http://writingfix.com/index.htm#
- *A collection of mentor text lessons that cover numerous writing skills, grades K-12.*

Books:
- *The Writing Thief: Using Mentor Texts to Teach the Craft of Writing*, by Ruth Culham, 2014. International Reading Association.
- *Write Like This: Teaching Real-World Writing Through Modeling and Mentor Texts*, by Kelly Gallagher, 2011. Stenhouse Publishers.
- *Mentor Author, Mentor Texts: Short Texts, Craft Notes, and Practical Classroom Uses*, by Ralph Fletcher, 2011. Heinemann.
- *Nonfiction Mentor Texts: Teaching Informational Writing Through Children's Literature*, K-8, by Lynne Dorfman and Rose Cappelli, 2009. Stenhouse Publishers.
- *Mentor Texts: Teaching Writing Through Children's Literature*, K-6, by Lynne Dorfman and Rose Cappelli, 2007. Stenhouse Publishers.

Resources About Citing Sources

- Quoting, paraphrasing, and summarizing:
  https://owl.english.purdue.edu/owl/resource/563/01/
- Paraphrasing:
  https://owl.english.purdue.edu/owl/resource/563/2/
- MLA Formatting and Style Guide:
  https://owl.english.purdue.edu/owl/resource/747/01/
- Overview of citing sources:
  http://libguides.mit.edu/c.php?g=176032&p=1159439
- Overview guides for APA, Chicago, and MLA formats:
  http://libraries.iub.edu/help-citing-sources

References

Achieve the Core. *The Common Core Shifts for English Language Arts/Literacy.* Student Achievement Partners. Retrieved from http://www.achievethecore.org

ACT (2004). *Crisis at the core: Preparing all students for college and work.* Iowa city, IA: Author.

Akhondi, M., Malayeri, F.A., & Samad, A.A. (2011). How to teach expository text structure to facilitate reading comprehension. *The Reading Teacher, 64* (5), 368-372.

Bangert-Downs, R.L., Kulik, C.C., Kulik, J.A., & Morgan, M. (1991). The instructional effects of feedback in test-like events. *Review of Educational Research, 61* (2), 213-238.

Benson, B. (1997). Scaffolding (Coming to Terms). *English Journal, 86* (7), 126-127.

Berne, J. (2009). *Giving feedback on student writing.* LDOnline. http://www.ldonline.org/article/36072/

Biber, D., Nekrasova, T., & Horn, B. (2011). *The effectiveness of feedback for L1-English and L2-English writing development: A meta-analysis.* ETS. www.ets.org/Media/Research/pdf/RR-11-05.pdf

Bloom, B. (1956). *Taxonomy of educational objectives, handbook I: The cognitive domain.* New York: David McKay Co. Inc.

Boscolo, P., & Gelati, C. (2007). Best practices in promoting motivation for writing. In S. Graham, C.A. MacArthur, & J. Fitzgerald (Eds.). *Best practices in writing instruction.* New York: Guilford Press.

Burke, J. (2008). *The teacher's essential guide series: Content area writing.* Scholastic Teaching Resources. http://teacher.scholastic.com/products/scholasticprofessional/pdfs/burke_contentareawriting.pdf

Common Core State Standards Initiative (2010). *Common core state standards for English language arts and literacy in history/social studies, science, and technical subjects.* Retrieved from http://www.corestandards.org/

Common Core State Standards Initiative (2010). *Appendix A: Research supporting key elements of the standards.* Retrieved from http://www.corestandards.org/

Graham, S., MacArthur, C.A., & Fitzgerald, J. (Eds.) (2007). *Best practices in writing instruction.* New York: Guilford Press.

Graham, S., & Harris, K. R., (2007). Best practices in teaching planning. In S. Graham, C.A. MacArthur, & J. Fitzgerald (Eds.). *Best practices in writing instruction.* New York: Guilford Press.

Graham, S., & Perin, D. (2007). *Writing next: Effective strategies to improve writing of adolescents in middle and high schools – A report to Carnegie Corporation of New York.* Washington, DC: Alliance for Excellent Education.

Graham, S. & Hebert, M. (2010). *Writing to read: Evidence for how writing can improve reading.* A Carnegie Corporation Time to Act Report. Washington, DC: Alliance for Excellent Education.

Graham, S., Bollinger, A., Booth Olson, C., D'Aoust, C., MacArthur, C., McCutchen, D., & Olinghouse, N. (2012). *Teaching elementary school students to be effective writers: A practice guide* (NCEE 2012-4058). Washington, DC: National Center for Education Evaluation and Regional Assistance, Institute of Education Sciences, U.S. Department of Education. Retrieved from http://ies.ed.gov/ncee/ wwc/ publications_reviews.aspx#pubsearch.

Graham, S., Harris, K., and Hebert, M. A. (2011). *Informing writing: The benefits of formative assessment. A Carnegie Corporation Time to Act report.* Washington, DC: Alliance for Excellent Education.

Hayes, J.R., & Flower, L. (1980). Identifying the organization of writing processes. In L.W. Gregg & E.R. Steinberg (Eds.), *Cognitive processes in writing: An interdisciplinary approach* (pp. 3-30). Hillsdale, NJ: Erlbaum.

Hayes J.R. (1996). A new framework for understanding cognition and affect in writing. In C.M. Levy & S. Ransdell (Eds.) *The science of writing: Theories, methods, individual differences and applications* (pp. 1-27). Mahwah, NJ: Erbaum.

Hayes, J.R. (2004). What triggers revision? In L. Allal, L. Chanquoy, & P. Largy (Eds.), *Studies in writing: Vol. 13. Revision: Cognitive and instructional processes* (pp. 9-20). Norwell, MA: Kluwer.

Hidi, S., & Boscolo, P. (2006). Motivation and writing. In C.A. MacArthur, S. Graham, & J. Fitzgerrald (Eds.). *Handbook of writing research.* New York: Guilford Press.

Klingner J.K., and Vaughn, S. (2004). Strategies for struggling second-language readers. In T.L. Jetton and J.A. Dole (Eds.). *Adolescent literacy: Research and practice.* New York: Guilford Press.

Lange, V. L. (2002). *Instructional scaffolding.* Retrieved from http://condor.admin.ccny.cuny. edu/~group4/Cano/Cano%20Paper.doc.

Lehr, F., Osborn, J., & Hiebert, E.H. (2005). *A Focus on Comprehension.* Honolulu, HI: Pacific Resources for Education and Learning.

Lipscomb, L., Swanson, J., West, A. (2004). Scaffolding. In M. Orey (Ed.), *Emerging perspectives on learning, teaching, and technology.* Retrieved from http://projects.coe.uga.edu/epltt/

MacArthur, C. A. (2007). Best practices in teaching evaluation and revision. In S. Graham, C.A. MacArthur, & J. Fitzgerald (Eds.). *Best practices in writing instruction.* New York: Guilford Press.

McKensie, L., & Tomkins, G.E. (984). Evaluating students' writing: A process approach. *Journal of Teaching Writing 3*(2) 201-212.

Murray, D. (2004). *The craft of revision,* 5th Ed. Boston, Heinle.

National Center for Education Statistics (2012). *The Nation's Report Card: Writing 2011*(NCES 2012–470). Institute of Education Sciences, U.S. Department of Education, Washington, D.C.

The National Commission on Writing (2004). *Writing: A ticket to work... or a ticket out – A survey of business leaders.* College Entrance Examination Board.

National Reading Panel. (2000). *Teaching children to read: An evidence-based assessment of the scientific research literature on reading and its implications for reading instruction.* Washington, DC: National Institute of Child Health and Human Development.

Newell, G.E., Koukis, S., & Boster, S. (2007). Best practices in developing a writing across the curriculum program in the secondary school. In S. Graham, C.A. MacArthur, & J. Fitzgerald (Eds.). *Best practices in writing instruction.* New York: Guilford Press.

Partnership for Assessment of Readiness for College and Career. *Writing forms.* www.parcconline.org/ samples/english-language-artsliteracy/writing-forms

Pauk, W. (1997). *How to study in college* (7th ed). Boston: Houghton Mifflin.

Pearson, P.E., & Gallagher, M.C. (1983). The instruction of reading comprehension. *Contemporary Educational Psychology, 8,* 317-344.

Peha, S. (2003). *Writing across the curriculum.* Retrieved from http://www.ttms.org/PDFs/06%20 Writing%20Across%20the%20Curriculum%20v001%20%28Full%29.pdf

Portalupi, J., & Fletcher, R. (2001). *Nonfiction craft lessons: Teaching informational writing K-8.* Portland, ME: Stenhouse.

Pritchard, R.J., & Honeycutt, R.L. (2007). Best practices in implementing a process approach to teaching writing. In S. Graham, C.A. MacArthur, & J. Fitzgerald (Eds.), *Best practices in writing instruction.* New York: Guilford Press.

Rodier, A. (2000). A cure for writer's block: Writing for real audiences. *The Quarterly, 22* (2).

Roth, A., (1999). *The research paper: Process, form and content* (8th edition). Fort Worth, TX: Harcourt College.

Russek, B. (1998). Writing to learn mathematics. *Writing Across the Curriculum, 9*, 36-41.

Saddler, B. (2012). *Teacher's guide to effective sentence writing.* New York: Guilford Press.

Sedita, J. (1989). *Landmark study skills guide.* Prides Crossing, MA: Landmark School Press.

Sedita, J. (2003, 2015). *The Key Comprehension Routine.* Rowley, MA: Keys to Literacy.

Shanahan, T., Callison, K., Carriere, C., Duke, N.K., Pearson, P.D., Schatschneider, C., & Torgesen, J. (2010). *Improving reading comprehension in kindergarten through 3rd grade: A practice guide* (NCEE 2010-4038). Washington, DC: National Center for Education Evaluation and Regional Assistance, Institute of Education Sciences, U.S. Department of Education. Retrieved from whatworks.ed.gov/publications/practiceguides.

Snow, C. (2002). (Chair). *RAND reading study group: Reading for understanding: Toward an R&D program in reading comprehension.* Santa Monica, CA: RAND

Strong, W. (1986). *Creative approaches to sentence combining.* ERIC Clearinghouse on Reading and Communication Skills. National Council of Teachers of English.

Troia, G.A. (2007). Research in writing instruction: What we know and what we need to know. In D.D. Deschler, M.F. Hock, M. Pressley, A.K. Billman, R.H. Perry, K.E. Reffitt, & J.M. Reynolds (Eds.). *Shaping literacy achievement: Research we have, research we need.* New York: Guilford Press.

Trupiano, C. (2006) Best classroom practices. In A. Horning & A. Becker (Eds). *Revision: history, theory, and practice.* Parlor Press.

University of Victoria English Department (2010). *Academic essentials.* Retrieved from http://www.uvicbookstore.ca/general/search.php?subject=acadwrit

Walberg, H.J. (1999). Productive teaching. In H.C. Waxman & H.J. Walberg (Eds.). *New directions for teaching practice and research.* Berkeley, CA: McCutchin Publishing Corporation.

Walker, B. (2009). A letter from Barbara Walker to President Obama. *Reading Today, 26*(4), pp 16.

Wiggins, G., & McTighe, J. (2005). *Understanding by design.* Pearson.

Wiggins, G. (1993). *Assessing student performance: Exploring the purpose and limits of testing.* San Francisco: Josey-Bass.

Wiggins, G. (2012). Seven keys to effective feedback. *Educational Leadership, 70,* (1), pages 10-16.

Witte, S. (2013). Preaching what we practice: A study of revision. *Journal of Curriculum and Instruction* 6(2), 33-59.

Take Away Activity

Use the right column to take notes.

Training Topic	• *What are the most important points to remember about this topic?* • *How can I incorporate what I learned about this topic in my instruction?*
Quick Writes *Consider:* *- different formats to reinforce content* *- to practice writing skills* *- sentence combining* *- use as formative assessment*	
Basic Text Structures *Consider:* *- types of writing* *- analyzing text samples* *- wall cards* *- introductions, conclusions* *- body development and organization* *- transitions*	

Writing From Sources

Consider:
- *providing sources*
- *tracking sources*
- *gathering information*
- *using two-column notes*
- *using notes to write a draft*
- *writing process*
- *text structures*

Set Goals Section of the WAG

Consider:
- *content and standards connection*
- *audience, purpose*
- *requirements*
- *writing process*
- *text structures*

Feedback and Revision

Consider:
- *collaboration*
- *feedback checklists, rubrics*
- *writing process*
- *text structures*

Providing Models and Scaffolds

Consider:
- *mentor models*
- *focus for analysis*
- *differentiating instruction*
- *scaffolds for stages in writing process*
- *scaffolds for text structures*

NOTES:

Keys to Literacy®

About Keys to Literacy

Keys to Literacy is a professional development and consulting company specializing in literacy instruction.

The importance of literacy and its connection to learning is widely recognized, yet many teachers do not receive sufficient preparation in teaching comprehension, vocabulary and writing skills. Keys to Literacy has literacy expertise across all grade levels and subjects to help teachers provide literacy instruction that is embedded in content instruction.

Keys to Literacy professional development programs are built upon the most current literacy research and best instructional practices. Keys to Literacy programs combine initial training with long-term follow-up support. Our instructional routines embed foundational literacy instruction across the curriculum while fulfilling many of the Common Core literacy requirements. Our programs are relevant to general educators as Tier I instruction and to special educators as Tier II support instruction.

Keys to Literacy Programs

The Key Comprehension Routine: Grades 4-12
The Key Comprehension Routine: Grades K-3
The Key Vocabulary Routine: Grades 3-12
Keys to Content Writing: Grades 4-12
Keys to Argument Writing: Grades 4-12
Keys to Close Reading: Grades 2-12
The ANSWER Key Routine for Performance Writing: Grades 3-12

Who We Are

Our staff of literacy experts has significant experience with K-12 literacy issues. We understand the reality of working in a school because we have been there as teachers and administrators. Our experience as educators has enabled us to develop instructional strategies that work because they are research-based, practical and effective. We are dedicated educators who share a passion for improving student literacy skills by improving teacher strategies and instructional methods.

Contact Us

To learn more about Keys to Literacy, visit our website at www.keystoliteracy.com, call 978-948-8511, or email us at info@keystoliteracy.com.